Invergordon Scapegoat

Admiral Wilfred Tomkinson

Invergordon Scapegoat

Alan Coles

ALAN SUTTON

First published in the United Kingdom in 1993 by
Alan Sutton Publishing Limited · Phoenix Mill · Far Thrupp · Stroud · Gloucestershire

First published in the United States of America in 1993 by
Alan Sutton Publishing Inc · 83 Washington Street · Dover · NH 03820

British Library Cataloguing in Publication Data applied for

Library of Congress Cataloging in Publication Data applied for

Typeset in 10/12pt Times.
Typesetting and origination by
Alan Sutton Publishing Limited
Printed in Great Britain by
The Bath Press, Bath, Avon.

CONTENTS

LIST OF
ILLUSTRATIONS

ACKNOWLEDGEMENTS

One of the major planks in the construction of *Invergordon Scapegoat* bears the secondary book title of *Those Damned Tomkinsons*, but after the assistance that the family has given me in my research I would rename it *Those Agreeable Tomkinsons*.

The late Admiral Wilfred Tomkinson's three surviving daughters were responsible for directing me to the right fountainheads, for giving approval to my copying their father's private diaries and providing me with their forthright comments on his character and demeanour after the Invergordon Mutiny and in his twilight years.

It is essential, therefore, that I list them: Mrs Venetia Hogan, of Bickley, Tenbury Wells, Worcestershire; Mrs Joyce Newbery, of Worton, Devizes, Wiltshire; and Mrs Susan Robinson, of Barton Stacey, Winchester, Hampshire. Without them I would not have been able to bring their father from out of the shadows of a disgraceful period of Admiralty history.

In-depth assistance was also given by the admirable research facilities at the Churchill Archives Centre, Churchill College, Cambridge, which safekeeps Admiral Tomkinson's papers, and its staff, archivists Elizabeth Bennett and Alan Kucia, and assistant Lesley James.

John Smith and Anique Skinner of the Naval and Maritime Library, Plymouth, were also extremely cooperative and aided me in tracing long-forgotten books, or many photographs produced herein. My niece, Valerie Wills, also gave invaluable help and advice with photographic work.

Similar cooperation came from staff at the Public Records Office, Kew, the British Library at the British Museum and the Newspaper Library, Hendon.

Thanks also to Roger Thorp and Simon Fletcher at Alan Sutton Publishing for their helpfulness and expertise.

Finally, I applaud the patience of my wife, Gay Coles, for reliving the Invergordon Mutiny during the past two years and for rummaging through my many photocopies and memoranda to produce the list of notes.

Alan Coles
Dartmouth

PROLOGUE

The Invergordon Mutiny was the turning point of a social revolution in Britain. If the rebels with a cause had succeeded, the structure of life in the Western world could have changed – just as Russian and German naval mutinies altered the face of those countries.

If Admiral Wilfred Tomkinson, the acting commander-in-chief of the Atlantic Fleet, had indulged in strong-arm tactics, instead of playing for time with a gentility with which many of his superiors did not agree, there is little doubt that Britain would have been plunged into a crisis deeper than the financial one which sparked the mutiny in 1931. If he had turned guns on the mutineers, called out the Royal Marines to obtain discipline or shot the ringleaders, as some of his juniors were on the point of doing, it is certain that revolution, bloody, bitter and unrelenting, would have spread from the ships of the Royal Navy to the civilian populace ashore.

Yet Tomkinson, by what in later years would have been described as 'playing it cool', averted all this. Similar tactics to those he applied have been used in the 1980s and 1990s for 'talking out' terrorists and criminals who have held hostages. He was one of the first officers in command to use psychology, even though it might have been unwitting.

In spite of his dexterous handling of the mutiny – and many Royal Navy officers even today refuse to call it that – he was made the scapegoat for the happenings of those three days in September 1931, when sailors turned their backs on their officers and went on strike, because their pay was about to be cut.

Within six months Tomkinson, who had been plunged into the cauldron of mutiny without being briefed of the possibilities of it by Their Lordships at the Admiralty, was to be made the scapegoat for it, to be thrown into the scrapyard of naval castaways, without a chance of explaining his actions to a public inquiry. The Silent Service had no intention of letting him break that silence, while he, too, wrapped up in his loyalty to the navy, was loath to cry out loud. It is because of this silence, and the shredding of many public records on the subject, that Tomkinson is a 'faceless' admiral. There are many references to him in Admiralty letters and memoranda; there are many asides about him in several books. But through them all there is no indication of what type of man he was. Was the occasion too big for him? Was he right to swim with the tide of mutiny? Was he a 'nice man' who should never have been an admiral?

No naval historian has attempted to excavate the ground Tomkinson trod, or to dive beneath the many seas in which he served. It was this which led to my attempt to determine what type of man he was. Was he a naval fool caught up in the whirlpool of mutiny, from which he had no answer because of his Victorian maritime upbringing; or was he a naval thinker, who after the First World War realized that the lower deck was far too distant from the wardroom and the quarterdeck?

This is not an attempt to absolve him from the sit-down strike at Invergordon. Instead, the facts are presented for readers to judge for themselves.

More to the point is the necessity to unveil Tomkinson from the mist of obscurity into which he was relegated after the mutiny. Many of the admirals who dealt with him were as grey as the dawn of their future, yet biographers turned to them and their private papers, ignoring Tomkinson.

The mutiny was just seventy-two hours of his naval life, yet it was the moment for which he will be remembered. Before then he had served with bravery and distinction in the Boxer Rebellion, in the submarine service, in the First World War, in the sublimely heroic raid on Zeebrugge, in HMS *Hood*, the world's biggest battle cruiser, in the Mediterranean Fleet during the puerile Royal Oak affair, and most of the time alongside Roger Keyes, a latter-day Drake of the high seas.

It was a career which without Invergordon would have excited the imagination of most naval officers, yet it was Invergordon that jettisoned Admiral Wilfred Tomkinson into anonymity. This is an attempt to rectify wrongs which were heaped on him, much misunderstood, much maligned, but a naval hero of the next century, when all that he did – or did not do – is examined against a social backcloth.

1
TOMKINSON DYNASTY

'Your mother learned to walk on the deck of a brigantine at sea . . .'. The words came from the lips of the mother herself; and, of the cluster of children around her, it was Wilfred Tomkinson, resembling her more than his seven brothers and five sisters, who caught the sea fever of her stories.

In the great house of Franche Hall, near Kidderminster in Worcestershire, Annie Tomkinson, a pretty woman from a Yorkshire family renowned locally for its comely daughters, would entrance young Wilfred with her passed-down maritime memories, and divert him away from her millionaire husband's carpet business to the Royal Navy. She had plenty to tell, for in 1850, aged nine months, she accompanied her mother and father, Matthew Stonehouse, a giant black-bearded captain of a 250-ton brig, on a seven-month voyage to Table Bay and back to Hull. It was a sea baptism which was not to be repeated, for on another trip from South Africa, eighteen months later, the ship ran aground on the Goodwin Sands and was wrecked, never to be salvaged. When Matthew returned to his wife Elizabeth, Wilfred's grandmother, he heard for the first time that his first son had died three months earlier, but that Elizabeth was due to give birth to another child in seven weeks. This decided him to turn his back on the sea, which had provided his living for six years, so at twenty-six he began a new career in worsted spinning.

It was from this date that Annie was to become immersed in a plethora of sea yarns, some true, some embroidered with fiction. Between 1846 and 1852 Matthew had skippered the *Ann*, owned by a benevolent godfather and uncle. She took cargoes to Montreal, Madras, Cape Town and Constantinople, where Matthew claimed to have penetrated a sultan's harem, although later he was writing to his wife Elizabeth that 'I only want my fat little wife in bed with me to make me the happiest of mortals.'

Annie's uncle, a Captain Lawson, had been butchered in the bunk of his ship by Chinese mutineers, who sold the vessel in Shanghai. This made Matthew, already a disciplinarian, more determined to batten down on any disorderly conduct on board his ship. The tale ran that only once did he have disaffection – a word Wilfred was to hear many times in the future – among his crew of ten. He dealt with it by asking for the spokesman and then punched him to the deck. 'And if there's anyone else who wants to speak up, come forward,' he demanded. That was the end of the trouble and the crew went back to work.[1]

1

This family fable passed on to an impressive Wilfred would no doubt have carved itself on his memory; there is no doubt also that another of his grandfather's escapades would have remained in Wilfred's mind, when several years later he was involved in the Boxer Rebellion. To trade along the Turkish coast a permissory document was necessary and, after the completion of loading, had to be surrendered at Constantinople before a ship was allowed to leave. When Matthew was ready to sail home in the *Ann*, the foreign trading office was closed, so he ignored the Turkish instruction and left immediately. The brig was fired on by Turkish forts on both sides of the Dardanelles but, with cannon-balls falling all around, he refused to return and pressed on unscathed until out of range.

If Annie had a favourite among her thirteen children – and she tried desperately not to be swayed – it was Wilfred. Yet it is improbable that he endeared himself to his self-made tycoon father, Michael, by keeping away from his carpet factory in Kidderminster. Like Matthew Stoneman, Michael was an adventurer, not on the sea but in landbound industry. His father, Wilfred's grandfather, also a Michael, described himself on his marriage certificate as a 'gentleman', but was by profession a mercer, or draper, in High Street, Kidderminster, and also an undertaker. His wife, Wilfred's grandmother, was a Miss Griggs, who came from the more fashionable area of Blakebrook in the town, where her father owned a confectionery business.

From this background it was not surprising that Michael Tomkinson II was to go into trade or industry. In 1854, at the age of thirteen, he was sent to London to serve a form of apprenticeship with James Schoolbred, lace dealers in Tottenham Court Road, where he was given a veneer of smart salesmanship and a taste for culture that he could never have acquired in his home town. His career in carpets began with Lea and Simcox, where he learned design, and continued with a clerkship at Pemberton Talbot, also in Kidderminster. But in 1867, when he was twenty-six, the company ceased trading. Michael stepped in to buy their surplus rugs, sold them at a goodly profit, and with this money he set himself up as an agent for carpet yarns. On his selling expeditions he met William Adam, a skilful engineer of carpet machinery and in 1869, with just £500, they bought secondhand equipment to make matching rugs and piece goods. Within two years they had expanded to the extent of employing 200 workers. It was then that Michael decided he could afford to take a wife – and that was Annie, whom he met through her father's worsted wool spinning business in Wakefield, Yorkshire. She was twenty-one and he was thirty when they married on 17 September 1871.

Within two months Annie was pregnant. Her first-born was a girl, Gertrude; then sixteen months later came Herbert, who was earmarked by his father for the Tomkinson carpet factory. Two more sons were born, Harry in 1875 and Gerald in 1876, also destined for a career with his father. The confinements of Annie continued with annual regularity, for within another six months she was pregnant again, with Wilfred being born on 15 November at Sunnyside, the Tomkinsons' rambling semi-Georgian white stuccoed house at Franche, with six bedrooms and staff quarters. 1877 was a landmark in the family's history, for it was the year Michael embarked on a pioneering entrepreneurial voyage, which was to ensure that the name of Tomkinson would be revered, and later envied, in the carpet industry.

Michael and his co-director William Adam had heard of a new spool loom being developed in America by Halcyon Skinner in conjunction with the world's largest carpet company, Alexander Smith, of Yonkers, New York. It was essential that the Kidderminster partners should remain ahead of their rivals, so Michael booked the first passage he could on a ship to New York, where he persuaded Smiths to sell him the patents of the loom for use in Britain. He was to write later:

There before me was the manufacturers' dream, realised by a machine producing carpets with any number of colours and all the wool in the surface. In a few days I returned to England and I carried in my handbag the patent right for Great Britain, which to a great extent revolutionised the trade. With the help of my partner William, with his great knowledge of weaving and his ability as an inventor we soon had the first loom running and the first piece of Royal Axminster carpet was woven in September 1878.

Before the production of Royal Axminster it took three machinists a day to produce one-and-a-half yards. The new spool power loom spewed out 25 yards of 27-in widths in the same time. Success was imminent; production built up in ten years to the point where 4,000 carpets, or rugs, were leaving the factory each week. The work force was expanded to 800, with a design staff of twenty-four. Fifteen tons of jute a week were woven into carpet backing; chenille weave of all widths up to church seating of 28 ft could be offered to customers in any length. Warehouses were opened in London, Manchester, Amsterdam, Hamburg, Melbourne and Montreal. Licences were sold at high prices for other companies to use the patent in Britain. The Tomkinson empire prospered.[2]

Young Wilfred wanted for little, for money meant nothing to his father; he seldom knew the state of his bank account and he was not interested in the total of his assets. In 1882, when Wilfred was five years old the Tomkinsons sold Sunnyside, beside the village church which Michael – as religious as Annie – had helped to establish. They moved to Franche Hall, just a few hundred yards along the road. The family, now numbering eight children (Marion had been born a year after Wilfred, while Raymond followed in 1880 and Geoffrey in 1881), settled like lords of the manor into this grandiose fourteen-bedroom Victorian mansion of dull red brick, with a slate roof and stone pillared porch in 16 acres. Their purchase also brought them the adjacent home farm of nearly 100 acres.

For the next nine years Wilfred was to witness the consolidation of the Tomkinson dynasty, one which was to acquire a second estate – mainly for shooting, fishing and farming at Chilton, near Cleobury Mortimer – and the complete side of the main street in Kidderminster. In all it was an administrative area of twelve properties in 5,000 acres. Franche Hall employed thirty staff, including a head gardener and four labourers, a coachman and groom, a farm bailiff and two head keepers. Each week a carcass of fresh meat was sent from Chilton for consumption at the hall, where business guests often demanded from fifty to a hundred meals a day. Michael and Annie were the forerunners of public relations officers and turned their mansion into an open house for business associates. Their table became famous in the area for its home-produced greenhouse strawberries, grapes, peaches, nectarines and orchids. Little was eaten which was not produced by the estates. Yet in contradictory fashion the Tomkinsons were not ostentatious for the times or for their wealth. Rarely was there a large ten-course meal, popular among Victorian socialites. A typical dinner would be of five courses: soup; fish or fowl; beef; apple pie, which Annie baked herself; fruit and cheese. Breakfast was bulkier, with porridge, eggs, trout, sausages, bacon and devilled chicken drumsticks.

All this would be recorded item by item in Annie's diary. She was meticulous about her larder and noted in 1886 that it contained 226 jars of seventeen different types of jams. Annie, who performed all the administrative tasks, such as working out the wages – she wrote the cook's salary in French for secrecy's sake – staff training, paying insurance, keeping accounts, was well schooled for it. She was one of the first women to sit for an external examination and at sixteen had passed the Cambridge senior local examination with distinction.[3] It was as well she was a gifted organizer, for she released Michael from all home problems to conserve his energy for business and recreation.

From his later diaries it does not appear that Wilfred was close to his father, although this was to be expected. Michael's business brain worked overtime on planning bold new ventures. Long spells of negotiations led to exhaustion and recurring headaches. Some of the photographs of him, which survive, depict him as a hollow-eyed, grey-bearded man with cadaverous cheeks and the look of a migraine sufferer. His major mental asset was the ability to think and speak clearly about a project; as a committee chairman he could quickly clarify and précis a subject for his associates. Wilfred was seven when his father was elected to Kidderminster Council; at eight he understood his father was a magistrate; a year later he became the son of the mayor. The honours continued; for six subsequent years Michael was to be mayor, with Annie, after twenty years of child-bearing, his mayoress; he also became high sheriff and deputy lieutenant of Worcestershire.

Although the children were told that they now had a great family tradition to live up to in the county, they were not pampered at home. Often Wilfred and his brothers and sisters would be designated jobs around the garden, and once all were required to help lift massive stones when a large rockery was being constructed. During lawn-cutting operations they would take it in turns to lead the pony, fitted with large, flat-bottomed leather shoes so that his shod hooves did not mark the turf on which tennis and cricket would be played. In the gazebo were stored flags of many nations, which were run up a fine pole to mark the visits of overseas customers.

Until the age of ten, Wilfred lived with his six brothers and three sisters (there were still three more children to be born) in the large day and night nurseries. Some of the younger ones were taught the rudiments of arithmetic and grammar by his eldest sister Gertrude, but after her came several governesses, whom Annie insisted on being old and disagreeable so that they could not be won over by her sons.

Childhood problems among her offspring were many. Geoffrey, four years younger than Wilfred, was so thin that a doctor's advice was sought. Starvation was the cause, Annie was told. It transpired that Geoffrey, as one of the youngest, sat some way from where the food was dished up, and Wilfred and his brothers and sisters had been eating his share. More serious was the condition of Harry, just over two years Wilfred's senior, who had heart trouble and was always delicate. He died at the age of eight, having told his mother 'God will take care of me.' The words were engraved on his headstone in Wolverley churchyard.

During 1884–6 the area experienced several epidemics. Wilfred caught whooping cough and chicken-pox, but smallpox and typhoid, which swept through Kidderminster, did not affect the residents of Franche Hall as the house had its own sewerage and water systems.

Once a day the children were paraded for parental inspection after being scrupulously washed. As a treat they would be quietly ushered into Annie's personal writing-room. There, alongside a marquetry, circular-topped pedestal table, a fine walnut davenport and chairs upholstered in red velvet, all set out on the inevitable blue ground Axminster carpet, those sea adventures of their grandfather would be related.

Forbidden territory was their father's study, with its large American oak roll-top desk, black Wedgwood bust of Shakespeare and several large bronzes – again all on a blue ground Axminster. Here he kept his collection of cameras and a chest-of-drawers containing smoking equipment. For many a leisure hour Michael would be closeted, examining and cataloguing his assembly of Japanese art, displayed in a museum gallery, which eventually built up into the most valuable in the world, with thousands of pieces ranging from netsuke and inros, to armour and sculpture.

Forbidden, too, was entry to one of the two libraries in the house. Here Michael, a fervent collector, allowed friends and students to browse over classic tomes, which included a ninth-century book, first editions of Caxton and Shakespeare, and letters by Washington, Louis XIV, Charles II, Prince Rupert and luminaries of Victorian literature. His friend C.W. Dyson Perrin, the owner of Lea & Perrins Worcester sauce, coveted one of the Caxtons so much that he swapped it for his motor car, a Delaunay Belville, which in turn became the prized vehicle of the Tomkinson children.

Many of Annie's household hours were spent arranging dinner parties for their growing circle of friends, which included Alfred Baldwin (the head of an iron and steel foundry in nearby Bewdley) and his wife, the parents of the future prime minister, and John Brinton, a Liberal MP and the popularly styled 'King of Kidderminster'. For example, her diary for February 1887 gives details of seven dinner parties, two dances and one soirée at Franche Hall. Neither was the children's entertainment neglected. Their birthdays were celebrated with parties of anything up to forty friends, followed the next day by a repeat for all pupils of Franche School.

All were encouraged in sporting activities, led by Michael. He was an enthusiastic cricketer and 'demon bowler' – if only underhand – and in the annual Franche Hall match against the borough police took nine wickets for eighteen runs. Old age did not stop his sporting prowess; he played his last cricket at seventy-nine, while seven years earlier he swam the River Severn. He was an accurate game shot and an expert fly fisherman. In this respect Wilfred was to follow him, loving the countryside and the sport it provided in shooting and fishing, as well as tennis, on four courts at the hall, and cricket. When Wilfred was eight, fifty-seven pheasants were shot by a small party in two days; the toll grew yearly until one day 403 pheasants were bagged with a selection of partridge, grouse, duck, woodcock, pigeon and hares, which abounded on the estate. From their own private waters at Chilton, trout were caught in prolific numbers. In one day 100 small specimens were hooked, only to be excelled several years later by the landing of 263 fish in four-and-a-half hours. For indoor pursuits there was a great organ at the hall and a telescope mounted in a swivelling dome.

There was little in the way of amusement that the Tomkinson properties could not provide. Nevertheless, holidays were considered essential; even for the winter they rented Sodington Hall, on the Shropshire borders, just 10 miles away. Summer vacations might be spent in Yorkshire – at Whitby or Scarborough – and moving the ménage meant chartering a third-class railway coach for the staff, a Pullman for Michael and Annie, a nursery carriage and a dining car, with lavatories and washing facilities alongside. When the children were older Michael and Annie would go abroad by themselves. Annie accompanied her husband to the United States in 1887, while Michael went on market research trips to Canada, Italy and Egypt. For weekends in London they would stay with the Baldwins. For the glorious twelfth they would reside with the Dyson Perrins at Ardross Castle, near Alness, where Michael, who had no qualms at bringing down dozens of grouse, refused to shoot deer.

At the age of eleven it was time for Wilfred to leave the cloistered, cared-for, if clamorous, confines of the nursery at Franche Hall, and go to Kidderminster Grammar School. It must have been a shock to his constitution, for in an entry in his diary many years later, when considering the development of his own son, he admitted that he himself was a late developer. Around this time his uncle John took him to a naval review at Portsmouth and from what he saw there, coupled with his mother's tales of the sea, he became determined to join the Royal Navy. His eldest brother, Herbert, was already at Winchester College, while Gerald, Wilfred's senior by fourteen months, was at Rugby. Both seemed certain to join their father to safeguard Tomkinson nepotism at the factory, and it was this, allied to his longing for the sea, which sent Wilfred on a different course.

2
FAMED FRIENDSHIP

When Wilfred Tomkinson clattered up the gangplank of the old wooden three-decker HMS *Britannia* moored on the River Dart at Dartmouth in Devon, with the even more ancient *Hindostan* tied alongside, he walked into a cauldron of controversy. The year was 1891, not a vintage one for the Royal Navy's training school, but a memorable one for the slight, blond, clean-complexioned Tomkinson, with a petulant lower lip resembling that of a latter-day Winston Churchill. He still had fifteen weeks to go to his fourteenth birthday and his callowness would have made him a target for the bullying which was fast becoming a national scandal for new entries.[1]

Diminutive cadets were threatened with physical violence by a gang, who demanded a penny protection money for what was called 'unmolested passage', which generally meant stopping them from using the bridge that linked *Britannia* to the *Hindostan*.[2] Although there is no record in the Tomkinson papers of Wilfred having been subjected to this blackmail – indeed there is little documentation of his early life in the navy – one of his contemporaries, Hugh Tweedie, who was to become an admiral and a knight later in life, made revelations of the bullying. The gang was exposed by an anonymous term-mate of Tweedie who, during a visit by his parents, stayed ashore and refused to return until the bullying was stopped. Eventually seven delinquents were expelled by the captain, Noel Digby.[3]

Newspapers obtained the story a month after Tomkinson joined, and this caused *The Times* to castigate the Admiralty for turning a Nelsonian blind-eye to the bullying, which was claimed to be rife. Their leader writer suggested that it was only possible in a training ship and implied that conditions in public schools were mild compared with the jail-like atmosphere of *Britannia*.[4] Michael Tomkinson and Annie read these comments and probably feared for their son, who had progressed through the more genteel hurly-burly of nursery and grammar school and finally on to a cramming course at Stubbington College. They could not have missed the correspondence columns of *The Times*, which in the autumn of 1891 were cluttered with letters about *Britannia*. One correspondent wanted Digby and his officers relieved; another suggested that the captain be replaced by a civilian headmaster who had ideas of training, other than those based on corporal punishment.

In spite of the expulsion of the gang, the penny blackmailing continued, with variations, until a new college was built ashore fourteen years later. Even without the bullying,

Wilfred was plunged into a spartan life, involving little education. The running of the ship was left in the hands – exceedingly tough hands – of a cadet sergeant nicknamed Skajjer. Rarely would Tomkinson have seen the captain or the commander, except in church. Often missing were two lieutenants, who kept day on, day off duty; it was rumoured that they only met at Paddington Station, where they exchanged notes.[5]

Naval instructors arrived onboard at 9 a.m., but left in the late afternoon. Little thought was given to modern training; instead there was an obsession for religion, and in the entrance examinations it was allotted 100 marks out of a total of 550. Annie, who always wore a large nun-like crucifix on a heavy chain around her neck, was delighted that Wilfred was required to study the scriptures every day, while after Sunday church an hour was devoted to answering religious questions, followed by another hour of New Testament instruction and a further half-an-hour studying the Old Testament. Yet this preponderance of the Bible did not sour Wilfred's religious upbringing, and for the rest of his life he remained a devout church-goer.[6]

Most senior officers of that day had not been educated in depth and were afraid that the embryonic officers would be blinded by new science. Academic work was pushed to the back of educational classes. Instead, an unnecessary emphasis was placed on seamanship, with lessons in rigging and sail drill, but there was a complete void in the sciences, although steam was rapidly replacing wind power. When Wilfred went to sea in the schooling vessel the *Racer*, a barque-rigged sloop of 970 tons, her auxiliary engine was used only for leaving and entering Dartmouth Harbour.[7] Cadets were not even shown around the engine-room. For most this was not a disappointment as they preferred to be out of the stuffy, oil-cloying engine-room and 'up top', where there were ladders to climb, sails to reef and furl in the fresh salt-tanged air. In the classroom they were not required to exercise their brains beyond professional subjects, like navigation and seamanship, all taught by non-commissioned officers, who were first of all professional ratings and secondly amateur teachers. Important guidelines on the conduct becoming to an officer, or how to treat the men on the lower deck, were ignored. The result was the creation of an officer class who generally regarded the men as servants in peacetime and cannon fodder in wartime.

In fact, the *Britannia* was a mental rest camp for cadets, such as Wilfred, whose brains had been overtaxed by the cramming that they had to endure to get into the service. Naval historian, the late Stephen Roskill, maintained that this ill-thought-out system of training was based on forcing cadets into a preconceived and rigid mould by the application of harsh, even inhumane, discipline. Any deviant who showed signs of independence, individuality or originality was stamped on. Sports and religion were the prime requisites; intellectuality was not sought. Toughness and self-discipline were essential.[8]

Although cadets grumbled about the regime – routine was carried out to the command of bugles or bells[9] – they had few complaints about the way they were fed. Wilfred's breakfast, for example, would consist of porridge, omelette, or buttered eggs, and ham and tongue. Cream, the bane of future generations, was served at least three times a week. There was always the sport, in which all-rounder Wilfred was to excel, especially at rugby (he eventually played for the navy and Harlequins), soccer, cricket and tennis, his first love.

The system ruined a great deal of potential officer material and many left disgruntled after a few years' service.[10] Wilfred, however, enjoyed it, and even in the gloomiest days ahead, with disgrace threatening, he never regretted joining, or bore the Admiralty a grudge for the ignominy they were to heap on him.

In the same year as his at *Britannia* were Dudley Pound, who headed the pre-entry examination list and whose brilliance propelled him to First Sea Lord in the Second World War; Frederic Dreyer, top in navigation, who by dogged paperwork was to become a sea lord; and George Chetwode, destined to be a rear admiral and naval secretary to the First Lord. All were to become his friends; two were to betray that friendship when he needed it most.

During the summer of 1893, having completed his cadetship at *Britannia*, Tomkinson went on leave to Franche. It was something of a surprise to him to learn that his mother was pregnant again at the age of forty-three. An even bigger surprise was the product of her confinement – twins Charles and Christine. And still in the nursery were Francis, aged ten, Dora, three years younger, and Margaret, just two. The twins were the twelfth and thirteenth and the last children for the Tomkinsons; yet their enlarged family did not prevent Michael accepting the mayoralty for the next three years, or Annie playing a major part in his success by being his mayoress. No other borough could have had a 'first lady' who had just given birth to twins at over forty.[11]

A month after the arrival of his new brother and sister, sixteen-year-old midshipman Tomkinson joined at Chatham the newly commissioned 14,150 ton battleship *Empress of India*, the Atlantic Fleet flagship of Rear Admiral Edward Seymour. Unfortunately, his midshipman's log, which every 'snotty' was required to keep, does not survive today. The first six years of his career followed the normal peacetime pattern. Young officers needed a colonial war to enhance their advancement, but the period from 1893 to the turn of the century was generally a peaceful one for the navy. In his two-year commission on the *Empress of India*, Tomkinson's life was spent in the transition from cadet to seagoing midshipman. His main duties were with the signal staff, but he also had to handle ships' boats, obey orders of seniors without question and generally act as a public school type of fag to everyone in the wardroom.

His next commission, prior to promotion, was a broader one. While his father was travelling to Naples and Egypt, Wilfred was further abroad, onboard the cruiser *Crescent*,[12] based in Bermuda, and calling at Martinique, Trinidad, Quebec and Halifax. His sporting skill – unusually, he played both soccer and rugby for the ship – made him a popular member of the gunroom. By the end of the two-year commission he had attained the rank of acting sub-lieutenant and was sent to the shore base, HMS *Excellent*,[13] at Portsmouth, where he requalified in gunnery and then took a pilotage course at the Admiralty.

By 1898 he had been in the navy for seven years, but like others of his age-group at *Britannia*, had yet to progress beyond sub-lieutenant, and like them, too, he knew that advancement would be slow unless he became involved in a war . . . and that war came in the unlooked-for theatre of China.

Tomkinson joined the destroyer *Hart*[14] in November 1898 at Hong Kong, and as first lieutenant, in name only, he soon found himself under the compelling leadership of the twenty-six-year-old Lieutenant Roger Brownlow Keyes. At first sight his new commanding officer was anything but prepossessing. He was inclined to initial shyness, stuttered when first introduced, was slight in stature, a little deaf and had a crooked arm caused by a break. He had scraped through the entrance examination to *Britannia*,[15] where he had passed out at a low grade six years ahead of Tomkinson. Since then most of his seatime had been spent in destroyers, the last being the high-freeboard three-funnelled *Opossum*. Destroyer skippers always had a reputation for dashing command and, although Keyes did not look the part, he fitted the archetypal role, and the more Tomkinson got to know him the more he knew he would follow him anywhere. Not that it seemed likely that there would be any derring-do in China, for Admiral Seymour, Tomkinson's first contact with a flag officer as a cadet in the *Empress of India*, now the commander-in-chief of the China Station, had made it known to the officers in his command that there was 'no chance of action with an enemy, no hope of promotion or distinction for war service',[16] although his squadron was on the brink of some of the most active service of any sailors in the navy's history. Few high-ranking officers knew of the political undertow lurking in Chinese waters, which was to boil into the Boxer Rebellion.

Foreign diplomats were astonishingly ignorant of the thunder of discontent rolling on through the countryside, as European interlopers carved up the corpse of China, bled white after the end of the war with Japan in 1895.[17] Germany stepped in first by taking over Shantung and transforming it into an oriental Prussia; Russia grabbed a lease on Port Arthur and the right to build a connection with the Trans-Siberian railway; France seized the safe anchorage of Kwangchownan on the southern coast, while Italy claimed a naval station in Chekiang province. Amid all the chicanery Britain was not a lethargic witness and was the forerunner of the dismembering of China by taking Hong Kong in 1841, the Kowloon peninsula in 1860 and the so-called New Territories behind the peninsula, up to a line from Mirs Bay to Deep Bay, in 1898. It had also staked out the Yangtze valley. China, even then with a population of 350,000,000, had little rich land remaining, as the 'foreign devils' insisted on trading and mining rights and concessions to build all the railways.[18]

Members of the Imperial Chinese Government, headed by the wily, old dowager Empress Tzu Hsi, were adamant that a stop must be put to the disintegration of their country into a patchwork of foreign provinces, and on 21 November 1899 they delivered a caveat to the viceroys and governors of all provinces that the position was getting out of hand and that 'there may occur incidents in which we are forced to face the situation.'[19] It was the first official encouragement by a government, woefully short of armed forces, to Chinese secret societies to start a guerilla war, and from it re-emerged the Fists of Righteous Harmony, interpreted by foreigners as the Boxers, an organization which was suppressed in 1808 but now revived for its stance against Christianity and missionaries and its belief in invulnerability against the colonialists' weapons.[20] At first the official Chinese army fought the Boxers, but eventually, with the off-stage blessing of the empress, they battled together side by side. For most of 1899 the Boxers slaughtered with impunity in the countryside, with the occasional execution for the murder of a European.[21]

10

These incidents should have been the harbinger of catastrophe for westerners, as they presaged Chinese national resentment caused by the creation of new railways, which brought unemployment to thousands of carters and boatmen; the opening of telegraph lines, looked on as an insult to the gods of the air and water; and the failure of two successive harvests, floods and a plague of locusts. Civil disobedience broke out in town after town; European churches were razed to the ground by fire.

Before this, during the first months of Tomkinson's introduction to Hong Kong, the social scene had continued apace, with dances, banquets, polo and horse racing beckoning ashore. As first lieutenant of the 275-ton *Hart*, which had been on the station for two years, he knew that soon she would be paid off. Nevertheless, when the time came in the New Year of 1899 she was one of the 'tiddliest' ships of the fleet, with white-painted hull and superstructure and two short yellow funnels, their copper cowls burnished like gold. Her replacement was the 30-knot, 310-ton *Fame*, which, with the *Whiting*, had been sent to Hong Kong in the previous year, but kept in reserve. Tomkinson now had the task of getting his charge shipshape, especially as Keyes did not like the original look of her. His captain's cabin, in particular, was cramped because of her low freeboard, and an exhaust steam pipe for the steering engine ran just over his bunk, turning it into a veritable Turkish bath when at sea.[22] She was also due for a three-month refit and this gave Tomkinson the chance to arrange for the extermination of swarms of giant tropical cockroaches, which had made their nests in every dark nook and cranny and which came out to gorge unprotected food. The fleet surgeon advised sealing the ship hermetically and fumigating with smoke charges. To carry this out, the ship's company were moved ashore; the fumigation process was successful, but for days afterwards the *Fame* stank of sulphur.

Keyes was able to pick his crew from the *Hart* and the *Fame* and he chose wisely, sagacity which he was able to apply throughout the rest of his illustrious naval career. Despite the fact that John Ham, the chief engineer, was years older than himself and also senior in rank, he persuaded him to stay in the *Fame* and his knowledge got her out of many mechanical mishaps. In contrast, Keyes' choice as the gunner was Warrant Officer Mascull, a young bachelor like himself and Tomkinson, who became a 'good messmate'.

While the *Fame* was being refitted, Tomkinson sampled the delightful climate and outdoor pleasures of Hong Kong. There was golf, cricket and swimming to satisfy his sporting appetite; there was good company in the officers of the Fourth King's Own, the Royal Welch Fusiliers and an introduction through Keyes to Prince Henry of Prussia, who commanded a German squadron from his flagship *Deutschland*. A strange link of affinity was forged between Tomkinson and his commanding officer. Keyes was a dashing horseman in point-to-point racing, polo and in the hunting field, yet his first lieutenant never got into the saddle, except to cycle. Indeed, for the next three months, while Tomkinson and Ham took up their responsibilities of ensuring that the *Fame* and her crew were on top line for service, Keyes, as he was to admit later, had 'a very happy and amusing time'.[23]

The duties of destroyers on the China Station were mainly as 'dispatch riders', or tenders to the flagships. In these pre-wireless days they raced to deliver long messages, pick

11

up mail, or transmit missives from the nearest telegraph station. They needed to be able to raise steam quickly and to slip into shallow waters denied to larger warships. Because they were often used to carry admirals or governors on diplomatic missions, it was also essential that paintwork and brasswork be impeccable and the crews immaculately turned out. Early in March, with her overhaul completed, the *Fame* went on gunnery and torpedo firing trials, with Keyes, full of charismatic leadership and burning ambition, determined she should excel in speed and smartness. He was not to be disappointed, for after a captain's inspection Keyes was able to write:

> Captain Bayly inspected the ship last Monday and gave a very flattering report.The men shot well and drilled well and I brought the ship in through about a mile of crowded shipping and junks at 20 knots and didn't alter the speed until I turned sharp round and went full steam astern, just stopping dead at the buoy by real good luck. Rather a gallery proceeding, but he was much impressed and very complimentary.But he was fairly on his toes with anxiety until we were safely tied up.

Keyes' braggadocio might sometimes be tempered by the quiet, more thoughtful, advice of Tomkinson, normally alongside him on the bridge, but the verve he displayed in speeding his ship into harbour came through reliance on Ham, who could bring the ship up 'all standing almost in her own length in response to an emergency signal for full speed astern'. Gunner Mascull had also trained the seamen to slide down a spar, jump on to a buoy with a hook rope and shackle swiftly on to a cable. But the pace of entering harbour through the jam of junks and sampans to the mooring off Murray Pier, almost under the window of the Hong Kong Club, shocked old-time mariners, as Keyes was proud to admit. This disregard of the threat to life was understandable to officers of Tomkinson's ilk, for the Chinese regularly ignored the maritime rule of the road, with the resultant drowning of many coolies. Life was cheap in China.

The first test of the *Fame*'s readiness for a quick mission came one Saturday early in April 1899. Keyes told Tomkinson and Ham that steam was to be raised for full speed, while he reported to Commodore F. Powell for immediate orders. On his return Keyes briefed his officers; there had been an outbreak of civil disobedience in the New Territories, with slogans displayed by Boxers inciting the populace to burn Britain's new buildings and drive out the 'foreign devils'. The *Fame* was to take the governor, Sir Henry Blake, to Canton to parley with the viceroy for protection of property and workmen, with the insistence that the agitators be arrested.[24]

The remainder of that day the *Fame* lay ready, with smoke curling from her funnels, as Keyes and Tomkinson waited to receive the diplomatic mission. Sir Henry did not arrive until 5.30 the next morning, together with the colonial secretary, Stewart Lockhart, his military secretary, Major Somerville, the aide-de-camp, Viscount Suirdale (later the Earl of Donoughmore) and Clive Bigham (later Viscount Mersey), then a young guardsman on his way to Peking to be a legation attaché.

To negotiate the River Canton, which would be at dead low water, a Chinese pilot was picked up. Sir Henry wanted to be in Canton by 10 a.m., which gave the *Fame* just five hours for a distance of 86 miles up a hazardous river. Soon after she left her mooring she worked up to 25 knots, but this had to be cut by several knots as she fairly planed along the river. Her wake churned the muddy water, sending a great wave against the banks and swamping several sampans. Keyes and Tomkinson on the bridge were anxious about grounding, but were still exhilarated as their little ship sped through, with the pilot, who had never travelled at more than 10 knots, shaking his head in fearful disbelief. While the diplomats breakfasted with Keyes, Tomkinson pushed the *Fame* on to such an extent that she covered 82 miles in four hours. Her progress was impeded by river traffic for the last stretch, which took nearly thirty minutes, but just before 10 a.m. she was tied up to a buoy off the British consulate, with Sir Henry congratulating Keyes for arriving on time, and Keyes congratulating Tomkinson for arriving without an accident. Within minutes Keyes, clutching a suitcase in which he had his full dress uniform, and the diplomats were being piped overboard, bound for the viceroy's palace.

Tomkinson waited patiently onboard for the party's return. After seven hours they appeared, with the sky darkening and Keyes eager to get back to Hong Kong. On the way he told Tomkinson that the negotiations had ended satisfactorily, with the viceroy undertaking to send 3,000 militia to keep order in the New Territories. Before the *Fame* could clear the river the searchlight had to be used to penetrate the darkness. On the bridge the pilot urged Keyes to anchor for a couple of hours. 'Catchee moon at 11.30,' he begged. Keyes replied: 'Catchee Hong Kong at 10 o'clock.' The *Fame* moored off Murray Pier at 9.55 p.m.[25]

Tomkinson and the *Fame* were involved in what was to become known as gunboat diplomacy for the next few weeks. Often it was triggered by the hot-headed vigour and unhesitant patriotism of Keyes and, although Tomkinson was more calm and meticulous in his approach, there was born a team spirit and *rapprochement* between them which survived all adversity and criticism in the fifty years of comradeship that lay ahead.

In the days following the *Fame*'s return to Hong Kong came several portents of the troubles that would turn Chinese provinces into battlegrounds. Within a few hours of the Canton mission, the ship's company were aroused at 1.30 a.m. and ordered to load 50 tons of coal and sail for Mirs Bay. Sixteen of the crew were on night shore leave and could not be recalled, so Tomkinson borrowed replacements from the battleship *Victorious*. The destroyer *Whiting* had already left, after embarking a general and 100 Welch Fusiliers.

The emergency concerned the chief of police at Mirs, who had managed to send a message calling for immediate assistance after being surrounded by hordes of hostiles. Soon after leaving at 5.30 a.m., the *Fame* ran into thick fog, which made the entrance tricky around two headlands into the bay. Here Tomkinson learned a valuable navigation lesson from Keyes. As the *Fame* ran adjacent to the shore, he made a note of the exact number of revolutions of the engines and blasted the siren in the direction of the land. 'When opposite each headland by dead reckoning we turned and stood slowly towards it until the echo of the siren came back,' Keyes reported later. 'On each occasion we were able to recognise the headlands less than a hundred yards off.' Nevertheless, for the last turn into the bay the dinghy had to be launched so that seamen could guide the *Fame* in. The fog

13

suddenly thickened and then lifted just as quickly. Ahead Tomkinson saw the *Whiting* anchored, but with water pouring out of her ejectors. The *Fame* stopped alongside and Keyes was told by Lieutenant Edward Kelly, the *Whiting*'s captain, that she had hit the last promontory head-on at 20 knots. All the damage was to her bows, but no one was hurt.

This mercy mission was in vain, however, for when the army and the *Fame*'s landing-party were put ashore they were told by villagers that the police had marched safely away and had reached Hong Kong almost at the same time as the *Fame* had arrived in Mirs Bay.[26]

It was disappointing for Keyes who, like his father, a fighting general on the North West frontier in Afghanistan, was thirsting for battle; but on 14 April he nearly got into one. Again there was unrest at Mirs Bay – this time by pirates. They had threatened to burn down the new police quarters at Tai-Po-Hei, so the *Fame* was ordered to embark the chief of police, fifteen Sikhs and two European sergeants to occupy the building. By the time they arrived, the police quarters was a smouldering ruin. From the handful of villagers remaining they elicited the information that 1,000 men had invaded, set the building aflame and chased off all the coolies. Keyes, who had landed with the police, was met with cannon fire, which they thought was due to firecrackers from a 'large body of men'. Keyes entreated the chief to allow him to order ashore Tomkinson and a detachment of bluejackets to put down the disturbance. However, the chief refused because he had no authority to use arms and could not ask the navy to attack unless they were fired on. Crestfallen, Keyes did as he was asked and the whole force retreated to Hong Kong.[27]

The next day he was disobeying orders to involve the *Fame* in her first encounter. Because of windy weather, a tug was unable to take guns and food to an encampment of Pathans of the Hong Kong Regiment, who were occupying part of the New Territories, where the governor was to unfurl the British flag. Instead, the *Fame* was to act as errand boy, deliver the stores and take with her seven Welch Fusiliers signallers and Major Long, a staff officer of the Army Service Corps. On the approach to Tai-Po-Hei, an army launch hailed the *Fame*. Keyes was told by the sergeant in charge that the Pathans had been attacked and were surrounded by masses of hostiles, probably the ones seen the previous day. Long opened a note from the Pathans' commanding officer which the launch was taking back to the general. Although it indicated that the Pathans were not in danger, they were hesitant about attacking until they acquired reinforcements and more ammunition. Long, like Keyes, was also looking for action, and added to the message that he and Keyes would drive off the enemy. Keyes also wrote a strong note to his commodore, stressing that he would not return until the matter was settled. 'Long and I agreed that we must finish the job before any generals or commodores could arrive on the scene,' he said later. 'Mercifully wireless was in its infancy in those days and had not been fitted in Her Majesty's ships.'

Tomkinson was ordered to send the men to action stations and to have a landing-party of sixteen men ready. Keyes had no intention of staying onboard. As soon as the *Fame* anchored, he was off in the dinghy with Long, the seven signallers and 3,000 rounds of ammunition. Tomkinson looked on admiringly, as for the last half mile they waded through shallow muddy water. Now all he had to occupy his time was to watch for the signal to open fire. During his vigil he heard the explosions of falling balls from the tiny Chinese cannon, called jingals, but no rifle fire. Then just before dark, a signaller reported a message from the shore, which gave the bearing of the Chinese batteries and the order to open fire. From a distance of 2,600 yards the first shell of the *Fame*'s twelve-pounder scored a direct hit on the largest cluster of jingals; shell after shell plummetted on the batteries. After seventeen shots, Tomkinson received another signal from Keyes to cease fire, so that the tiny British force could attack. He was also ordered to lead *Fame*'s landing-party ashore.

By the time Tomkinson and his men had squelched to the rescue, the impatient Keyes had led a charge of fifty shrieking Pathans as the Chinese retreated down a hill. Not content with this Keyes and Tomkinson joined up with Long's force to attack a Chinese entrenchment of about fifty. By now it was dark, but the British officers and the Pathans clambered up the hill and fired a volley into the trench. Bayonets were fixed, but when the Pathans raced into the line, the Chinese abandoned it. The operation was called off and the force returned to the original camp, where for the next three hours Tomkinson had the *Fame*'s crew turned to and wading with loads of supplies through 800 yards of clinging mud up to the camp on the hill.

It was agreed to start flushing out the Chinese again at 4 a.m., with Tomkinson returning to the ship to land a mountain gun to defend the camp while the raiding party were away. Such was Keyes' magical power of leadership that everyone wanted to join in. He finally decided to command it himself, accompanied by Tomkinson and twenty men; again not an executive officer was left onboard the ship.

At dawn the march began to mop up the hostiles, but the enemy, having tasted the cordite of the *Fame*'s shells, failed to form up again for an attack. The contingent trudged on into two more villages, which had defensive positions, but as they approached the rebels ran off. After four hours without firing a shot the detachment returned to their base, where a squad of Indian Mountain Artillery had arrived with the news that another 400 soldiers of the Hong Kong Regiment were due to bolster defences.

When the situation had stabilized, the *Fame* was dispatched the next day to patrol one side of the narrow neck of land, which connected Kowloon with the New Territories, to prevent a large force of Chinese attacking Kowloon itself. But also in the area was a Chinese gunboat which Keyes illuminated with the *Fame*'s searchlight. She was crowded with excited troops, so he tried to keep them awake all night by occasionally turning the beam on them.

By now the British had decided to drive out the Chinese rabbles completely, and the entire Hong Kong garrison was turned out to push them away. On the left flank, the *Fame* linked with the Welch Fusiliers to provide cover with her guns, but the enemy faded away and there were no casualties. At the end of the skirmishes the *Fame* returned to Hong Kong, where Tomkinson and Keyes read with amusement the reports in the Canton newspapers of the uprising. At first it was claimed that the *Fame* had been sunk, only for it to be refuted the next day with the statement that she had been forced to withdraw to Hong Kong. Another account described the *Fame* as being in league with the devil by using 'his

15

evil eye [the searchlight] and got him to drop burning things, which could not have come from the ship, as they fell from the sky.' Tomkinson attained some credit for his gunnery from the report, which said that fifteen Chinese were killed by naval shells.[28]

For the next six months Tomkinson was involved in the routine of showing the British flag, as the fleet sailed around the Far East. When in harbour, he virtually ran the ship, while Keyes indulged in his passions of polo and horse racing whenever he could, even to the extent of ignoring sailing orders from his admiral so he could attend the races at Shanghai and transport one of his ponies.

The *Fame* was the tender of the battleship *Barfleur*, flying the flag of Rear Admiral 'Rough' Fitzgerald, but she did not arrive until June, later to be joined by David Beatty, newly promoted to commander for his part in the Nile expedition, and in the future to become an ally of Tomkinson.

With enmity towards the Western powers growing, the entire China Squadron met at Wei-Hai-Wei and sailed in company across the Yellow Sea to Port Hamilton, for a show of strength. The grand tour then began, with the *Fame* scurrying in and out of difficult harbours to send, or collect, telegrams. Korea, Korniloff Bay, Vladivostock, Possiette, Hakodate (in Japan's north island), Yokohama, Kobe, Nagasaki and Shanghai . . . most of the prestigious ports and safe anchorages were visited and not without adventure. Many places were still uncharted and Keyes and Tomkinson often went ashore to look at the lie of the land for future reference. In the China Sea strong southerly winds forced the squadron to give a wide berth of the low and unlit Samarang Rocks. The *Fame* was ordered to take up a look-out position on the port bow of the *Barfleur*, with the *Whiting* on the starboard. As the *Fame* surged a mile ahead, her look-out sighted breakers on the port beam; they were so close that Keyes had to put the helm hard to port to avoid going aground. Tomkinson fired Very lights and blew the siren as a warning. The *Barfleur*'s helm was jammed over for an alteration of 16 points and the rest of the squadron followed her to clear the rocks.

There was no escape, however, for the cruiser *Bonaventure* a month later when exercising in Korniloff Bay. Keyes and Tomkinson were on the *Fame*'s bridge when they saw the cruiser's bows bounce upwards and remain there. As she listed heavily to starboard, Keyes, showing all his usual disregard to regulations, ordered full speed ahead to the rescue, passing dangerously through the lines of the remainder of the squadron. But soon after, Tomkinson handed him a quick confirmation of the approval of Admiral Seymour, who had signalled '*Fame* close *Bonaventure*' minutes later, when the *Fame* was well on her way. On inspection, they discovered that the cruiser had been speared by an uncharted rock. She was stuck on it for four days until she was unloaded and floated clear.

The *Fame* herself was fortunate not to be sunk on her way back alone from Vladivostock to rejoin the fleet at Korniloff Bay. Later Keyes was to relate:

In order to shorten the trip I decided to go through the narrow eastern channel, which I had not used hitherto, owing to fog and darkness. As we were running in at about 20 knots, yawing at least three points each way, owing to the following swell, we saw right ahead of us, as we yawed to starboard, a great black pinnacle of rock. I put the helm hard a starboard and we went through two or three agonising seconds, wondering if she would swing enough on the yaw to port to clear the rock. We tore past on the crest of the next great swell as it broke with a roar on the rock almost alongside us, and Tomkinson and I looked at each other speechless with relief.

Again, this rock was uncharted and when its exact position was confirmed and noted it was called Fame Rock, a name that remains today.[29]

In all his adventures, Keyes wrote Tomkinson into the scenario, almost as though he wanted his friend to be able to corroborate the many tight spots they were in together.

Like most fleet cruises, the social and sporting occasions were many. Often both men shot and fished together. One Sunday they discovered a little salmon river, but the fish would not take fly, so Tomkinson used a spoon to catch a 17-pounder. It was sent with his compliments to Admiral Fitzgerald, who returned the courtesy by dispatching to the *Fame* half a sheep and then dining Tomkinson and Keyes in the flagship. Several days later they landed a great 50 lb salmon, but they kept this fish for their wardroom.

Pheasants were hard to bring down because there was no dog to flush them out, but this was compensated for when Tomkinson, very much the amateur ornithologist, spotted hundreds of rock pigeons flying out of several caves. It was impossible to land, so they went out in the dinghy and although 'not conducive to accuracy' they shot sixty-two pigeons from the boat.

On one occasion Keyes' fondness for horses led to his complete disregard of orders and brought both him and Tomkinson in contention with Admiral Seymour. At Wei-Hai-Wei Keyes purchased a polo pony for a bargain price; not content with that, he and Tomkinson hoisted the animal onboard the *Fame*, with the intention of taking it to Shanghai for shipment to Hong Kong. Unfortunately for them, when they arrived at Woosung there were new orders. Keyes was stopped by Lieutenant-Commander Kelly, of the *Whiting*, from going up the Yangtze to Shanghai. Instead, the *Fame* was ordered to wait for the arrival of the *Empress of India*, which Tomkinson was required to board with 'one petty officer and five ABs and 20 rounds each, to be joined by a similar number of men from the *Whiting*.' He was instructed to protect one of the passengers, Kang Yu Wei, a refugee reformer, regarded as dangerous by the Chinese government. 'He is to be constantly watched by day and night by at least two ABs,' Tomkinson's written orders stated. 'You are to signal should any attempt be made to molest this man.'[30]

This put Keyes' plans into disarray because his pony was running out of fodder and needed to be landed. 'So I turned a blind eye to the signal and went up to Shanghai, exceeding the speed limit, I fear,' he confessed afterwards. The pony was led off at Shanghai and the *Fame* returned to Woosung in time to intercept the *Empress of India*. Tomkinson, complete with cutlass and revolver, boarded her, but was told by the captain that the Chinese reformer was not among the passengers. Still Keyes was determined not to let naval business interfere with a polo tournament being played at Shanghai; the *Fame* returned there – again contrary to orders – and stayed for several days, Keyes knowing that Admiral Seymour was away cruising in his yacht, the *Alacrity*. But when Keyes was at the races, Tomkinson, who stayed onboard, was startled to see the *Alacrity* going up river. A messenger was landed to find Keyes, who hurried back. He reported himself to Seymour, who wanted to know why the *Fame* was still at Shanghai. Keyes admitted the races had kept him there, but this was the last day. Seymour admonished sarcastically: 'Then perhaps Mr Keyes you won't mind sailing tomorrow.'[31]

By the time the *Fame* reached Hong Kong she was due for a long overhaul and went into dockyard. Because of the continual coal-dust, heat and flies, Tomkinson spent as much time as he could ashore with the many friends he and Keyes had made. Both were envious of other colleagues who were with the Naval Brigade, fighting the Boers ashore in South Africa. It was this envy which was to lead Keyes into his own blood-and-thunder escapades in China, but for the moment the two young friends had to wait for their war. They also had to wait for the *Terrible*, which was bringing out reliefs for the ships' companies of the *Fame* and *Whiting*, who were becoming aggrieved at being on the China Station for more than three years. However, the *Terrible* had been diverted to the Cape to land every available fighting hand to stop the Boers. When she did arrive at Hong Kong on 8 May 1900, she was seven months overdue. Consequently, the new crew of the *Fame*, although looking very young and immature compared with the veteran two-badge ABs and stokers they replaced, were veterans of actions from Colenso to the relief of Ladysmith.

The *Fame* and the *Whiting* were now sent north to Wei-Hai-Wei, where other units of the Royal Navy were assembling in order to be on hand to counter any Chinese hostility in Peking. On the way to Shanghai, the *Fame*'s newly overhauled engines broke down, mainly due to the inexperience of her artificers and stokers, and she limped into Swatour for emergency repairs. Next morning the two destroyers sailed again, but 400 miles on the *Whiting* broke down. The two crawled to Shanghai, where repairs took three days. During the last stage of the voyage to Wei-Hai-Wei, the *Fame* lost contact with the *Whiting*, first through a fog and then because of a gale. At one stage Keyes and Tom--kinson 'turned to' themselves as a short, steep sea sent all but six of the young crew to their hammocks with seasickness. When the *Whiting* rejoined, her steering became faulty and her new temporary captain, junior to Keyes, sought permission to return to Shanghai, escorted by the *Fame*. Remembering his last clash with Admiral Seymour, Keyes decided he had best not go back to the attractions of Shanghai, so turned down the suggestion and struggled on without further incident to Wei-Hai-Wei. There the *Fame*'s engines were virtually taken to pieces to remedy the defects. While Keyes stayed ashore with James Bruce, the new admiral in the *Barfleur*, Tomkinson remained onboard to organize the painting of the ship. One side was still mottled with red lead patches, while the other gleamed in white enamel, when the emergency signal came: 'Prepare for sea at once.'[32]

For the next two months in the Boxer Rebellion, the *Fame* looked a different ship, depending on which side she was seen.

3
BOXER REBELLION

The reign of terror of the Boxers began to grip the countryside of northern China in the early summer of 1900. Every adversity suffered by China was blamed on the foreigners – some of it with good cause. The signs of a massive uprising were there for the Western diplomats to see, yet they were disastrously ignored, or at least not comprehended. As early as April 1900 a Boxer placard posted in Peking exhorted the people: 'The will of heaven is that the telegraph wires be first cut, then the railways torn up and then shall the foreign devils be decapitated.'[1] Three weeks later the *North China Herald* published a letter detailing a plot to crush all foreigners, which had the approval of the Chinese royalty, Manchu armies and the Imperial Guard.[2]

The uprising began just as the poster ordered – with the burning of railway stations on the lines to Peking; throughout nearby provinces riots increased; Christian churches were destroyed. By now even the over optimistic British minister in Peking, Sir Claude MacDonald, began to fear for the lives of nationals and sent a telegram asking for a naval guard to Admiral Seymour, now with the China Squadron in the *Centurion* at Wei-Hai-Wei.[3]

Within two days the cruiser *Orlando*, the sloop *Algerine* and thirteen vessels of other friendly powers arrived off the Taku forts at the entrance to the Pei Ho River, the umbilical cord to Tientsin, whose railway was, in turn, the lifeline for supplies and reinforcements to Peking. A combined allied landing-party of 337 was hastily collected. Surprisingly, they arrived in Peking without incident – but this increased the optimism of MacDonald that the Boxers would not dare attack the Western legations there.

It was in this climate of uncertainty and lack of reliable intelligence that the *Fame* was ordered on 30 May to sail to Taku. Although her engines were in pieces, the new engineering officer had them quickly assembled and she was able to steam out of Wei-Hai-Wei that evening, arriving the next day. She was to become a vital link in the communications of the British fleet.

Protecting the entrance to the river, 12 miles offshore, was a sand bar, over which there was only 2 ft of water at low tide, and 17 ft at high water. Because of the odd construction of her stern, the *Fame* drew just 8 feet of water, 2 ft less than her sister, the *Whiting*, and could negotiate the bar for two hours each side of high tide. For efficient communications, the sloop *Algerine* was anchored upstream in the Pei Ho, beyond the three Chinese-held forts, to receive telegrams and telephone calls from Tientsin, which had lines to Peking. All messages were then signalled to the *Whiting*, anchored 3 miles inside the sand bar, which in turn telegraphed messages to the *Alacrity*, which lay another 3 miles outside the bar, which relayed the information to the *Centurion*, the commander-in-chief's flag-ship, another 5 miles further out. In consequence when there were long orders or papers, the *Fame* was used as a dispatch rider again, constantly on the move backwards and for-wards across the bar, almost on every tide, night and day.[4]

Keyes and Tomkinson, who were on the bridge during these errands, became the local naval experts on navigation of the river. Under a trade agreement, pilots had to be employed for the 9 miles of water from the bar to the railhead town of Tongku. Tomkinson and Keyes made careful notes and fixed positions of all alterations of course, but it struck them that never were the plots the same; often one pilot altered his route. Over a tot of whisky one night they asked a sympathetic river navigator why was it neces-sary to vary the course; his reply was that 'pilots had to live'. Nevertheless, he gave the two officers several hints, which in the action ahead were invaluable.

Every movement of shipping was watched by the Chinese army, stationed in three modern forts, two on the north side of the river and one on the opposite edge of the mouth. Recently rearmed with rapid-firing 5 and 8 in Krupps cannon, they made formida-ble opponents for any navy in the world.

On 5 June the *Fame* was due to ferry 100 bluejackets to Tongku, where they would be entrained for Tientsin, as a standby force for Peking. Keyes was told that this defensive build-up must be kept secret and, if seen by the Chinese, might lead to a bombardment from the forts. Everyone, except Tomkinson, Keyes and the helmsman, was sent below deck as the *Fame* steamed up river; high on the bank, the batteries were trained on them as they went by. It was obvious to both men that if it came to a war, the forts would have to be destroyed by gunfire, or captured by an infantry assault.

For the next three successive days the *Fame* was employed in this manner, with Keyes becoming 'accustomed to looking down the muzzles of the Chinese guns, which followed us in and out of the river like the eyes of portraits in a gallery.'[5]

All the time the crisis in Peking was deepening, and on 9 June came news that the European ministers, their missions and families were sheltering in the British legation, with little hope of holding out for more than forty-eight hours, unless more troops were sent. Seymour, also the senior officer of all the navies afloat off Taku, called a conference of admirals onboard the *Centurion*, where every nation agreed to land detachments, all under his command, to help relieve Peking.[6]

Keyes was ordered to embark sailors from the sloop *Endymion* and then wait for Seymour, who wanted to cross the bar at the first tide. All other craft had left two hours ahead, and when Seymour arrived the *Fame* went full speed in the dark towards the pilot depot schooner anchored just outside the bar. No pilot was available, the tide was falling fast and, to make the passage more hazardous, all lights marking the mudbank were extin-guished. Keyes was told by Seymour that he and the bluejackets had to be in Tongku as soon as possible in order to board trains for Tientsin before the line was cut, but ques-tioned whether it was worth the risk. Showy Keyes would never have retreated, although he, too, had his doubts as the *Fame* edged over the bar, slithered like a sailor's squeegee through the mud into the deeper water and then kept to the courses that Tomkinson had jotted down on their earlier trips. Both young officers on the bridge had never seen the river so shallow as the ship passed adjacent mudbanks, which previously had not been exposed to them.

Confidence in their borrowed navigational tips evaporated when they sighted a steamer that had grounded. Keyes hailed her and found she had onboard a pilot, who was willing to take them to Tongku. The remainder of the passage was uneventful, and before the bluejackets trooped ashore Keyes pleaded with Seymour to be allowed to go with them, assuring him that Tomkinson could easily command the *Fame* in his absence. He was turned down courteously, but firmly, and told he would be of more use helping to ferry in the foreign contingents. The next day all communications with Peking were cut.[7]

As the *Fame* went down river again to join the fleet her two young fighting-cocks were envious of the 915 Britishers landed. One of them was determined to get into the war.

Keyes was soon pestering senior officers to capture the Taku forts. He and Tomkinson had surveyed them from the shore in secret expeditions and knew their history. Nearly forty years earlier British and French gunboats had attempted to force their way up river, but had been compelled to retreat with heavy losses;[8] but a year later they had been captured from the rear by a large Indian army. From the seaward the forts, now rebuilt with low tops and profiles, were impregnable and out of range of the cruisers and battleships, and because of the river shallows only small gun vessels could enter, generally in line ahead, passing the north and south forts at the river-mouth at a range of 200 yards. Every one of the forts' batteries could bear on the upper reaches and, with central pivot mountings, commanded all the approaches from inland. Keyes was certain that the only way to take them was by bombardment and then by a foot assault, first on the north-western fort, which was up river and then on the northernmost fort.

One afternoon he convinced the *Alacrity*'s commander, Kit Cradock, later to be killed in the Battle of Coronel in 1914, that the forts must be knocked out if the Western powers were to maintain supply lines and relieve Peking. The two of them landed from the *Fame*, while Tomkinson stood the ship off, and reconnoitred around the two northern forts. There and then they formulated a plan which was to be enacted four days later.

Before then came the alarming news that Seymour's relief force, swollen to 2,000, had been surrounded, while the railway line of retreat behind them to Tientsin had been cut.[9]

The next day, 15 June, Keyes left the *Fame* in the hands of Tomkinson, having been directed by Admiral Bruce to go to Tientsin alone and report on the situation. Keyes was away for more than twenty-four hours. When he returned he had an intrepid tale to tell – he had arrived alone in Tientsin in a train packed with hostile Chinese troops; he met Captain Bayly, the senior naval officer there, who said that the situation was desperate, with no news of Seymour's force; then rode back 28 miles from Tientsin to Tangku on the footplate of the only available locomotive; commandeered a tug and steamed out to Admiral Bruce to implore him to capture the forts; begged him to give command of the strike force to Cradock; and returned to the railhead in the tug, laden with guns, ammunition and supplies for Tientsin.[10]

Tomkinson and the *Fame* had been inactive during this time, but this was the intention of Keyes. He wrote later: 'I simply did not dare take the *Fame* out, as the fight inside might start at any moment and if once we got outside we might not be allowed in again. There were the four Chinese 35-knot destroyers, which I had marked down as my own.'[11] To ensure that the *Fame* would not be required he lied by reporting that her engines once again needed a brief overhaul.

The destroyers had claimed the attention of Keyes and Tomkinson on the first day the *Fame* arrived at Tongku. They were berthed at a Chinese dockyard, 2 miles below the town, and their white hulls and yellow-painted funnels glistened in the sun, in smart contrast to the *Fame*'s unpainted side. They were the fastest ships in the area, each with two torpedo tubes and four quick-firing six-pounders, having been built by Schichau in Germany. Meanwhile, the admirals of the newly allied navies had agreed, with the exception of the United States, that as the Chinese Imperial troops appeared to have joined the Boxers and their forts were menacing all Western shipping, a base had to be secured at Tongku and that meant knocking out the forts.[12]

An ultimatum was sent to the commanding officers of the three bastions that the allies intended to occupy them at 2 a.m. on 17 June; if there was no resistance, they would be handed back when Peking was relieved.[13] The conference broke up, but was followed by a council of war made up of Cradock, who was to be in charge of the foot assault, and the captains of the *Algerine* (Britain), *Iltis* (Germany), *Lion* (France) and *Atago* (Japan), which were all in the river under the guns of the north-western fort. Before they met, however, Keyes had the temerity to tell Captain Johnston Stewart, of the *Algerine*, that Admiral Bruce wished him to make certain there was no risk of the four Chinese destroyers escaping and creating havoc among the allies' older vessels. 'I asked him to assure the council of war that the *Fame* and *Whiting* would guarantee the capture of these destroyers in time to prevent them interfering with any vessels in the river, or outside', Keyes later revealed.[14]

There were no specific written orders for this, in fact, but the council of war accepted it as an integral part of the plan. So it was agreed that at 2 a.m., under the command of Keyes, the *Fame* and *Whiting* were to seize the destroyers, to clear the river of their threat, then signal the result. Meanwhile the allied 'infantry' was to land at 2.30 a.m. to occupy a long ditch 1,000 yd from the north-western fort and to attack it after it had been bombarded.

The allies now began scouring their ships for manpower, because many of their seamen had already gone with the relief force. Cradock's contingent of 321 was made up of a few lieutenants, midshipmen, quartermasters, boatswains' mates, blacksmiths, armourers, carpenters, stokers and even boys and bandsmen who had volunteered. Their weapons, which were in short supply, too, included axes and boarding pikes. The Japanese provided 244 sailors, the Russians 159 soldiers from Tongku, the Germans 2 officers and 20 men and the Italians 24 seamen and an officer.[15]

In the river alongside Tongku wharf, out of range of the two northerly forts, were the *Iltis*, a modern German gunboat, armed with six 4-in quick-firing guns and pom-poms; the *Lion*, an old French gunboat, with two 5.5-in breech-loading guns; Japan's *Atago*, another ancient gunboat, with one 8.2-in muzzle loader and one 4.7-in breech loader; two Russian torpedo boats and the American *Monocacy*, a wooden paddle steamer, used as an accommodation vessel for refugees.

Below the dockyard and within 200 yards range of the north-western fort were three Russian gunboats – the *Gilyak*, a new ship, with seven quick-firing guns, one 4.7-in and six twelve-pounders; the old *Bobr*, which possessed just two big guns, one 9-in and the other a 6-in but both breech loaders; and the *Korleytz*, with three breech loaders, two 8-in and one 6-in.[16]

The most active vessel on the river that evening was a steamboat, which Keyes had borrowed for spying on the Chinese destroyers. He took with him Tomkinson and MacKenzie, of the *Whiting*, and at dusk went up river to look at the enemy. All four destroyers were in line, about a ship's length apart, moored ahead and astern alongside the dock. They did not appear to be preparing to sail, so the three officers returned to the *Fame* to make plans for their attack.

It was decided that the *Fame* and the *Whiting* would each tow a whaler. There would be boarding parties of eight men in each, with similar numbers on the bows of the two British destroyers. The *Fame* would get under way at 1.30 a.m., followed by the *Whiting* 300 yards behind. To give the impression they were heading for Tongku, they would keep well out in the river, and then, when *Fame's* bows were adjacent to the first destroyer and the *Whiting* abreast of the third, Keyes and MacKenzie would steer towards them, with the trailing whalers veering in towards the second and fourth destroyers. As every man in the boarding parties was to be armed with a pistol and a cutlass, with a covering squad of six riflemen on the parent ships, the armouries of the British vessels were low, so a protection party of stokers, formed to prevent a counter-attack by the Chinese, could only be armed with iron bars and pokers.

Tomkinson piped the ship's company to muster just after 9 p.m., when Keyes explained what was expected of them, sorted out the volunteers and selected his teams. Finally, he called for a volunteer to leap onboard the first destroyer to secure a hawser around the mast when the vessels touched. Among the first to step forward and get the task was Henry Brady, a young able seamen, who for nearly twenty years was to be Keyes' coxswain and personal servant.

It began at 12.50 a.m. But it was not the allies who fired the first shot. The Chinese were not as gentlemanly as the Western powers and the stillness over the River Pei Ho was broken by a single shot from the south bank fort more than an hour before the ultimatum was due to expire. The batteries of all three forts then began to pound the exposed ships below. Plumes of mud and spray spattered the decks as shells plunged close to the warships, few of which were armour plated. Fortunately for some, the tide had fallen a great deal since daylight, when the Chinese would have worked out the range, and many salvoes went over the top of the allies' ships, only to send up muddied omelette-like bursts into the sky. Relishing this moment of lone command, and with it the responsibility for the success or failure of the entire naval action, Keyes signalled the *Whiting* to start the operation immediately.

With shells whirring overhead, it was also imperative that the *Fame* should be on the move. He shouted to Tomkinson to get his men into the whaler and then ran forward himself to weigh the anchor, before returning to the wheel. As Tomkinson made sure his boarding party were all present and correct, a tremendous explosion emitted from the old *Korleytz*, a few feet away from the whaler. She had been hit in her combustion chamber. Tomkinson and his men were spattered with soot from the black smoke which spiralled up, making them look more forbidding. Keyes was into his role now and as the *Fame* steamed past the other anchored ships he cheered each one. Tomkinson heard men on the crippled *Korleytz* yell back enthusiastically; the *Bobr*, yet to be hit also replied, but there was no response from the *Gilyak* which, having rashly switched on a searchlight, already had lost most of her ship's company when her ammunition exploded after she was struck on the waterline.

At the bend of the river, hidden from the look-outs in the Chinese destroyers, the *Fame* stopped to wait for the *Whiting*. Tomkinson reckoned she was probably sunk, for he had seen a shell splash right over her, followed by a massive eruption. After about fifteen minutes in midstream, Tomkinson heard Keyes hailing him. The operation would go on without the *Whiting*, Keyes ordered, but instead of Tomkinson taking the second destroyer, he was to capture the fourth one, leaving the *Fame* to take the third in line. The first two were then to be sunk by the *Fame*'s twelve-pounder. Within minutes, Keyes had to cancel the new orders, for around the bend appeared the *Whiting*.

The Chinese destroyers' crews were all awake by now, watching the bombardment, but had little idea of the impending boarding, as the outlines of the *Fame* and *Whiting* held the centre of the river, as if bound for Tongku. Then, just as planned, Keyes veered the *Fame* over towards the first destroyer; Tomkinson's whaler also swung over and bumped into the side of the second. As he clambered up the side and sprang over the guard-rail an officer ran towards him firing a revolver; bullets hissed by him, but there was no chance for the Chinaman to fire again. Tomkinson was after him with a cutlass; he disarmed him and drove him overboard.

There were shrieks of pain and shouts of success all around him now as each destroyer was taken over. Tomkinson's men herded the remnants of the crew below deck and battened down the hatches, while he ran to the bridge to take the wheelhouse. Hand-to-hand skirmishes lasted momentarily and after five minutes Tomkinson had secured the ship. There were no hold-ups for the other boarding parties and Keyes was able to signal his success well inside the zero hour for the allied bombardment, which strangely had yet to reply to the Chinese.

It was Keyes' intention to leave a guard of bluejackets on the dockside and to join the *Lion* and *Iltis*, which were now able to come down from Tongku to help with the shelling of the forts. Until now he had not lost a man, but the whole mission was endangered by his typical English good sportsmanship. Although several Chinese had been killed on the destroyers, he had issued strict orders that the many who had been rushed overboard and who had escaped up the bank, should not be fired on. 'It was a mistake which no foreigner would have made, but one is rather squeamish about these things,' he stated later.

Soon the survivors had rallied and rearmed inside the dockyard walls. Snipers' bullets began to make positions untenable on the upper decks of the six ships. Suddenly a large gun, set up closer than the forts, opened up on them. Tomkinson's prize was hit by a 5 in shell on the forecastle, but without casualties, while the *Whiting* escaped with another shell through her boilers, which did not detonate.

By now Keyes had abandoned his plans and decided that the destroyers must be towed to Tongku and out of range. But it was difficult to untie them because of the snipers' fire. Keyes never asked his men to do anything he could not achieve himself. He rounded up a raiding party, shouted to Tomkinson to organize a covering broadside from the captured destroyer's port gun and the *Fame's* twelve-pounder, and then raced off towards the dockyard. Tomkinson watched in amazed admiration, as Keyes ran into the dark, amid the flashes of rifle and battery fire.

While the shelling continued, Tomkinson and the other boarding parties were unsuccessfully trying to raise steam on the destroyers. Suddenly the snipers' bullets stopped pinging on the ironwork, although the shelling continued. It enabled the boarding parties to cut the wire hawsers securing the destroyers to the dockside and to start preparing tows. As this was going on, a breathless Keyes emerged to claim that the Chinese seamen did not possess the fanaticism of the Boxers and that a British flag now flew over the dockyard. Tomkinson's party had managed to secure their prize to one side of the *Fame*; while Keyes' capture was lashed on to her other side. In this ungainly way they manoeuvred into Tongku.

Whiting's first lieutenant eventually had more success with his charge's engines and she got under way with the parent ship, which was towing the third destroyer astern. But after a few hundred yards she broke down, was anchored and eventually picked up by a tug.

The shelling followed them and continued at Tongku, for they were now directly in line with the southern fort's batteries. As dawn broke the position looked desperate. Tomkinson could see through his binoculars that all three forts' guns were flinging shells over the allied ships. None of the bastions appeared to have been damaged by the counter bombardment; neither did the foot assault seem to have succeeded.

As the *Fame* brought in her captives, now flying white ensigns, to tie them up at the wharf near the *Monocacy*, one of her American officers jeered jokingly: 'Just like you British – bagging all the most valuable prizes.' Soon after, the *Monocacy*, crowded with refugees, was hit by an 8-in shell, which pierced her upper deck and came out of her side above the waterline, without exploding.

Keyes and Tomkinson were impatient to return to the fight and to join in the razing of the forts. They left the Chinese destroyers in the odd command of a naval chaplain and an instructor, who had sheltered the night in the *Monocacy* and at 5 a.m. were under way again. By then, however, the British and Japanese flags were flying in triumph over the north-western fort. The southern bastion was still wreaking its revenge on Keyes' little force and one of its accurate shots started a fire on the *Whiting*'s forward mess-deck. Mackenzie's men managed to put it out, but the ship ran aground.

Again Keyes had to bury his fervour for the fight, to take the *Fame* to her rescue. With the aid of a tug they managed to pull her off. At last the *Fame* headed down river again, towards the battle, only to be signalled by a midshipman on the tug *Fawan*, bound for

Tientsin with ammunition, that her Chinese crew refused to go up river more than 12 miles beyond a fort at Hsi-Cheng. No one on the *Fame* knew of this obstacle, so Keyes took her alongside the *Atago* and asked the captain if he had any knowledge of it. He came up with a book, which revealed that the fort had forty-three guns. This did not deter Keyes. He instructed the *Fawan* to proceed at full speed, then followed in the *Fame*, with the *Whiting*, surprisingly still operable, close behind. Abreast of the fort, the two warships stopped menacingly as the *Fawan* went on unmolested. On the fort, which was 400 yards away, Tomkinson could make out 6-in gun embrasure parapets, crowded with men, but there was little indication that they would fire on the fleeing *Fawan*.

For half an hour the *Fame* remained a sitting target, but not wishing to 'stir up a hornets' nest' – as Keyes put it – they returned to Taku, now silent, but with the dust of battle hanging over the three forts – and a British flag over each.[17]

The *Fame* was the first warship to cross the bar in the afternoon to carry dispatches from Commander Johnston Stewart to Admiral Bruce in the *Barfleur*. As she sailed through the ships of the allied fleet they sounded their sirens in salutation of victory. When Keyes reported onboard the *Barfleur*, he was told that the *Fame* was to go to Nagasaki, where news of the successful storming of the forts could be relayed to the Western world, via a Canadian Pacific steamer. Keyes and Tomkinson could see themselves being sidelined from the undeclared war, with Tientsin and Peking still to be relieved. They pointed out to the admiral that the *Fame* was undamaged and was an important link in the chain of command, whereas the *Whiting* could be temporarily repaired and then take the dispatches to Japan, where she could go into dockyard for a more thorough overhaul. Their argument prevailed and that evening they were back in Tongku, attending to the release of the Chinese prisoners from the captured destroyers.

The next day Tomkinson was overseeing the return of possessions to the Chinese sailors. As first lieutenant of the capturing ship, it was naval tradition that he should command one of the prizes. Keyes, who had been instructed by Admiral Bruce to keep the best destroyer, chose the *Hai Loong*, with the other three being allocated to Germany, France and Japan. The *Hai Loong* had been the flagship of the commodore and when a Chinese officer returned the next day for his gear he explained to Keyes that the commodore, wounded by one of the boarding parties, had run to the dockyard, but when retreating in the face of Keyes' assault was killed by Boxers for losing his ships. In the commodore's cabin was found his full dress sword, made by Wilkinsons, of London, and similar to that used by Royal Navy officers, but with a dragon engraved on it. This was handed over by Tomkinson to Keyes, who was to wear it on all future ceremonial occasions. Yet although tradition was on Tomkinson's side, Bruce did not appear to be.

After the ceremonial towing of the *Hai Loong* out to the fleet – again to a great ovation from the assembled vessels – she was anchored alongside the flagship. Onboard Keyes was told by Bruce that it had been decided to rename her the *Taku* and that Lieutenant Phillimore, from the *Barfleur*, was to command her. Loyalty to his officers and crew was a bigger priority to Keyes than deference to the orders of an admiral; he argued that in line with tradition Tomkinson, although only a sub-lieutenant, should be given the privilege of captaincy. 'I'll be content to have even a midshipman act as my second in command in the *Fame* if a more senior officer cannot be spared,' he said. He got his way. Bruce agreed to appoint Tomkinson as the new commanding officer of the *Taku*, with Sub-Lieutenant Stephen Newcome joining the *Fame* as his deputy.[18]

It was an immediate parting, but only a temporary one for Tomkinson and Keyes. The next six weeks were quieter for Tomkinson, while Keyes' lust for adventure took him ashore to blow up the fort at Hsi-Cheng and led to brushes with the Chinese in Tientsin.

By the end of July a new British expeditionary force had arrived; at its head was General Sir Alfred Gaselee, an old friend of Keyes' father. Through dint of persuasion, Keyes was seconded as naval liaison officer to the general's headquarters. On the afternoon of Sunday 29 July, Tomkinson was recalled from the *Taku* to command the *Fame*. It was a proud moment for him as he waved goodbye to Keyes, now on the starry mission of the relief of Peking, with an allied army of 19,300. As Keyes' boat was about to shove off from the *Fame*, he suddenly had the extravagant idea of ordering Tomkinson to haul down the white ensign and union jack and pass them down to him.[19]

Four days later the commander-in-chief, Admiral Seymour, now back in the flagship *Centurion*, after the first relieving force had been severely mauled and forced to retreat, countermanded the orders and insisted that Keyes return to the *Fame*. In his new bivouac at Hsi-Ku, Keyes ignored the telegram he had received and marched out with the army. Nearly three weeks later he was to claim to have been among the first men to force their way into the British legation at Peking. He had with him the *Fame*'s white ensign, which an army officer hoisted over the beleaguered haven of foreigners.[20]

While ashore Keyes was bringing to life a *Boys' Own Paper* type of yarn, on the water Tomkinson was back to the everyday fetching and carrying for the fleet and, even as a passive partner in Keyes' decampment, was not endearing himself to the commander-in-chief. Seymour had telegraphed the Admiralty to ask for another captain for the destroyer, although Their Lordships had just extended Keyes' two-year appointment in her to 'indefinitely'. Seymour blamed Keyes for thrusting himself on General Gaselee and leaving his ship at a crucial time in Tomkinson's inexperienced hands. His anger could be understood for Tomkinson was still a sub-lieutenant and only twenty-two.

With the relief of Peking achieved and a new captain already on his way from England, the *Fame* was released from her duties in the Pei Ho and sailed for Wei-Hai-Wei, with Tomkinson wondering not only about his future, but when he would see Keyes again. They were reunited, however, when the *Barfleur* sailed in. Onboard was his commanding officer, looking old, hollow cheeked and 2 stone under weight after contracting diphtheria in Peking. Keyes wanted to rejoin the *Fame* immediately, but although he had found an enemy in Seymour, he had discovered a friend in Admiral Bruce, who insisted that he stay in the more comfortable *Barfleur* until he was fully recovered.

By now the *Fame* was in poor shape outwardly and internally and in dire need of repairs after weeks of rough usage, churning her way through the Pei Ho mud-bar. She had also been damaged when at anchor off Taku by a Chinese vessel, which drifted into her and badly bent her bows. Nagasaki was the only suitable dockyard where she could be hauled up on a slipway, and it was there she was sent with the *Barfleur*. Keyes hoped to be left behind when the *Barfleur* parted company after ten days, but the ship's doctor found he was still suffering from the after-effects of diphtheria and Bruce ordered him to stay onboard.

Keyes feared that he would never take the *Fame* to sea again and at the first chance made his peace with Seymour when the *Centurion* was in harbour. Nearly three months after his hot-headed disobedience of orders, Keyes was told by the Admiralty that his reappointment to the *Fame* had been approved and his relief was to go to the *Taku*, still commanded by Phillimore. Tomkinson and Keyes reformed their partnership off the Pei Ho River on 3 November and within ten days sailed into a new crisis.

Typhoons in November were rare in the China seas, for as the old mariners' saw ran: 'July stand by. September remember. October all over.' Yet the weather was exceptionally grim on 12 November, when the *Fame* and the *Taku* were within four hours' sailing of Hong Kong. At dawn, as they steamed along the coast at 15 knots, the sky was a funereal indigo, with no sign of the sunrise. The barometric pressure was at its lowest, as a great long swell swept in from the south-east. Tomkinson made his rounds of the ship to ensure that everything was secure, with lifelines rigged fore and aft to prevent anyone being washed overboard. Yet even as he joined Keyes on the bridge at 5 a.m. the monsoon-like wind had eased, to be replaced with sudden gusts from the east, whipping the sea into the *Fame* and foaming over her deck. Soon it was hurricane force, yet when the two friends conferred they reckoned that, by the direction of the wind and the sudden fall of barometric pressure, the eye of the storm would be to the south. Nevertheless, if it approached up the Formosa Channel they would still be too close on a lee shore to ride it out comfortably in vessels barely over 300 tons. But the nearest shelter was 50 miles away and the *Taku* had only enough coal for twelve hours. They decided to steer into the wind to get plenty of sea room and then be prepared to take the *Taku* in tow if her fuel ran out.

The *Fame* lurched through one gigantic wave after another; at times it seemed to Tomkinson she would not right herself, as momentarily she would almost pose on each crest, with a third of her displacement out of the water, before shuddering headlong into another trough, with her propellors gyrating ineffectively for a split second. Looking across to the *Taku*, Tomkinson doubted whether she could survive, particularly after one spectacular plunge, when she reappeared with her anchor and 18 ft of cable dangling from her bows. When she climbed the next crescendo of water, the anchor swung towards her keel, so close that it looked as if she would transfix herself on it. But when the bows dipped down again the anchor sank rapidly and did no damage. All day it remained, swinging there like a maritime metronome.

Because the *Fame*'s propellors were deeper set, Keyes had trouble in keeping the *Taku* in sight, especially as the torrential rain and spume restricted visibility to 100 yards. Soon the *Fame*'s sounding machine was smashed and because she was in shoal water they had to resort to the perilous and old-fashioned method of working a lead line, with seamen secured by ropes, passing it from hand to hand, fore and aft.

By afternoon there was no abatement and little progress for both ships as they were steadily lashed towards the shore, with soundings reduced from 13 to 11 fathoms. If she were to make Hong Kong, it was essential that the *Taku* obtained more knots from her boilers. Keyes ordered Phillimore by flag: 'Increase speed of engines.' But before the

Taku's signalmen could read it, the flags were blown to tatters. Other flags were hoisted, but these, too, were shredded.

Keyes then allowed the *Fame* to draw astern and closer to the *Taku* and was able to signal by semaphore: 'Nearly onshore. Increase speed of engines. Follow me.' The course was altered to bring the sea on to *Fame*'s bows, accompanied by a tremendous and sickening rolling, to shield the *Taku* and enable her propellors to dig deeper. To everyone's relief, the soundings deepened too.

When the tempest was at its fiercest Tomkinson had gone down to the forward messdeck to find it breast high in water. Dozens of rivets were not holding and as the bows bumped into each trough, the plates buckled in three sections and gaped so wide that he could almost put his hand into the sea. Then as she bucketed out of a trough they closed for a few seconds, only to open again to swallow another great gush, like a gargantuan gorge. Steam pumps could not cope, although they were used to keep the water down in other compartments where rivets had been sucked out. Luckily the coal in the forward bunkers had gone, otherwise her buoyancy would have been impaired more. Tomkinson reported it to Keyes and commented it was as well that hundreds of faulty rivets in the after part had been replaced at Nagasaki.

The high point of the crisis was passed by mid-afternoon and at 5 p.m. the barometer began to rise and the wind died down. Keyes ordered both ships to steer towards Hong Kong again; with the *Taku* having 2$\frac{1}{2}$ tons of coal left, a tow was not necessary now. Eerily, with not a whisper of wind disturbing their halyards, the two destroyers increased speed to 20 knots.

By 9 p.m. Keyes and Tomkinson, drenched, shivering and hungry after sixteen hours without sleep, saw the approaches to Hong Kong harbour. As the *Fame* tied up at a buoy an officer from the guard-ship boarded her with a letter from the commodore. It congratulated both commanding officers and enclosed a copy of an Admiralty telegram, promoting Keyes to commander – at the incredibly early age of twenty-eight – for his services in the rebellion, and awarding the DSO to Phillimore.

That night the mainbrace was spliced in the sodden *Fame*. But Tomkinson could well wonder why Phillimore had been decorated and not he.

For five days and nights the ship was pumped out. When she was docked it was discovered she had sprung 1,300 rivets.[21] It was not a repair job that was to concern Tomkinson. At the end of November he was on the *Duke of Wellington*, bound for Britain and a long leave.

4
BRAVEST MAN OF YEAR

Tomkinson found a family welcome awaiting him at Franche Hall. Not only was he returning as a hero, but he also arrived on leave on New Year's Eve, to the usual house full of relatives. None of the children had yet married and all were allowed to live at the hall, if they conformed to the rules of Michael and Annie. It was the home comforts of their ever open house that persuaded six of them to remain single all their lives. While Tomkinson spoke modestly of his exploits in China, most of his brothers' conversation was of the business and of sport. Herbert and Gerald were in a form of apprenticeship which was to lead to their heading the carpet business, while Francis, always known as Tommy, was about to leave Eton to qualify as a solicitor with a Birmingham practice. Geoffrey, then at Winchester, and Tommy had played against each other in the annual cricket match between the two public schools. As for the girls, Gertrude, the eldest, was at Lady Margaret Hall, Oxford, while Marion was studying music in Dresden. There was also Dora, then fourteen, still at school, destined to go to Oxford University, too, Margaret, still only nine, and the twins, Charles and Christine, just seven.[1]

For two months of joyous leave Wilfred relaxed in the sport of the countryman, which always remained at his heart, as he shot, fished and savoured the green softness of the countryside around Franche and Chilton. It was the type of squire-like life he always returned to when on leave from the navy, for the Tomkinsons were the aristocracy of the area, where villagers curtsied, or touched their forelocks to them.

Tomkinson was expecting some share of the prize money for the seizure of the Chinese destroyers, but was informed by the Admiralty that at the time of their capture Britain and China were not officially at war, so it could not be granted him.

The next ten years were fairly uneventful for him, and one of the first of the many letters preserved in his private papers, written from onboard HMS *Hibernian* at Invergordon – coincidentally, mentioned in the last of his papers, too – was a plea forwarded through his commanding officer for promotion to commander. His service had composed two years at HMS *Vernon*, where he qualified as a torpedo lieutenant; just eight months in the battleship *Royal Sovereign*; more than three years in the *Crescent*; sixteen months in the *Hannibal*; and another fifteen months as first lieutenant in the *Hibernian*.[2] He felt that promotion was long overdue, particularly as he was now married with a son and a daughter.

It was while with the *Crescent*, in which he served earlier as a midshipman, but then on the Cape of Good Hope station at Simonstown, that he met the lovely Joan Bittleston, whose father was commanding officer of the Royal Artillery, based at Simonstown Castle. For a year the couple were engaged, and at the end of the *Crescent's* commission both returned to Britain. They were married on 12 June 1907, at All Saints' church, Ennismore Gardens, Kensington,[3] 'round the corner' from where Joan's grandfather lived. A year later, with Tomkinson on the battleship *Hannibal*, based at Devonport, close to Ashleigh, the home of Joan's father just outside Tavistock, their son was born and, in Tomkinson tradition, he was named Michael, although always called Peter by the family. Eighteen months later their first daughter, Elizabeth, but known as Betty, was born.[4]

With these extra commitments and the upkeep of Somerset Place, Plymouth, the impatience of Tomkinson for promotion was understandable and was exacerbated by the enviable progress of Keyes, who in ten years had been second in command of the Devonport Destroyer Flotilla, assistant to the First Sea Lord, Prince Louis of Battenberg, in the Naval Intelligence Department, and naval attaché in Rome and Vienna, where at the age of thirty-two he was promoted to captain, the youngest in the navy.

Tomkinson and Keyes visited each other's homes regularly. In 1906 Keyes had married Eva Bowlby, an attractive Scottish woman whom Tomkinson was to admire in a strictly platonic friendship. So it seemed perfectly natural for Tomkinson to ask Keyes to press his case for promotion. In a constant stream of letters, Keyes, always a prolific, if often ungrammatical writer, reassured his friend that he was doing everything in his power to further his progress, as the following succession of correspondence shows.

When Keyes was about to leave the British Embassy in Vienna he wrote to Tomkinson on 3 October 1907, saying 'I am going to sea in January . . . I will certainly do all I can to get you appointed first lieutenant – unless something better turns up – and thank you for wanting to come. I certainly will not rest till I get you promoted.'[5]

Instead, Tomkinson went to the *Hibernian* in the Channel Fleet. Then on New Year's Day 1908, Keyes, who had just recovered from a head injury after a hunting accident, reassured Tomkinson, whose wife was pregnant: 'I hope very much to be able to put you into my ship before long . . . in the next two weeks.'[6]

Tomkinson lingered on in the *Hibernian*.

Ten months later Keyes, now in command of the cruiser *Venus* in the Home Fleet, boasted of putting in a 'strong recommendation – on two sheets of foolscap' to his commander-in-chief, Admiral Sir William May. 'I recited all your doings,' he wrote Tomkinson, 'including a word about the Kowloon (Taku) show and fairly ladled it out . . . and that Sir Edward Seymour and Sir James Bruce would testify to the good you had done when in command of *Taku* and *Fame*. I rather fear you might not get it this time.'[7]

Tomkinson remained in the *Hibernian* until the summer of 1910. But he was not to join Keyes. He was promoted to commander, and to his annoyance was appointed commanding officer of the 310-ton destroyer *Mallard* . . . and she was based in the Mediterranean as a tender to HMS *Orantes* at Malta. With a two-year-old son and a nine-month-old daughter to look after, it was impossible for Joan to join him. Tomkinson, always very much of a family man and father, left England full of misgivings, despite the three gold bands on his sleeves. But within three months Keyes had answered his appeal for help. In November 1910, Tomkinson heard from his friend: 'I have a billet here, if you care to take it on. You can't do better from a service point of view, only don't do it against your will because you feel your right to oblige me.'[8]

Surprisingly, Keyes had been called to the Admiralty and offered the post of inspecting captain of the Submarine Service, which was just nine years old.[9] It was surprising because, valiant and dashing though he was, he was not renowned for his intellect nor his technical knowledge.[10] Unknown to Keyes, the appointment was to beget controversy, for he was to succeed Captain Reginald Bacon, a friend of the megalomanic former First Sea Lord 'Jacky' Fisher, who had doubted, and who was always to doubt, Keyes' ability. The appointment offered to Tomkinson was the command of the Portsmouth Flotilla of Submarines and HMS *Mercury*, a hulk moored off the submarine depot at Fort Block-house, Haslar Creek. With it went a small cottage. 'You would have to go out with boats in a tender three days a week,' Keyes told Tomkinson.[11] Chains of command were fettered in odd, if understandable, ways in the Royal Navy up to the start of the Second World War. Keyes had a reputation for taking on any job enthusiastically, if not having the technical knowledge, and he knew that Tomkinson, who also had little working experience with submarines, would not outshine him, but with an expertise in torpedoes would help meticulously to make the service more efficient.

Keyes need not have warned Tomkinson 'don't do it against your will.'[12] He accepted smartly and was back in England for Christmas. Because of his minimal experience of submarines, he needed to 'mug up' on their operation and tactical usage.

Submarine development in Britain began in 1902 with five American Holland designs, built under licence by Vickers Maxim at Barrow-in-Furness. Despite primitive periscopes and poor performance on the surface, these were never involved in a serious accident.[13] This encouraged the Admiralty – and Admiral Fisher in particular – to order, in 1907, a bigger model, the A type, which was 105 ft long and displaced 185 tons. By the time Tomkinson joined the service, and with the appearance of the 550–600 ton D type, Britain possessed sixty-one submarines; eight more were under construction and the biggest, the 600–800 ton E type, was about to be laid down. But the service could not be deemed a success, for the classes up to the Ds were unreliable, primitive and, worst of all, highly toxic and explosive because of their petrol engines.[14]

Keyes' appointment came at a difficult time, when Germany, a late entry into the underwater armament race, was beginning to catch up, mainly through the introduction of diesel engines. On top of this, the First Sea Lord was now Admiral Sir A.K. Wilson, no adherent to submarine policy and who, eight years earlier, had called submarines 'underhand, unfair and damned un-English'.[15] Keyes knew that Britain could, and must, do better and, with his enthusiasm brimming over to the brink of unpopularity with his seniors, he looked abroad to break the Vickers monopoly and for improvements – especially towards Germany, with its superior periscopes and engines. He was quick to insist to Tomkinson that good training and leadership were not enough unless 'the machinery and weapons are maintained in the highest state of efficiency'[16] – and that was the department in which he relied heavily on Tomkinson.

For the next two years at Portsmouth, Tomkinson was to help to turn a pioneer service into a more efficient fighting unit, but even then only as scouts to seek out the enemy. In a similar mould to their leader, the submarine captains took chances with the earlier craft, which led to notoriety and tragedy.

The worst disaster for Tomkinson came on 2 February 1912, when one of his flotilla, A3, collided with his seagoing depot ship, HMS *Hazard*, and sank off the Isle of Wight. There was not one survivor among her crew of fourteen.[17]

In 1912, as part of the reorganization of the Home Fleet, Rear Admiral John de Robeck was appointed as admiral of patrols, responsible for flotillas of destroyers and all submarines not allotted to port defence. Keyes, as inspecting captain of submarines, continued to control all flotillas in home waters, although still being responsible to the commanders-in-chief of home ports for training.[18] It was under this new system that Tomkinson was moved to Devonport in command of the depot ship *Forth*, and in charge of all training of western ratings. It suited his domestic arrangements because the cottage at Portsmouth was too small for Joan and their two youngsters; a move to the West Country also enabled them to be closer to their own home and Joan's father and mother.

Within a year, Tomkinson found himself being headlined as the bravest man of 1913, after being awarded the Royal Humane Society's Stanhope gold medal for a 'deed of great gallantry'.[19]

On 20 November 1913 Tomkinson, in the destroyer *Wolf*, was supervising a routine exercise with the submarine B4 in Bigbury Bay, Devon. There was a heavy sea running, which buffeted the tiny submarine, ridiculed for its unseaworthiness in rough weather. Tomkinson, who was on the bridge, was handed the signal 'man overboard' from the submarine. He ordered full speed, and as the *Wolf* raced towards B4 a look-out spotted a man in the sea. When the destroyer approached it was impossible to lower a boat, so Tomkinson threw off his heavy clothes and dived in over the side. Always a powerful swimmer, he clawed through the waves and managed to grab the man, Able Seaman Bill Ball, and haul him back towards the *Wolf*. A roped lifebuoy was thrown out to enable them to be hoisted inboard. Tomkinson grasped it and as he and Ball were being pulled up the side, the rope broke and both were pitched back into the seething sea. Tomkinson spluttered to the surface and managed to cling to another line, which had been thrown to him. There was no sign of Ball, who had been sucked under the ship. But Tomkinson refused to be brought inboard until the destroyer look-outs had tried to spot Ball. When all hope of saving the seaman was given up, Tomkinson, who was close to freezing, allowed himself to be lifted inboard.[20]

The next two months were full of unwanted incident for Tomkinson. Four weeks later, when exercising the 1st Flotilla, he received another SOS; this time it was for a submarine smash. In poor visibility, as the flotilla streamed out between Drake's Island and Devil's Point in Plymouth Sound, C14 collided with an Admiralty hopper. Her pressure hull was pierced, but she sank slowly and, with the rest of the flotilla closing in to help, all twenty men onboard jumped clear and were picked up. Six weeks later came a more disastrous sinking, when A7 foundered in Whitesand Bay, a few miles from the C14 accident. All eleven men in her perished and no one knew why, because it was decided to designate A7 as a maritime grave and no attempt was made to raise her.[21]

It was the fear of tragedies like these – Britain lost nine submarines up to the start of the First World War[22] – which turned Tomkinson against the submarine service. But if they were worrying times for him, they were equally as anxious for Joan, who as well as being pregnant again was continually concerned for her husband, who spent most of his days at sea.

Tomkinson's career now seemed shackled to that of Keyes, who, like him, was coming to the end of his three-year term with submarines and yearned for a surface appointment, possibly in a cruiser. Meanwhile, Keyes was making plans for both of them. Rear-Admiral David Beatty, whom he had met in Tientsin during the Boxer Rebellion, was on the brink of being given command of the Battle Cruiser Squadron in 1913. Keyes begged Beatty to earmark him for the captaincy of the battle cruiser *Queen Mary*, due to be commissioned that summer. Beatty acquiesced and Keyes was provisionally noted for the appointment, with Tomkinson pencilled in as his second in command, only to be told by the Admiralty that his work was so valuable with the submarine service that he must stay for another year. Disappointment for Keyes was tempered by promotion to commodore, but he still desired a battle cruiser and it was agreed that he and Tomkinson should 'have' the new speedy and powerful *Tiger*, scheduled to be ready for trials in September 1914.[23]

Again the two friends were to be disappointed, but not separated.

5
DESTROYER CAPTAIN

Joan and Wilfred had just returned from a walk to the Hollies, their home at Mannamead, Plymouth when the noise of a motorcycle interrupted their August Bank Holiday reverie. On it was Bennett, one of the *Forth*'s officers. He saluted and then announced: 'Urgent telegram, sir.' Tomkinson was expecting it; most of the fleet was mobilized in preparation for the declaration of war against Germany and he was awaiting his orders. The telegram read: 'Appointed *Lurcher* in command. Join forthwith at Harwich.'

He had dreaded going to war in the depot ship *Forth* and 'being shut up all the time in her, kicking my heels'. Although delighted with his appointment to the two-year-old, 760-ton, 32-knot destroyer *Lurcher*, it did not make his leave-taking from the Hollies any easier.[1] Like thousands of other servicemen that day he packed his personal gear, hurried to the *Forth* in Devonport to pick up his uniforms, signalled the Admiralty that he would be in Harwich the next day and caught the midnight train from Plymouth to Paddington. He was peeved that he could not get a sleeper, so shook down in a first-class carriage[2] overflowing with other officers. Although he pondered over whether war with Germany was probable, but not certain, he wondered more about his new job and whether Keyes was behind it. The answer came next afternoon in Harwich.

When he arrived he could not find any sign of the *Lurcher* – he learned later his telegram had not been received – but the *Maidstone*, Keyes' depot ship, was in harbour. He boarded her and was welcomed warmly by his old friend,[3] who, as enthusiastic as ever, explained his manoeuvring during the past week. Six days earlier he had been called to the Admiralty, to receive a secret package containing war orders for the 8th Submarine Flotilla.

In the first of many clashes with the Admiralty over operations, he was annoyed to discover that the flotilla and the *Maidstone* had been ordered to the Humber instead of to Harwich – and this was too far north for him. In a flurry of activity he asked for it to be switched to Harwich, but although this was agreed, permission could not be obtained until 10 p.m. from the commander-in-chief of the Home Fleet, Admiral Sir George Callaghan, who was to be succeeded by Admiral John Jellicoe within a week.

Keyes caught the last train to Grimsby, then at 5 a.m. to Immingham, where he found the *Maidstone, Adamant*, the other depot ship, and ten submarines. In true Keyesian style he immediately hoisted his broad pennant in the *Maidstone* and ordered the flotilla to

Harwich, where it arrived on 31 July. Then he dashed back to the Admiralty to plead for two fast destroyers for his command. Two days later he was given the sister ships *Lurcher* and *Firedrake*.[4] Until then Keyes had no particular job for Tomkinson, but when he discovered that the *Lurcher*'s commanding officer, Harold Campbell, a junior lieutenant, was to be relieved by a more senior officer, he asked for Tomkinson, with Campbell staying on as first lieutenant.[5]

If Keyes was confused about the muddle of command at Harwich, he did not show it. Although, in fact, he was Senior Naval Officer at the port, there were three independent commands – Commodore Reginald Tyrwhitt, in the light cruiser *Amethyst*, who controlled the 1st and 3rd Destroyer Flotillas, comprising forty ships with their attached light cruisers *Fearless* and *Amphion*, and Captain Cuthbert Cayley, who administered the port and the nearby boys' training establishment, HMS *Ganges*. The third command, of course, was Keyes' 8th Destroyer Flotilla.[6]

He had good reason to be optimistic about cooperating amicably with Tyrwhitt, because the 1st and 3rd flotillas had worked with the 8th just four months earlier, when destroyer officers, including Tyrwhitt, had embarked in submarines for manoeuvres.[7] What Keyes did not reckon with was that his very good friend Tyrwhitt was, like himself, a seagoing adventurer who led from the front, and this was to bring problems in the months ahead.

Keyes explained to Tomkinson that the task of Tyrwhitt's flotillas was to make sure that the Narrow Seas – the area south of the line from Flamborough Head to Heligoland, Germany's naval nerve centre, was clear of torpedo boats and minelayers. In support, to tangle the command complexity even more, was Cruiser Force C, formed by the five old warships *Bacchante, Aboukir, Euryalus, Cressy* and *Hogue*, whose guns had not been fired for years,[8] manned by reservists and cadets from Britannia Royal Naval College.

Keyes' submarines were to guard the entrance to the Straits of Dover and scout the Heligoland Bight. He intimated to Tomkinson that he interpreted his own command as an active and roving one, leading his men wherever they were needed, in which he would be flying his broad pennant at sea in the *Lurcher*, even though he had an office at the Admiralty.[9] Because the visibility of submarine commanders was restricted by their low position in the water and lack of speed, Keyes, mistakenly in many eyes, decided that his destroyers should work with them by scouting ahead – and this was how he wanted to use the *Lurcher* and *Firedrake*, mainly to promote his own daring schemes. Already, he had put his ideas on paper to Tomkinson in this way:

> I do feel that it will be in the best interests of the Service – if the German fleet comes out to dispute the passage of the Expeditionary Force – that I should be out in a destroyer and in a position to lead the submarines into the most favourable place between the High Sea Fleet and the Channel Squadron. I have declined to send more than two on the service the Admiralty are most keen about, as I consider it a minor operation, in comparison to the safe passage of our Expeditionary Force. They have given me a free hand.[10]

Winston Churchill, then First Lord at the Admiralty, was later to reveal the sheer ama-teurism of the initial orders, which he and Prince Louis of Battenberg, the First Sea Lord, had approved on 28 July, when he wrote: 'The original War Orders were devised to meet the situation on the outbreak of hostilities. They placed the pieces on the board, in what we believed to be the best array and left their future disposition to be modified by experi-ence.'[11]

With the channels of command far from clear, Keyes interpreted his orders almost as he wished; some officers failed to comprehend what was expected of their forces; others received no written orders, but acted on original verbal instructions. Tomkinson was going into war with a navy slap-happily convinced of its own invincibility.

As he left the *Maidstone*, the signs of war were all around the harbourside. Commanding officers had been signalled to paint out all their ships' upper-deck bright-work and funnel bands and to land spare gear and woodwork; great piles of officers' 'ashore clothes' were dumped in heaps on Parkeston Quay. Onboard all vessels young officers had been issued with hypodermic syringes and morphine; soon most would be practising on each other with a water, or saline, solution. Tomkinson found the *Lurcher* alongside an oiler and, after completion of the fuelling operation, he moved her in closer to the *Maidstone*, as if in expectation of new, immediate orders from Keyes.[12]

That evening the commodore received a signal telling him that an ultimatum, expiring at midnight, had been sent to Germany. Keyes immediately assembled his submarine crews and in his faltering, yet believable, style, made a fighting speech, virtually telling them they were already at war.[13] The cheers that rang out were heard by Tomkinson, but he chose to wait until the ultimatum had expired. The next day, 5 August, he had *Lurcher*'s ship's company paraded aft and told them that war had been declared, although it was obvious most of them knew already. He also attempted to explain that it was for 'such a very war that the Royal Navy owed its very existence', before asking for three cheers for the King.[14]

In spite of being instructed by the Admiralty that he was not to go to sea in the early stages of the war, Keyes could not resist a patrol on that first day.[15] Tomkinson watched Tyrwhitt's force leave harbour early for a sweep towards the Heligoland Bight, followed by E8, escorted by the *Amethyst* and *Ariel*, and then four other submarines. Soon after, he had Keyes piped onboard the *Lurcher* before she sailed in pursuit. It was a wet morning, but such was the fervour and patriotism spread abroad that every ship was cheered by boys from the *Ganges* on the foreshore.

The *Lurcher* rendezvoused with the *Bacchante, Aboukir* and *Euryalus* off the Kentish Knock Light, where a boat was lowered for Keyes and Tomkinson to meet Admiral Campbell in the *Bacchante*, to make arrangements for a submarine escort. Both were appalled by the *Bacchante*'s dirty condition, caused by recent coaling, and the seemingly inefficient ship's company.[16]

On their way back to Harwich, the *Lurcher* intercepted a message, telling of Britain's first triumph of the war by the *Amphion* and the 3rd Destroyer Flotilla – the sinking of the minelayer *Königen Louise*. The next afternoon another message was received that the flotilla was 'engaging scouting cruisers near the Sink lightship'. Keyes boarded the

Lurcher in Harwich and Tomkinson ordered full speed to the north to intercept the enemy. Could this be 'The Day', as they termed it, of Agamemnon, when the German High Seas Fleet clashed head-on with the British? Both sides believed that the enemy would appear quickly in large numbers and the war would soon be over. This was to be the first of many such false alarms, mainly through poor signalling and decoding.

It transpired that the flotilla had fired on the neutral steamer, *St Petersburg*, carrying the German ambassador back to Holland. Flying a German flag, she resembled the *Königen Louise* and, in haste, thinking she was another minelayer, the flotilla blazed away at her. Paradoxically, the order was countermanded by Captain Fox in the *Llewellyn*. Unknown to Keyes, the *Amphion*, with twenty prisoners on board, had run into a mine laid by her victim, the *Königen Louise*, on her way back to Harwich. Fox had been saved by the destroyer *Llewellyn* and stopped the sinking of the *St Petersburg*.[17]

For the next week Tomkinson was at sea in the *Lurcher* on patrol in support of the transportation of the British Expeditionary Force to France. With the *Firedrake* and every available submarine, the line of defence was planned to be between the Galloper and Hinder lightships, north of the Goodwin Sands, but it was too large a section to defend, so the thirteen submarines moved south to an area off the North Foreland and the Sandettie Bank, with the *Lurcher* and *Firedrake* guarding just to the north. 'August the 13th will be the day the enemy will come out,' Keyes predicted to Tomkinson – but neither forecast, nor threat became a reality.[18]

Tomkinson could not see the point of the *Lurcher* guarding submarines at night, and had written peevishly in his diary – the keeping of which by officers was banned by the Admiralty – 'Spent the night at sea with submarines. This is a bad plan. They should be by themselves at night.'[19]

Even in good weather there was difficulty in communicating with submarines. Normally boats were sent across, until Ranken, one of Tomkinson's officers, fitted up a cask, which the *Lurcher* towed astern for a submarine to pick up. On 9 August, after a mishap with this method, Tomkinson wrote sarcastically in his diary '. . . the cask with all secret orders in it was put over the side by some genius and, of course, the hawser carried away. The said genius didn't report it. . . . However, we eventually sighted it and picked it up.'[20]

Mistakes similar to this were commonplace in the early days of the war, when identification signals were often misread. Once, when the *Lurcher* failed to reply quickly to a challenge from the 1st Destroyer Flotilla she was nearly fired on. Tomkinson, never one to ignore slackness, was always concerned about the dilatoriness he observed in Cruiser Force C, which often failed to rendezvous. It seemed obvious to him that it was only a matter of time before the old cruisers were 'bagged by enemy subs', if the Admiralty persisted with their orders to remain on the Broad Fourteens, close to enemy shores.[21]

After a week at sea, with just two refuelling trips for the *Lurcher* at Dover, the patrol line was disconnected and all returned to Harwich, where Tomkinson found the atmosphere not to his liking. The *Maidstone* had set up a beer canteen on the jetty, which was open for three hours each evening. 'I'm not sure this is a good thing', he commented. There was also 'rather a superfluity' of wives and girlfriends staying at the Station Hotel, who had been gossiping about naval movements. 'It cannot be good for anyone to have his friends staying so close,' he complained in his diary. 'They naturally want to be with him until the last minute whenever he goes to sea and his ship must suffer to some extent.'[22]

Keyes was also not finding the set-up to his liking. After Jellicoe, the commander-in-chief, reported to the Admiralty that he was having difficulty in keeping in communication with forces in the southern area of the North Sea, it was decided that Rear-Admiral Christian, in the *Euryalus*, would take under his wing all Tyrwhitt's destroyers and Keyes' submarines, in addition to the five old cruisers of C Force.

6
BATTLE OF HELIGOLAND

As Keyes became increasingly impatient that the war was not being prosecuted efficiently or industriously, he took naval policy into his own hands on 18 August after four submarine commanders had returned with information that there was an abundance of targets in the Heligoland Bight. He cast off the role of shepherd of submarines, borrowed four destroyers from Tyrwhitt and, in the *Lurcher* accompanied by *Firedrake* and three submarines, pushed deeper into the Bight than anyone else had achieved in the war so far, but unfortunately his force was not big enough to charm out the enemy.[1]

Because of his submarines' ceaseless activity in the Bight it was known that many enemy destroyers patrolled the western approaches to Heligoland to prevent minelaying and to harass British underwater craft. Their night patrols returned at dawn and were relieved by a big daytime flotilla, which stayed out until dark.

On his return from the three-day mission with Tomkinson, he wrote his famous letter to the Director of Operations, in which was the question: 'When are we going to make war and make the Germans realise that whenever they come out . . . they will be fallen on and attacked.' This he followed with an ambitious plan, hammered out with Tyrwhitt, to raid the German patrols off the western Ems with destroyers, while two lines of submarines would lie in wait – one submerged to attack any defensive action by German cruisers; the other on the surface as decoys for enemy destroyers. The War Staff were not enamoured with it, however, so Keyes went directly to First Lord Churchill who, like himself, wanted to make war, and forced the plan through the Admiralty.[2]

Before Tomkinson, in the *Lurcher*, departed on the first phase of the attack, with *Firedrake* and nine submarines, he was told that apart from the battle cruisers *New Zealand* and *Invincible*, 30 miles to the north, no other Grand Fleet vessels would be involved, therefore any large ship not resembling Tyrwhitt's flagship, the new light cruiser *Arethusa* (which had three funnels and one mast) or the older cruiser *Fearless* (with four funnels and one mast) would almost certainly be German.[3]

The two destroyers and the submarines left Harwich on the night of 26 August and were in position before dawn two days later. After searching for U-boats, at 4 a.m. the *Lurcher* and *Firedrake* steamed towards Heligoland in the wake of the surfaced submarines, with the intention of tempting the Germans to chase them westwards. The closer to land they went, the poorer the visibility became, until it was down to approximately $2^1/_2$ miles. In the *Lurcher*'s WT room, Tomkinson heard from intercepted signals that the *Arethusa* and Tyrwhitt's thirteen destroyers of the 3rd Flotilla, and the *Fearless*, leader of the 1st Flotilla, were being engaged to the north-west of Heligoland. At 7 a.m. firing was heard ahead, followed fifty minutes later by the misty silhouettes of two light cruisers with four funnels and two masts, resembling the German Rostock class. They were so close that Keyes and Tomkinson were of two minds whether to attempt to torpedo them, or to turn out of range. Instead, they shadowed them for fifty minutes and reported intermittently to Tyrwhitt and his destroyers, until they were lost in the mist.

The *Lurcher* continued to try to track them to the north-east before firing was heard again. Immediately ahead were sighted four cruisers, two of the class first seen, while the others were unidentifiable. Keyes switched the *Lurcher* to the north-west, with the intention of luring them towards the battle cruisers *Invincible* and *New Zealand*. Fortunately, the mist lifted and Tomkinson suddenly became aware that all four were similar to ships of the 1st Light Cruiser Squadron. They were challenged by light signal at 9.50 a.m. and back came a friendly answer from Commodore William Goodenough, in the *Southampton*, who also revealed that Vice Admiral David Beatty's 1st Battle Cruiser Squadron was in the area.[4]

Battle plans had been changed and not a word of the new strategy had reached Keyes.

His main concern now was that his submarines might attack their own countrymen; this was exacerbated nearly two hours later, when, in trying to contact the destroyers, five British battle cruisers were sighted heading towards Heligoland at top speed. Tomkinson was given the hopeless order by Keyes to get ahead of them in an attempt to warn the submarines of their approach, although communication would have been virtually impossible, because once any unidentified ship was sighted a submarine normally dived. Instead, the *Lurcher* ran into the final stages of the first sea battle of the war.[5]

At 12.37 p.m. the sound of heavier firing began ahead, and the mist was punctuated by gun flashes, followed by yellow smoke and fumes. The German light cruiser *Mainz*, which earlier had scored hits on the destroyers *Liberty*, *Laertes* and *Laurel*, was herself in her death throes, as she was ringed by Goodenough's light cruisers and cannonaded with their 6-in shells. Remarkably, after being hit aft and unable to steer a straight course because of a damaged rudder, she fought on, until a torpedo skewered in. Her main mast collapsed and two of her funnels crashed into interlocking positions as cruisers and destroyers used her for target practice.

There was a sudden silence, as if her tormentors wanted to give a mark of respect; then came the crump of larger calibre shells as Beatty's battle cruisers, the *Lion, Princess Royal, Queen Mary, New Zealand* and *Invincible*, all five times her size, took up the barrage.[6] By the time the *Lurcher* crossed her track, the *Mainz* was a tangle of iron and steel, with all her adversaries, except the *Liverpool*, seeking other quarries. Around her were dotted survivors in lifebelts, or supported by lashed hammocks. On her upper deck the critically wounded squirmed their last agonies alongside the dazed uninjured.[7]

With his thoughts going back to the prizes he had taken in China, Keyes' first intention

41

was to capture her. Then he put chivalry before avarice and concentrated on saving the defeated. At first Tomkinson had ordered the whaler to be lowered to pick up survivors, although some German officers were insisting that the dispersed crew should not surrender. It was reported to Tomkinson that an enemy officer was shooting men who had jumped overboard. Even in rescue Keyes was adventurous. He ordered the accompanying *Firedrake* to pick up the swimmers and instructed Tomkinson to lay the *Lurcher*'s bows alongside the *Mainz*'s quarterdeck.[8]

Confusion was caused, however, by Captain Edward Reeves, of the *Liverpool*, which was lying off and collecting survivors in three boats. He had ordered his rescuing crews to keep clear of the *Mainz* because he feared she might explode. Not realizing that the *Lurcher* was flying a broad pennant, which marked Keyes' seniority over him, he also signalled the *Lurcher* to keep away. Typically, Keyes ignored him.[9]

In the middle of his approach, with the *Lurcher* 100 yards off, Tomkinson saw a group of enemy officers scramble through the wreckage to a starboard gun and swing it round to bear on the destroyer's bridge. 'They're going to fire at us,' he warned. Keyes reached for a megaphone and shouted at them: 'Don't fire, damn you. I'm coming alongside to save life. Get your fenders out at once.' They understood his intention and secured the *Lurcher*'s port bow, with her forecastle abreast of the *Mainz*'s starboard part of the upper deck.

The German cruiser had settled by the bows, with the result her stern area was jammed with men, many mutilated or dying. Her batteries were twisted shambles; from amidships came spumes of smoke from burning paint, and most of her structure was daubed saffron from the fumes of British lyddite shells.[10] The wreckage exuded such a degree of heat that even on the *Lurcher*'s bridge it scorched Tomkinson's face. He watched as the wounded were hauled in over the bows. 'Some of them were quite hopeless cases, legs blown off, arms blown off and one or two almost disembowelled, but still alive,' he later recorded.

The orderliness of the uninjured surprised him, because they did not attempt to climb down on to the *Lurcher* until all the wounded were hoisted inboard. In all, 224 Germans were rescued, dangerously outnumbering the *Lurcher*'s crew by almost two to one. As the *Mainz*'s list to port increased Tomkinson could see her starboard propellor under his ship so it was imperative that the *Lurcher* should disengage soon to avoid damage or, at the worst, a capsize.[11]

He noticed that there were just three officers left on the *Mainz*. One was in the foremast, making a futile effort to hoist an ensign to signify she had not surrendered; another was marooned on the forecastle by the fire raging amidships and a third – he later turned out to be the son of Von Tirpitz, the commander-in-chief of the German Navy – was still on the poop, near Keyes, after organizing the evacuation of the wounded. When Tomkinson reported the ship's dangerous position, Keyes told this officer that nothing more could be done and the *Lurcher* was casting off. He preferred his hand to help his enemy jump onboard. Instead the officer drew back to attention, saluted and rejected the offer.[12]

'Full speed astern,' Keyes ordered. Tomkinson edged the *Lurcher* away warily at first and then into full power to clear the rapidly rolling *Mainz*, which she had been propping up. The cruiser sank in three minutes, at 1.08 p.m., with her starboard propellor showing last of all.[13] The rescue operation had taken just fifteen minutes, but during that time Beatty had ordered all his ships to withdraw.

Captain Reeves, in the *Liverpool*, had already hoisted his boats and with eighty-seven survivors onboard retreated at high speed to regroup with his squadron. Tomkinson was well aware that although the firing had stopped his ship now faced a new danger – the threat of being captured by the prisoners. The *Lurcher* was within 20 miles of enemy coast and with a crew of seventy – of whom twenty were needed to run her – had just fifty to control 165 fit, if cowering, Germans herded on the forecastle. But when the *Mainz* had gone down all had jumped up and given three cheers for the Kaiser. It appeared that this ritual might have been a signal for an insurrection, but they were ordered to sit down again and obeyed.

Once the *Lurcher* and *Firedrake* had retrieved their rescue boats, which had been picking up Germans over a wide area, Keyes also gave the order to withdraw at top speed of 33 knots. Soon the engineer officer was reporting to Tomkinson that this was unattainable because the condenser inlets were clogged by surface scum from the *Mainz*. The most that could be obtained was 25 knots.[14]

On the way home the Lurcher met the destroyers *Liberty*, with a dead captain onboard, and *Laurel*, which after the engagement with the *Mainz* could not manage more than 16 knots. *Lurcher*'s speed was reduced to escort them to Harwich.

For the next few hours Keyes was relying on keeping out of range of any scattered enemy force. Although the prisoners were quiet and obedient, it was doubtful whether they would remain in this frame of mind if the *Lurcher* were in action against their comrades, now expected to emerge from the River Jade. The ship was in no condition to fight. Only one of her 4-in guns could bear, because the other housing was jammed with prisoners. Of the four vessels, only *Firedrake* could offer efficient resistance. After three hours of tension on the bridge there came in sight five lumbering ships of Admiral Christian's Cruiser Force C, welcome now, but previously regarded as a hindrance to fast destroyers.

The *Lurcher*'s boats were launched to ferry to the *Cressy* 165 fit, or walking wounded, prisoners. But the cruiser's RNVR surgeon told Keyes that the other fifty-nine were too badly wounded to be moved in the mounting swell. Instead, the doctor and a sick-berth attendant remained in the *Lurcher* – at this stage of the war destroyers did not carry medical officers – as, with the *Firedrake*, she made for Harwich, leaving the maimed destroyers with the cruiser force.[15]

Efforts to alleviate the pain of the wounded and dying were amateurish, because of the sparseness of the ship's medical-chest, although Tomkinson was interested to note that the enemy were better prepared, with each man issued with a first-aid packet of lint and bandages and a mouth pad against fumes. Sheets and shirts were shredded for extra dressings and blankets were taken from officers' bunks and ratings' hammocks. Lieutenant Ranken and Lieutenant Harold Campbell became volunteer doctors, with Ranken gruesomely and gratingly amputating stumps of limbs with a carving knife from the galley. Within an hour, however, twelve prisoners had died. Their bodies were sewn up in hammocks, weighted down with 4-in shells and dropped into the sea. Such was the compassion in this first month of the war that Tomkinson, as captain, felt compelled to read a short burial service.[16]

The passage to Harwich had now become a matter of mercy, but Tomkinson was forced to cut speed when the *Lurcher* ran into fog. She crept into port at 3.05 a.m., grazed a lighter because of the poor visibility and eventually Tomkinson was forced to anchor her in the harbour, instead of alongside. Not until 6 a.m. were all the wounded taken to a hospital ship and by then two more had died.[17] Tomkinson was in no doubt that the traditional chivalry of the Royal Navy had been upheld, although within a few days he was reading neutral contradictory press propaganda of Britain's brutality in the Battle of Heligoland.

There was still a deal of concern and depression about the navy's possible casualties, even though it was nearly twenty-four hours after the action. What had happened to Tyrwhitt and his destroyers? How many ships had gone down in the fleeting skirmishes? Few people at sea that day had a clear picture of the battle. It was not until he obtained information from Captain Arthur Waistell, in the *Maidstone*, that Tomkinson realized it had been a British victory. Germany had lost three light cruisers, the *Mainz*, *Kolb* and *Ariadne*, all decimated by the battle cruisers, and a destroyer (V. 187), while three other cruisers were damaged. Personnel losses amounted to 781 killed and 381 taken prisoner, among them Von Tirpitz's son, and the other two officers Tomkinson had seen in the *Mainz*'s last minutes afloat. British casualties totalled thirty-five killed and forty wounded, with no ships lost.[18]

From the convolution of mislaid signals – the news that Beatty was intervening lay in someone's in-tray at Harwich until the *Lurcher* returned – wrong identification, scattered salvoes and general pandemonium, Tomkinson was later to disseminate how Tyrwhitt escaped in the *Arethusa*. His first encounter was at 7 a.m. when a sequence of mazey attacks and counters occurred. But three hours later he was enmeshed in a web of superior forces, represented by the *Frauenlob, Stettin, Strasburg, Koln* and *Mainz*, all rushed out in defence when the Germans anticipated the raid because of excessive British radio activity. Not only was the new and unsettled *Arethusa* outranged, but three of her guns jammed, a fourth was put out of action and her forward engine-room was awash. In anguish, Tyrwhitt called for help and received immediate reaction from Beatty, 40 miles to the north. His five battle cruisers turned east and swept into the Bight at high speed to save the light forces and hurl out thirty minutes of destruction. In fact, it was Keyes' signal at 9.45 a.m. which stated he was being chased by four enemy cruisers, that menaced Tyrwhitt's force. For half an hour Tyrwhitt turned his flotilla sixteen points to help Keyes, but after signalling to *Fearless* he guessed that Keyes had wrongly identified the 1st Light Cruiser Squadron as the enemy. Instead, Tyrwhitt turned to the west again and into the Bight for a confrontation with enemy reinforcements, arriving after an hour's respite. At the end of the battle, of all the separated ships, the *Arethusa* was in the most parlous plight. With eleven killed and eighteen wounded and only one gun working, she turned for home just before her engines broke down. Fortunately for Tyrwhitt she met the old cruiser *Hogue* and was towed to safety.[19]

44

Of the senior officers involved, the names of Beatty and Tyrwhitt were emblazoned at once as the navy's new heroes. In Tyrwhitt's words, Churchill 'fairly slobbered' over him.[20] It depressed Keyes at first to know that he had played the out-of-character part of stretcher-bearer, rather than the warrior. If he were envious of Tyrwhitt, he did not show it, but soon the friendship of the two men was to sour; afterwards there was to be an undercurrent of jealousy of Tyrwhitt, who although two years older than Keyes, was still his junior in service terms.

Tomkinson, who was to continue his friendship with Tyrwhitt, tenuous though it was to become, seldom envied any of his contemporaries and was content with this mention in dispatches for his role of a saviour in the battle: '*Lurcher* was skilfully handled by Commander Tomkinson, when she was laid alongside the *Mainz* to save life at a time when the latter was sinking rapidly, heavily on fire and the risk of explosion was considerable.'[21]

7
DISENCHANTED BY BLUNDERS

For the next two months Tomkinson was relegated to the role of an 'ordinary' destroyer captain, unable to fly the broad pennant of the commodore because Keyes was banned from going to sea.

When submarine commanding officers had reported that, despite the Battle of Heligoland, enemy destroyer patrols were being maintained as previously, Tyrwhitt and Keyes colluded again to suggest at an Admiralty conference that another raid should be made with the 1st and 3rd Destroyer Flotillas, the submarines and Goodenough's cruiser squadron. Keyes pressed for a cruiser to accommodate him and was given one 'for a few minutes'. When the offer was withdrawn he had to backtrack quickly or not go on the raid, so he intimated he would be happy to stay in the *Lurcher*.

The Keyes/Tyrwhitt plan was adopted, but two days later the Chief of Staff, Admiral Frederick Sturdee, objected to Keyes going to sea at all and 'barging about' in the Bight on his own again, as he had just a week earlier to cause confusion – through no fault of his own – with wrong identification. In spite of Keyes' protests, Sturdee buttonholed Prince Louis, the First Sea Lord, who put it in writing on 6 September that 'the commodore is not to go in a destroyer'. As a sop, Sturdee told Keyes he had a free hand to go anywhere to advise on submarine tactics and policy but, realizing there was a loophole in the Prince's order, added: 'You are not to go afloat.'[1]

For the first time in a large operation Tomkinson was in lone command of the *Lurcher*, as at daylight on 10 September a rendezvous was made with the light cruiser *Amethyst* and Cruiser Force C, off Terschelling. The *Lurcher* proceeded ahead of them towards the Ems, as a backup for the 1st Flotilla, which was aimed at wiping out enemy coastal patrols. At the same time the 3rd Flotilla was sweeping the Heligoland Bight, supported by Goodenough's cruisers. The third tier was formed by Beatty's battle cruisers, while the entire Grand Fleet hovered 100 miles away in case this was 'The Day' the German High Seas Fleet ventured out.

But Tomkinson saw nothing;[2] neither did other eyes in the fleet, for the German Navy, after its earlier mauling, had been ordered by the Kaiser to go on the defensive in the North Sea to avoid further losses.

It was the last attempt by surface vessels to bring out the enemy for three months. Instead, at Keyes' instigation and after Lieutenant-Commander Max Horton, in E9, had torpedoed the old cruiser *Hela*, more submarines were sent to the Baltic.[3]

For the remainder of September Tomkinson and the *Lurcher* were involved in the monotony of patrol work until the 22nd, one of the most catastrophic and incompetent days in British naval history.

At 1 a.m. with *Firedrake* in company, he picked up two submarines off Smith's Knoll with the intention of towing them for a mission in the Kattegat.[4] Seven hours later the plan was changed. A wireless telegraphy (WT) message from Keyes, in Harwich, instructed him to leave the submarines and meet him off Terschelling at 6 p.m. to try to intercept U-boats returning from the Broad Fourteens. Tomkinson was mystified by the message until the *Lurcher* intercepted another from Tyrwhitt, in the cruiser *Lowestoft*, that the ancient cruisers *Aboukir, Hogue* and *Cressy* had been torpedoed and sunk by a U-boat. But Tomkinson and Keyes never kept their rendezvous. Not until he returned to Harwich was Tomkinson given the full story.

In the early hours that morning Keyes, in the *Maidstone*, had been woken by his secretary with an urgent letter from the Admiralty, informing him that his suggestion to send younger men to Cruiser Squadron C to replace the old reservists, and therefore to make it more efficient, had been approved. At 7 a.m. a servant was shaking Keyes again with this more dramatic message from the *Cressy*: '*Aboukir* sunk. *Hogue* sinking.'[5]

For four hours he waited for further news from Tyrwhitt who, in the *Lowestoft* and with eight destroyers of the 3rd Flotilla, had also waited for a gale to subside before going out to screen the unprotected cruiser squadron. The long-delayed signal from Tyrwhitt said: 'Loss due to submarine. Send destroyers to cut sub off at Terschelling.' Keyes was intent on summary revenge. He telephoned the Admiralty and told the Director of Operations that he was going out as a 'passenger' with Captain Blunt, in the *Fearless*, to hunt submarines. The director hesitated and put him through to Sturdee. Keyes repeated his intention, but Sturdee refused permission. Keyes argued: 'Surely there is no one better qualified than I, the Commodore of Submarines, to hunt submarines.' Sturdee relented.[6]

Keyes knew that there was little chance of intercepting U-boats at this stage of the war, when there were no listening devices or depth charges. He now saw himself in the role of an approved knight errant and it clouded his judgement. By noon he was at sea in the *Fearless* with eight destroyers of the 1st Flotilla. It was not enough for him and he began to signal every destroyer within six hours' sailing time of Terschelling, where he had agreed to meet Tyrwhitt's force and Tomkinson. After an hour's signalling, he had rounded up seventeen destroyers to 'sink, burn and destroy the enemy' – as Lord Fisher had prescribed for battle years earlier. Until then he had not communicated with his commander-in-chief, Admiral Jellicoe, who with the Grand Fleet was at Scapa Flow. As the Admiralty had supported his plan, Keyes could assume Jellicoe had been informed, so flamboyantly he transmitted his intentions to the ultra-cautious commander-in-chief.

'Propose to attack light patrol off Ems River at dawn with 1st Destroyer Flotilla,' Keyes signalled, ignoring the fact that he was supposed to be a U-boat hunter. Jellicoe, normally hesitant to commit his warships, surprisingly signalled his approval, with the rider: 'In view of weakness, leave before daylight.' Keyes' enthusiasm was as infectious as ever, for Jellicoe joined in by sending two cruisers.

The Commodore of Submarines had taken care to ensure that the Admiralty was not notified of his change of tactics. But other ears were listening and his signals to Jellicoe were intercepted by a vigilant officer at the Royal Navy base at Ipswich and passed to Whitehall. With ships speeding towards Terschelling and then to the Ems, the Admiralty called 'enough'. They were ordered to return to their previous positions and Keyes was peremptorily instructed to 'Report to Admiralty immediately.' He admitted later: 'I hadn't the courage to disobey such a definite order.'[7] Tomkinson heard from his friend: 'The War Staff of course were simply furious, but so was I, for I had travelled up from Harwich with a trainload of survivors from who I had learnt that the navy had lost over 1,400 lives.'[8]

His anger was echoed by this entry in Tomkinson's diary: 'No doubt by leaving these ships in the south part of the North Sea we have simply been asking for this. It is, of course, [all] very well to say "I told you so," but it is a fact. I know that the War Staff have been warned about this for the last six weeks and I think the loss of these three ships and about 1,000 lives must be laid at their door. It is really monstrous that the enemy should be given such a cheap victory – victory it is and there is no point in belittling the performance of the submarine.'[9]

Keyes' disenchantment with the Admiralty began to rub off on Tomkinson, for around this period his diary proliferated with comments such as: 'I cannot see the point of patrolling and wearing out our good destroyers in bad weather.' Or: 'He [Admiral of Patrols George Ballard] doesn't seem to at all grasp the submarine situation – the reason being probably that he is too pigheaded to take advice from those who know, and understand, their capabilities, functions and weaknesses.'[10]

The efficient Tomkinson also fumed about the inefficiency of Whitehall civil servants. When he asked for matting to protect the *Lurcher*'s bridge from shell splinters he was sent 200 potato sacks and instructed to fill them with coal. He wired back that they were unsuitable, but was told they were being dispatched 'as requested'.[11]

He was also irritated by the many false alarms for raising steam, ready to go into the Bight. Impatient as he was to get at the enemy, he enjoyed his days ashore, golfing or walking.

The old partnership with Keyes was re-formed for four days during October, when the *Lurcher*, E4 and E11 were needed to cover the cross-Channel transportation of the 7th Army Division and the 3rd Cavalry to Zeebrugge, then virtually an unknown port, but later to be linked inextricably with Keyes. The Admiralty feared an enemy attack on the harbour from the seaward, but at first did not endorse Keyes' plan to use the submarines in shallow seas close to minefields as a ploy to prevent the chances of bombardment by the German fleet. But his persistence was rewarded and eventually he was told wearily by Sturdee: 'Yes, do as you propose.'[12] It was a decision that in the future was to help embroider the Keyes' legend and bring honour to Tomkinson. Such was the confidence of Keyes that he said later: 'I felt very strongly that the navy should do everything in its power to ensure that the Army gets over and sufficiently far from the coast to be safe from the enemy's fleet – so I went myself.'

During the successful operation, with the *Lurcher* moored alongside the main mole, Tomkinson spent a great deal of time noting the docks and the topography, as he had done with Keyes in China. There were no large-scale charts of Zeebrugge, but the facilities available – a mole 1 mile long by 100 yards wide, connected with the continental rail system by a huge steel viaduct, excellent roads, lock gates and electric cranes – surprised both men. If they had known that within a few days the port would be in the hands of the enemy, then 15 miles away, their optimism of using its docks for disembarkation to the front would have been dulled and more thought would have been given to destroying the lock gates, which gave a canal passage to Bruges.

Soon Zeebrugge was awhirl with army activity as transports unloaded men, horses, mules and ammunition. By the second day 15,000 had landed; they belonged to crack regiments like the Household Cavalry, Royal Horse Guards, Life Guards, Hussars, Lancers, Dragoons, Scots Guards, Gordons and Scots Fusiliers.[13] With their arrival Tomkinson was introduced to a new circle of comrades by Keyes.

Alongside a passenger ship early one morning he chatted to an unknown bewhiskered and medal-bedecked lieutenant colonel of the 1st Life Guards. Tomkinson left him to breakfast onboard the *Lurcher* and then returned to the mole with Keyes to greet a group of officers. Among them was the hirsute colonel, who was introduced to him as the Duke of Teck, the eldest brother of Queen Mary. With him was his brother, Prince Alexander George, later the Earl of Athlone, second in command of the 2nd Life Guards.[14] The Duke had a fad for collecting medals, but was not familiar with one of the ribbons Tomkinson wore on his chest. When he explained it was the Stanhope Gold Medal for his attempted rescue in Bigbury Bay, the Duke pointed it out to all of his entourage, to the embarrassment of the retiring and shy Tomkinson. In turn, Teck was embarrassed when his own medals were examined, and apologized for wearing his civil GCB, or Knight's Grand Cross, on military uniform.[15]

It was during the trips in and out of Zeebrugge that Tomkinson began to feel severe stomach pains, from which he was 'fairly doubled up most of the day'. He had experienced twinges before, but now feared he would have to get medical advice. Nevertheless, on his return to Harwich he found that Joan had sent him 'some of our grapes' and, being an inveterate fruit lover, he could not stop himself eating them. That afternoon he called in a naval doctor from Shotley, but despite being warned it might be an ulcer, put it down to indigestion.[16]

The pains did not diminish, however, and a week later he told Keyes, who made an appointment for him to see the specialist Sir Berkeley Moynihan in Leeds. 'If ever I have anything wrong with my inside I shall go straight to Berkeley Moynihan,' Keyes had said. 'He saved those two brothers-in-law of mine.'[17]

The outcome of the examination Tomkinson kept to himself, but it is fairly certain from what was to happen before the end of the war that he was told he had a duodenal ulcer, which could be treated temporarily with medicine. There is no mention in his diary at this time of the diagnosis, but instead there is the ecstasy of his being able to arrange for Joan to meet him in London after his return from Leeds for her birthday weekend at the Windsor Hotel, near St James's Park, where on the first evening they did not go out but 'spent a very nice and happy time'. This was followed by the guarded, yet tantalizing, entry next morning 'Rather late for breakfast!'[18] The varied events of that weekend – lunch at Scotts, shopping at Selfridges, a visit to London Zoo, an Alahambra show and a sermon by Dean Inge at Westminster Abbey – were all described as 'delightful' and underlined that although he always had an eye for a pretty woman, his love for Joan was unquenchable. His diary is full of mentions of her, even when she was not with him. For example, on a fine autumn day he wrote: 'Would love to be blackberrying with Joan.' His thoughts were seldom of himself and it was to be another three years before the serious-ness of his stomach disorder recurred.

Meanwhile, the restless Keyes was constantly thinking up 'stunts' for the *Lurcher*, most of which, including a sortie into the Kattegat, were rejected by the Admiralty. There were continuous reports of floating mines, laid by the Royal Navy, which broke adrift easily. 'Our mining is rotten and it seems a pity that we ever started it,' Tomkinson com-plained. This led to Keyes' idea of fitting out the *Lurcher* and *Firedrake* as minelayers, which was eventually accepted.[19]

The commodore, however, was making a nuisance of himself at the Admiralty, and some of his belligerent suggestions remained in pigeon-holes to be dusted off fifty years later by historians and researchers. As his right-hand man, Tomkinson inevitably found himself drawn into unwanted controversy, although his loyalty never wavered. During most planned operations now, the *Lurcher* and *Firedrake*, as 'Keyes' ships', were left in Harwich with whatever glory available in the North Sea – the cruiser *Undaunted* sank four torpedo boats in one action – being left to Tyrwhitt's force. When Tomkinson's destroyer was just one of six left in port one day he moaned: 'I suppose Tyrwhitt doesn't want us.' With plenty of time on his hands most afternoons he was able to work out his frustration of inactivity on the golf course. When he was offered the captaincy of the depot ship *Maidstone*, he rejected it because the *Lurcher* gave him a 'better chance of a show, while *Maidstone* means no fighting'.[20]

The Admiralty expected a German attempt at invasion during the late days of autumn and this was reflected by the number of false alarms, when the *Lurcher* was signalled to raise steam for full speed and leave harbour immediately – only for the order to be coun-termanded at the last moment. 'It really is pitiful the state of panic that some people, naval and military, get when any ships of the enemy are reported in the North Sea,' Tomkinson criticized.[21]

At the Admiralty, important changes were being made, which eventually, although obtusely, were to divert Tomkinson from the North Sea. When Prince Louis resigned as First Sea Lord at the end of October – mainly through controversy over his German birth and a succession of naval failures – Lord Fisher, the founding father of the modern navy, but now a supercilious, over-critical old man, was recalled to office. This was to have several repercussions for Keyes, who had crossed swords with him about submarine poli-cy before the war.[22] Fisher was the first admiral to realize the potential of the submarine, and as soon as he took office again he began sniping at Keyes' handling of the service, particularly the building programme. One of his first moves was to bring in Captain S.S. Hall to supervise construction policy.[23]

Tomkinson could see the danger signals and wrote:

I am afraid the new regime at the Admiralty has very much upset him [Keyes]– it is wicked to bring back Hall as submarine adviser. I doubt if RK [Keyes]will stay on. . . . He was very perturbed about the state of affairs at the Admiralty. It is a bad business that there should be discord up there at such a time as this [it was just after the sinking of the *Good Hope* and *Monmouth* at Coronel]. It was bound to come with the return of Lord Fisher and his unscrupulous methods. I shouldn't be surprised if he got Winston out of it and became First Lord himself.[24]

A prime example of those unscrupulous methods came at the beginning of December 1914, when this 'extraordinary' signal from Tyrwhitt was received by Keyes: 'Admiralty informs me that I am appointed Commodore First Class from tomorrow.' It outraged Keyes that he should be told in this way by an officer junior to himself and who was now promoted over his head. He wrote to his wife: 'Lord Fisher is really a ruthless, unforgiving old villain and he is so vindictive. . . . I really think Tomkinson and Waistell were more angry than I was.'[25]

At the same time, Vice Admiral Henry F. Oliver, the new Chief of Staff, was asked by Fisher why Keyes did not go to sea more, like Tyrwhitt, knowing nothing of the order by Prince Louis that Keyes was to confine himself to shorebound duties.[26] Now the position had become even more invidious for Keyes, because Tyrwhitt's new seniority was in the way. He could hardly go to sea and take charge of operations with just two destroyers, while Tyrwhitt had four cruisers and forty destroyers at his disposal. In the first stages of the war Tyrwhitt was content to serve under Keyes, but now he was the swashbuckler of the North Sea. Tomkinson could not understand Tyrwhitt's unprecedented advancement, because Goodenough and Keyes were first in the promotion list of seagoing officers. 'I don't know why, unless it is Fisher's method of slighting our commodore,' he wrote.[27]

Keyes managed to establish a truce with Fisher by writing a letter, which bordered on the obsequious in praising his ability and ruthless energy. Although this momentarily touched the narrow, generous streak of Fisher's nature,[28] Keyes was still sidelined and 'kept out of it'. The worst slight came during the bombardment of England's north-east coast by German battle cruisers on 16 December. Naval Intelligence, who through the Russians possessed the German Navy's cipher and signal books after the cruiser *Magdeburg* was wrecked in the Baltic, had pieced together enemy plans two days before the incursion.

A strategy to trap the Germans was evolved between Jellicoe, Beatty and Tyrwhitt. Beatty's battle cruisers and Goodenough's light cruiser squadron, supported by battleships commanded by Admiral Sir George Warrender, were to be stationed off the southeast of the Dogger Bank, while Tyrwhitt and his two flotillas were to be off Yarmouth. The target was expected to be Harwich or the Humber; in case it was aimed at a more southerly objective, Keyes was ordered to have the *Lurcher*, *Firedrake* and eight submarines spread out on a 30-mile line north-north-west of Terschelling.[29] But the detailed information that Naval Intelligence had disseminated was not given to Keyes. He met Tomkinson onboard the *Lurcher* at 5 p.m. on 15 December not knowing that the German force was expected to comprise four battle cruisers, several cruisers and two, or three, destroyer flotillas; neither was he informed of their date of departure or the strength of the intercepting forces.[30] Like his commodore, Tomkinson was annoyed about the orders and was later to grumble about the War Staff's idea of a submarine patrol line: 'We think it useless and very difficult to carry out.'[31]

The futility of what was to happen in the next thirty-six hours was presaged as soon as they left harbour with the *Firedrake* and eight submarines. The *Lurcher*'s steering jammed, forcing her to anchor for repairs. It was two-and-a-half hours before they were under way[32] – precious hours which might have avoided a serious mix-up. Because the submarines went on independently in abysmal weather, with strong tides, it was difficult for their positions to be established accurately and in the storm it was virtually impossible to contact them if new orders arrived. The commanders had also been told that if the enemy were not seen and they received no fresh instructions, they should return to Harwich the next evening.[33] After a night of torrential rain and a severe westerly wind, only one submarine, the French *Archimede*, could be found. Then at 10.30 a.m., for the first time, Keyes and Tomkinson realized the enormity of the operation. They were out of range on destroyer band wireless, but the WT room picked up a faint signal from the 2nd Battle Squadron that the enemy were off Scarborough. Unable to ask for new orders, Keyes sent the *Firedrake* at full speed towards Yarmouth to set up a new line of communication through the submarine tender *Adamant*, which had a telephone link direct to the Admiralty. In this way he was eventually able to tell Chief of Staff Oliver that he was rounding up the submarines and awaiting new orders. Meanwhile, Tomkinson set up a series of look-outs to search for the scattered submarines.

By the end of the day only four were contacted. At 3.30 p.m. *Firedrake* conveyed this answer from the Admiralty: 'High Sea Fleet is at sea and at 12.30 p.m. was in lat 54.38N. 5.55E (near Dogger Bank). They may return after dawn tomorrow. Submarines should proceed to Heligoland and intercept them. They will probably pass west of Heligoland, steering for Weser light vessel.'[34]

On a howling, black December evening it was 5 p.m. by the time Tomkinson had contacted four submarines with written instructions that they were to reach their new position by 3 a.m. to attack from the surface before daylight. After discussing the altered strategy with Tomkinson, Keyes was tempted to dash into the Bight with the *Lurcher* and *Firedrake* in a stopping operation of his own; but he had been accused in the past of intervening on missions of self-aggrandisement so this time he smothered his impetuosity and for the next three hours *Lurcher* and *Firedrake*, by using searchlight signalling, endeavoured to round up the missing submarines.[35]

In the Admiralty War Room there was complete dejection, for the sprung trap had not been closed. No one had anticipated a raid on the north-eastern coast, and the first news of it came at 8 a.m. with the German battle cruisers bombarding the open towns of Hartlepool, Scarborough and Whitby. The British ships were 100 miles to the south and still seemed certain to cut off their retreat, when the plan began to fall apart. In high seas and poor visibility, Tyrwhitt was forced to send his destroyers back to Harwich and press on with his four light cruisers unescorted.[36]

As the weather worsened to 2,000-yard vision, the interceptors had only fleeting glimpses of the enemy. At 11.30 a.m. Goodenough's four light cruisers, 5 miles ahead of Beatty's battle cruisers, fired on their German counterparts, the *Stralsund, Strasburg* and *Grudenau*, which were the probing force for Admiral Franz von Hipper's battle cruiser squadron of *Derfflinger, Moltke, Von der Tann, Seydlitz* and *Blucher*. But because of mistaken orders, the British cruisers disengaged. Thirty minutes later Warrender, in the *King George V*, sighted them again, then lost them in a rain squall. Hipper was warned of the presence of battleships and altered course to escape them and Beatty's squadron.[37]

Then at 2 p.m. in the War Room came the belated, astonishing report that the whole German High Seas Fleet had been sent out in support – and this with Jellicoe's Grand Fleet still more than 200 miles away off Scapa Flow.[38] Suddenly the situation changed yet again. Admiral von Ingenohl had heard from his advanced screen as early as 5.45 a.m. that they had met British warships. Strangely, at this moment only, he remembered the Kaiser's orders that actions which could involve heavy losses must be avoided – and turned for home.[39]

By now, in the general alarm, Warrender and Beatty had been warned not to venture too far to the east and that there was no opportunity of catching the raiders. All that remained between them was a handful of submarines, the *Lurcher* and the *Firedrake*, now 200 miles away from Heligoland.

At 8 p.m. in the War Room, the strategists knew they would be sending the *Lurcher* and *Firedrake* to certain destruction by diverting them to Heligoland with orders to attack the returning huge German force. Fisher, Oliver and Sir Arthur Wilson agreed that, although they were virtually sending Keyes to his death, there was no alternative. The message was sent at 8.12 p.m.[40] But fate was on the side of Keyes, the fatalist, and Tomkinson, his more religious shipmate. Instead of dispatching the signal through the line of communication Keyes had taken the trouble to set up, it was sent through ordinary destroyer channels and he did not receive it until five hours later, when the *Lurcher* was returning and 50 miles from Harwich. Keyes wrote later: 'I got the signal at 1.20 a.m., when I was too far off the objective to carry it out. The only thing is one must regard it as Kismet. All the same, Tomkinson and I were, are still, too sick for words – for there was much merit to be acquired.'[41]

8
BATTLE OF DOGGER BANK

It was two days before Christmas, when at dusk Tomkinson heard overhead the roar of nine seaplanes from the Naval Air Station at Felixstowe. He knew then that his Christmas Day would be spent at sea in the first ever air–sea operation.

Churchill had been keen for the newly born Naval Air Service to raid Zeppelin sheds at Cuxhaven, more than 350 miles from Harwich, which was out of range for land-based aircraft. Three cross-Channel passenger steamers, the *Engadine, Riviera* and *Empress*, were fitted with steel hangars to house three seaplanes each. They were to be escorted by Tyrwhitt's destroyers to 15 miles from Heligoland, where they would take off. After the attack they were to reconnoitre Wilhelmshaven and river anchorages, fly westward along the coast to Norderney Gat and then turn seaward to be picked up by the carriers 20 miles out.[1]

Keyes, who this time took part in the planning of what was known as Y operation, was providing support with eleven submarines, escorted by the *Lurcher* and *Firedrake*, who would be stationed in a follow-my-leader formation to point the way back to the carriers. His commanding officers were warned that they were expected to help the planes 'regardless of all other considerations'.

Several of the War Staff, who had no faith in some of Churchill's rash ideas, went along with this one in the far-fetched hope that it might provoke a German surface ship reaction, for which the Grand Fleet would be concentrated in the middle of the North Sea. The December weather had not been favourable for the attack until the 23rd, when the forecasters promised a bright, calm Christmas Day.

Early on Christmas Eve Tyrwhitt's force steamed slowly out of Harwich, careful to keep speed down to 22 knots, the maximum of the three cumbersome carriers.[2] Few officers had confidence in the raid and when the destroyer captains Mackworth, of the *Ferret*, and Freemantle, of the *Badger*, parted earlier they shook hands solemnly and agreed they would be lucky to meet again. Some stewards, who had landed to collect turkeys and geese for the festivities, wisely decided to stay ashore until the last of the strange looking cavalcade had sailed.[3] The *Lurcher* and *Firedrake* left at 6 a.m. and by next morning were 10 miles from the enemy coast – the closest of all the surface vessels. At 7.30 a.m. on

54

Christmas Day Tomkinson passed on the message from Tyrwhitt that seven seaplanes had taxied off, but the remaining two could not get away and had been hoisted in again.[4]

For the next three hours the *Lurcher* was shadowed in turn by two Zeppelins, hesitant to attack, although the destroyer had no anti-aircraft weapons or guns which could bear on them. Several German seaplanes were also buzzing busily without bothering the *Lurcher*. At 9.30 a.m. Tomkinson saw a British seaplane heading towards the ship, just above the waves. It landed nearby and taxied alongside. The pilot, Lieutenant Robert Ross, shouted across that he had run out of petrol; he was taken onboard and his machine was tethered and towed along by the destroyer.[5]

The *Lurcher* steamed on to rendezvous with Tyrwhitt's pick-up vessels and on the way spotted two more British seaplanes and a German aircraft. After an hour they met the *Engadine* and handed over Lieutenant Ross and his plane. Only two others had been recovered. Tyrwhitt waited until 11.45 a.m. and then ordered a general withdrawal, for it was known that long before then the missing planes' fuel would have been exhausted.

Keyes had no intention of retreating and ordered Tomkinson to turn the *Lurcher* back to the original marker point, with the idea of drawing enemy vessels away from the 'retriever' ships, slowly heading for Harwich. Both were relieved to see the sterns of the dawdling carriers and felt sure that at any moment a counter-attack force would be steaming out. But not one enemy surface vessel did they see as they searched for the missing airmen.

At 2.20 p.m. the E11, skippered by Lieutenant Martin Dunbar-Nasmith, destined to win the VC in the Sea of Marmara, was able to signal by wireless that he had picked up the pilots and mechanics of three seaplanes, but had been forced to submerge because of a Zeppelin attack. At 20 fathoms the crew of E11 shared their Christmas turkey and pudding with the survivors.[6] This still left one plane to be found. The *Lurcher* pressed on deeper into enemy waters, only to run into a German seaplane, which approached from astern. It was so low that the layer of the 4-in gun could only get his sights on it with a few degrees of elevation in hand. Keyes, who was standing nearby, urged him to give the gun a swing up as he fired, just as he would for a rocketing pheasant. 'She looked like a frightened bird and disappeared,' Tomkinson reported later.[7] It was the first time a gun on the *Lurcher* had been fired in anger.

Although the search was given up at dusk, Keyes was still not satisfied. Tomkinson was given new orders to cruise between the Ems and Terschelling to look for enemy craft which might be hunting homeward-bound submarines. But the Germans were not stirring that Christmas night, and at 8 p.m. the *Lurcher* turned for Harwich, with the delayed festivities now piped for the crew.

Back in port Tomkinson heard that the pilot of the last missing plane had been picked up by a Dutch fishing-boat – and so ended the first air–sea raid in history.[8]

It had been a bombing failure, however, for the pilots failed to spot the Zeppelin sheds, because of a dense frost–fog, but their appearance caused such surprise over Skellig Roads that, in their haste to get under way, an enemy battle cruiser and light cruiser were badly damaged in a collision.[9] It was still unbelievable that seven primitive seaplanes could fly a total of 120 miles around fortified bases without a human casualty and that a

British force could occupy German waters for sixteen hours without seeing an enemy ship.[10]

The *Lurcher* moored at Harwich on Boxing Day morning and that afternoon Keyes dispatched tins of bull's-eyes, which his wife had sent, to all ships in port. 'Tomkinson was most awfully pleased,' he told her.[11]

Any chance of Tomkinson distinguishing himself depended on the attacking ability of Keyes, who chased every forlorn chance now that the situation had diametrically changed and he was expected by Fisher to be at sea whenever the weather permitted. When the submarine C31, commanded by Lieutenant G. Pilkington, one of the flotilla's brightest and most popular officers, was several days overdue after a patrol off Zeebrugge – she was never heard of again and her loss has remained a mystery – Keyes, who described himself at the time as being 'bloodyminded', decided she had probably been sunk by enemy trawlers. On 10 January in the *Lurcher* and with Tomkinson's constant companion, the *Firedrake*, they arrived 5 miles off Zeebrugge at high tide in order to clear the minefield. They could see the main hotel and government buildings, but ventured no closer because they knew there was a battery of 6-in guns on the breakwater. No patrol craft were out, however, and with the weather roughening they headed for home. So tempestuous did it become that Tomkinson vomited up the cocoa that his steward brought him. Keyes, who had only been seasick once before in his thirty years in the navy, also threw up his cocoa. 'I was awfully pleased Tomkinson told me his cocoa had the same fate,' he wrote to his wife. 'He is a very stout sailor.'[12]

In the New Year it was intimated to Keyes by 'friends' at the Admiralty that he was to be given a light cruiser to operate with the *Lurcher* and *Firedrake* and the submarines. 'There seems to be just a chance of my going in command,' Tomkinson confided only to his diary. Both men were soon to be disillusioned.[13]

Another air attack in the Bight was about to be launched and, on 23 January, the *Lurcher, Firedrake* and eight submarines left at 1 a.m. to support Tyrwhitt's flotillas again. Within an hour they were recalled because four German battle cruisers, six light cruisers and twenty-two destroyers were expected to sail that night on a scouting mission off the Dogger Bank. It was 4 a.m. before Keyes had rounded up his submarines and returned to Harwich, where awaiting him was a War Staff message – sent by slower telegram, instead of wireless – which told him to take the *Lurcher, Firedrake* and four submarines to a point near the Borkum Riff light vessel and listen for further orders.

That night he was instructed to dispatch the submarines into the Bight. From the blurred wireless signals received in the *Lurcher* next morning it was clear that a big action was in progress to the north. The *Lurcher* and *Firedrake* were sent at top speed across the German line of retreat – but yet again they were too late by those few hours lost in the recall, and an opportunity of intervening in the Battle of the Dogger Bank was lost. There was a chance, however, of sinking a U-boat, which was about to attack the *Firedrake*. Tomkinson ordered his helmsman to steer towards 4 ft of periscope, which was 100 yards ahead on the port quarter. Full speed was obtained as the *Lurcher* went in to ram. A collision seemed certain, but the U-boat's periscope plunged under the destroyer's bows and she raced over without crashing into it.[14]

For the remainder of that night the *Lurcher* scouted in vain for crippled German ships at the edge of the biggest naval action so far in the war, in which the German battle cruiser *Blucher* was sunk, while the *Seydlitz, Derfflinger* and *Kolberg* were damaged. On Britain's debit side Beatty's flagship, the *Lion*, was severely damaged, forcing him to transfer his flag; yet British casualties were only 15 killed and 80 wounded, against Germany's 954 killed and 80 wounded. The Germans had learned the lesson, however, that magazines were vulnerable to the flash of bursting shells and burning cordite. It should have been a major British victory, but again a signal blunder prevented a complete *coup de grâce*.[15]

Tomkinson and Keyes were later to shake their heads over the gunnery mistakes of the *Tiger*, which they looked on as 'their ship' having been promised her just before the start of the war. Despite being the only battle cruiser fitted with a director fire-control system, she had not registered a single hit. Her commanding officer, Captain H.B. Pelly, came in for searing criticism from Fisher, who considered that his failure to engage the *Moltke* was inexcusable and that he was a 'poltroon' for not charging the enemy, when the *Lion* was forced to steer out of line.[16] Caustic words were also being said of Keyes.

Within a few days the future of Keyes and Tomkinson changed, mainly because of the attitude of Tyrwhitt.[17] There had been an alteration in plans and now Keyes was offered the cruiser *Penelope*; because she had a full four-ring captain in Hubert Lynes, there would be no room for Tomkinson, still a commander. But Tyrwhitt objected to another cruiser being added to the Harwich Force, particularly as it would improve Keyes' status. It appeared that Tyrwhitt, although liked by both men, was playing a two-faced game and was something of a cat's paw for Fisher, who preferred to consult him, rather than Keyes.[18]

By the end of January, Keyes was ready to patch up the quarrel by writing another of his friendly letters – this time to Tyrwhitt. After Tomkinson had been shown a draft of it, he recorded: 'I hope they will manage to settle matters amicably. It seems to me the main points are: 1. Admiralty expect Commodore S to go to sea. 2. A destroyer is not suitable for an officer in his position, quite apart from her limitation with regard to accommodation, personnel and WT capabilities. 3. If he does have a cruiser, the choosing of his captain is his business and no-one elses.'

On the last point, Tomkinson was concerned that Keyes was putting his loyalty to him first and insisting on his being given command. 'I don't like to think that I have become in any way a bone of contention,' Tomkinson said,[19] not realizing that for the next four months under the Fisher regime, anyone whom Keyes wished to appoint became a bone of contention, and seldom got the job.[20]

Within a week Tyrwhitt and Keyes appeared to have shaken hands and forgotten the controversy. But Tomkinson had not. He sounded out several officers, with whom he had social contact at golf, or tennis, and was able to state:

From what I hear through these destroyer commanders, I am afraid Commodore T [Tyrwhitt] has been acting a double part with Keyes – it is very regrettable. I understand that he thinks submarines are no good and have done nothing and is tired of hearing, I suppose from Keyes, what fine fellows they were. Well, granted they have not done as much as they would have done had they had more targets – they have done more than the destroyers have. As far as I know, one hundred, or so, destroyers have accounted for one destroyer and have assisted *Undaunted* to sink four small torpedo boats, armed with three four-pounders each. A lot of 21-in torpedoes have been expended, but in no case is there clear proof that one from a destroyer has hit.[21]

Tomkinson, too, was playing a double part, for socially he, Tyrwhitt and Keyes were great friends, dined together, walked together and knew each other's wives. Intrigue in their professional careers never brimmed over into their private or domestic lives.

Although the blame for the blunders of the Battle of the Dogger Bank was being thrust by Fisher on to the shoulders of several senior officers, Keyes, who was blameless himself this time, found he had not been absolved. During the early stages of the battle the Admiralty had signalled him a warning that the German High Sea Fleet was coming out. It was intercepted by the *New Zealand*, but was reported as being sent by Keyes to her Admiral, Sir Archibald Moore, who promptly withdrew. When at the Admiralty, Keyes saw that this had been noted in official reports of proceedings at the War Room, so he tackled one of Fisher's naval secretaries about it. 'I suppose your chief holds me responsible for the failure of the Battle Cruiser Squadron to continue the pursuit, after Beatty fell out of the line,' he questioned, half in jest. The secretary agreed that the point had not escaped Fisher's notice. This led to Keyes writing a denial to the Admiralty.[22]

Keyes knew these altercations must lead to his removal from the submarine service. Two months earlier he had received this sardonic rebuff from Fisher: 'I have not mastered on what basis our submarines harm the enemy more than themselves.'[23] By the beginning of February he was being talked of as becoming the commanding officer of the *Tiger*, or the *Princess Royal*, but realized that they were just 'sop' offers. Finally he asked Churchill for a change of appointment, because 'I am against a very wicked, vindictive, old man, who was absolutely determined to jab a knife into me on every possible occasion and I really think I'm better off out of it.'[24]

Fisher, for his part, was making sure that any support Keyes received from fleet officers was undermined. To Beatty he wrote: 'But Keyes is a fancy man. Why, I don't know. He has made a d . . . d mess of the submarines in the last three years.'[25] To Jellicoe he intrigued ungrammatically: 'Keyes is very shallow and has not shined so far.'[26]

Although Keyes was spending a lot of his time at the Admiralty, he was often at Harwich to keep a fretting Tomkinson up to date. The rumours were affecting him, too, for his old stomach pains began nagging again. Tomkinson's acrimony towards Fisher, whom he called 'that poisonous cunning and wicked, old First Sea Lord', is written vitriolically across the pages of his diary in February 1915.[27]

Although happy to continue as commanding officer of the *Lurcher* without Keyes, he was determined not to stay if Hall took over.[28] Keyes' frequent absences from the *Maidstone* and the *Lurcher* signified that a new appointment was soon to be announced. It came on 9 February, when it was promulgated that he would be chief of staff to Rear-Admiral Carden, commanding the allied naval squadron off the Dardanelles. He had not time to say goodbye to his wife, his family at Fareham, or to his submariners,[29] or to Tomkinson. About the time that his letter of farewell to Tomkinson was delivered, Keyes was crossing the Channel, bound for Marseilles and heading for one of the world's bloodiest and most controversial amphibious operations. But as ever, in his letter to Tomkinson allegiance came first, with the promise that he, too, might be wanted in the Mediterranean and to stand by for his call.[30]

Tomkinson wrote this entry in his diary that night:

> I shall be very glad, indeed, to be with him, but I hope it will be a useful appointment as I don't want to leave the *Lurcher* to go to an indefinite sort of job. Also I should very much like to have a scrap in *Lurcher* before leaving her . . . I must take it as it comes. He has always been very good to me and I would do anything he wants and I know he wouldn't want me to go anywhere unless he thought there was bound to be good out of it. It was perfectly disgusting and contemptible the way that JF [Fisher] and his accomplices have got rid of Keyes and Addison [Commander Percy Addison, Keyes' principal technical assistant in submarines] and made it look as if they were being shot out for mismanagement – after all the good work they have done the last four years or so. Perfectly iniquitous, I call it. There is no end to the meanness and blackguardism of that crowd.[31]

Tomkinson need not have worried about leaving the *Lurcher* immediately. Keyes had planned for him to be given the command of the destroyer *Foresight* in the 'first rush', but although her commanding officer was ill, the Admiralty stopped the appointment. Within a week Keyes had sent Tomkinson a cable from Malta saying there was 'no good billet' available.[32]

Instead, Tomkinson was to concern himself about the organization of the submarines at Harwich. Waistell had, in effect, taken over from Keyes, although in the lower grade of captain of submarines, with Hall in the deskbound appointment of head of the service. Tomkinson was still showing antipathy towards Tyrwhitt's command, and it was aggravated in February 1915, when the *Undaunted* and a division of destroyers all fired on the British submarine E14, when she was off Ymuiden, Holland. Waistell had told Tyrwhitt that the submarine would be in the vicinity, but no one else had been informed. 'Bad work, I call it,' Tomkinson grumbled.[33]

Since Keyes' departure, liaison between the two forces had not improved and Tomkinson was determined to sort it out. He suggested that when Waistell was away he himself should deputize. He sought an official designation, such as assistant to captain of submarines, but although he was expected to stand in, there was no Admiralty recognition of his position.[34]

A month later, Tyrwhitt went to Tomkinson's cabin in the *Lurcher* and had an off-the-record chat with him in a successful effort to win him over. 'He is a most charming person to talk to and it is hard to believe he could do anything that was not absolutely above board,' Tomkinson noted. 'But although I have the greatest admiration for him as a fighter and as a Commodore T, it is impossible to forget his attitude towards Keyes, although it was very short lived . . . he is very ambitious and does not intend to let anything stand in his way.'[35]

Tyrwhitt was keen on trying another seaplane raid, with the target this time the Norddeich wireless station, near the Frisian coast. During the next six weeks seven attempts were made, but on each the destroyers, submarines and makeshift carriers were hampered by bad weather and returned to Harwich without a plane taking off. During the third 'retreat' the *Landrail* ran into the bows of the *Undaunted* in thick fog, killing three stokers and seriously injuring four. On another occasion the destroyer *Lennox* was put out of action when she was rammed by a carrier. The futility of these continual sorties annoyed Tomkinson, who considered that the destroyers would have been better employed on convoy work than on 'these abortive air raids'.[36]

Admiralty confidence in the ability of submarines to operate in the North Sea was diminishing, and it was thought that there were better opportunities in the Dardanelles. It was there that E11, E14 and E15 were diverted in the spring of 1915. Tomkinson's escort duties were therefore curtailed. He had high hopes of going out to the Mediterranean himself when he heard that the commander-in-chief, Admiral Sir John de Robeck, through Keyes, had asked for him and other officers for 'transport and minesweeping duties'. His diary on that day read: 'I don't want to go out for transport, but would not mind the minesweeping, if I was to be in charge, but it would be no good being No. 2 or No. 3 in a job like that. However, I feel sure Keyes would not have me wired for unless there was a good job and if I am asked what I want to do, I shall go.'

But when he went to seek more information about the post from Rear-Admiral Tommy Brand, naval assistant to the Second Sea Lord at the Admiralty, he was told that Fisher was 'dead against' anyone going whom Keyes had asked for.[37] The next day this prediction was confirmed when Fisher refused to let any officer join the Mediterranean staff. Keyes' concern for his old colleague was underlined when he wrote to him soon after saying 'I would do anything to get you here.'[38]

Several times the *Lurcher* and *Firedrake* were left alone in harbour now while other destroyers took on their role as escorts for submarines, which led Tomkinson to suppose that Tyrwhitt 'didn't like the idea of anything being done without him'.[39] This seagoing attitude of Tyrwhitt rebounded on him during his absence, when King George made a surprise visit to Harwich on Thursday 25 March 1915, to present him with the CB. Again, the *Lurcher* and *Firedrake* were the only warships in harbour when the King made an informal inspection of officers and men lined up on the jetty and 'talked with me for a bit', as Tomkinson was to report. The day was made even sweeter for him when Joan arrived to spend two nights with him at a local hotel.[40]

Tomkinson's first long leave of the war at Franche, with Joan, son Peter, daughters Betty and Rachel, and his father and mother, ended in tragedy. On the first day of his holiday, tiny Rachel contracted meningitis. Her first convulsion came the next day, but she seemed to improve during the following twenty-four hours, only to relapse, convulse again and be given chloroform on the last day of his leave. When he returned to Portsmouth, where the *Lurcher* was in dockyard, she was still in a coma. Twenty-four hours later she died, with Joan holding her hand. Tomkinson mourned in his diary: 'What a blank it has left – and I had been so looking forward to playing with her and seeing her just beginning to walk, as I really had seen so little of her. It does seem very, very hard to bear.'[41]

Out of the shadow of personal tragedy, Tomkinson's life took on a more pleasant routine, normally with escort duty, or exercising in the morning, followed by golf or tennis every afternoon. Towards the end of May came Admiralty changes which he applauded. Admiral Sir Henry Jackson, the complete technician and one of the brains of the navy, replaced the devious Fisher as First Sea Lord, while Arthur Balfour, the Prime Minister from 1902 to 1905, and a former Foreign Secretary, took over from Churchill as First Lord. 'Two gentlemen for a change,' Tomkinson approved.[42]

Yet the prosecution of the war by British submarines in the North Sea did not improve, despite fair weather. In one tour of duty in the Bight, D3 met the German battle fleet and missed any target. Tomkinson expressed his disappointment as being 'sickening and to me inexplicable that we have not been able to get a hit when the chance has come. It is so jolly hard to explain in the report to the Admiralty also – and the submarine service do want a success now to buck things up a bit.'[43]

More embarrassment followed a week later when E17, while exercising with the *Lurcher*, collided in fog with the new destroyer *Tipperary*, captained by Barry Domville, one of Tomkinson's golfing partners. She was holed aft and all officers' cabins were flooded.[44]

It was a week of incident for him, not the least being when a look-out reported sighting a U-boat near the Galloper light vessel. Tomkinson ordered the *Lurcher*'s helmsman to 'go for it', but it dived immediately. For some time he stayed in the locality, then its periscope was spotted. Again the *Lurcher* was turned to ram and this time she caught it with her starboard propellor. When she was turned again to look for oil, or debris, Tomkinson discovered all she had hit was a big spar, eight inches in diameter, floating vertically and rising and falling like a periscope. Several hours later, however, came confirmation that there had been a U-boat in the area, when a large collier, which had been torpedoed, was seen bottom up in the last throes of sinking.[45]

To Tomkinson's chagrin the success of enemy submarines became more evident when the *Lurcher* came across the survivors of two British torpedo boats, which had fallen victims after one had stopped to aid the other. The consequence next day was that 'three over-zealous and rather stupid torpedo boats' tried to attack a British submarine, with which Tomkinson was exercising, despite a red warning flag being flown.[46]

The submarines needed constant practice, particularly with torpedo runs, and in early July Tomkinson registered his exasperation at having to go on this placid duty while the *Firedrake*, the light cruisers, destroyers and carriers went on yet another attempted raid of Norddeich. His disgust turned to the contemptuous ejaculation 'What a farce' when out of seven seaplanes two turned round immediately, three failed to take off, another was interned in Holland and only one reached the target zone.[47] For the remainder of that summer the *Lurcher* was mainly confined to escort work as U-boat commanders tightened their grip on the seas around Britain. On two other occasions he had evidence of the menace of German torpedoes. The first came when the *Lurcher* answered an SOS from the destroyer *Mentor*, hit during a minelaying operation, and escorted her at 12 knots into Harwich;[48] the second was when the *Lurcher* picked up survivors – 'two Dutch women, a Chinese lady, two Dutch children, a fox terrier and five men' – from the torpedoed *Königen Emma*. Although there was danger of a lurking U-boat, Tomkinson put the *Lurcher*'s bows along the forecastle of the merchant ship, so that a woman and her husband, who had refused to get into a lifeboat, could step aboard.[49]

Conversely, the closest the *Lurcher* came to being damaged was from the air. When Zeppelin raids were at their height in August, Tomkinson ran up to one of the *Lurcher*'s new anti-aircraft guns to aim it at an enemy airship. But a probing searchlight prevented an accurate shot, apart from five seconds when it caught in its beam the Zeppelin, which immediately dropped two bombs. One sprayed the *Lurcher* with fragments; the other blew shrapnel into the nearby *Firedrake*, wounding a sailor asleep in his hammock. Tomkinson lamented, however, that in nearby Parkeston the eight-year-old daughter of his coxswain was killed by a bomb and his wife seriously injured, just three days after arriving there.[50]

Once during the next month, when on escort duly, three German Taube seaplanes dived on the *Lurcher*, only to veer away as her 4-in guns and $1\frac{1}{2}$-lb pom-poms opened up. Tomkinson reported critically: 'They were at least 60 miles from Borkum and flying well at the time, which seems to be more than one ever gets from our aircraft service here at Felixstowe.'[51]

His sojourn at Harwich came peacefully to an end in September with a shooting party – '30 brace of partridge and some hares', blackberrying expeditions – 'officers picked over 41 lbs for jam', and a meeting with the author Rudyard Kipling, a friend of the family, who was allowed to go out in E5.

Tomkinson's farewell to the *Lurcher* and Harwich was tinged with disappointment, for he was given just twenty-four hours to pack his gear and hand over to the new commanding officer, Harold Dawson, who was only a lieutenant, and report to the Admiralty. 'I am very sorry to leave her and disgusted at being turned out without any warning,' he wrote, 'and without letting me know even where I am going to.'[52]

Next day, a Sunday, somewhat optimistically, he went to the Admiralty to see Hall, who was not on duty. Instead he was interviewed by the Chief of Staff, Admiral Oliver, who told him that he was being sent to Venice to operate a flotilla of British submarines alongside the Italian allies. Once again he was disgusted with the appointment and failed to see 'why I should be taken out of a good seagoing job and dumped into a shore job with absolutely no chance of going to sea'. To his mind it was 'evidently Hall's work'.[53]

In a three-day flurry of packing and farewells, he went home to the Hollies at Tavistock, then returned to the Admiralty to protest in vain to Hall about his new job. By the end of the week he had arrived by train in Venice.

9
VENETIAN VENTURE

Tomkinson entered a confused theatre of war in Venice where, although only a commander, he became the senior British naval officer. Until 26 April 1915, Italy had remained neutral; then she withdrew from the Triple Alliance with Germany and Austria, waiting a month before declaring war on Austria and another two before naming Turkey also as an enemy. Italian liaison with the British and French was fragile because Germany was still a 'friendly power', although U-boats operated from Austrian ports in the Adriatic.

The Allies had welcomed the entry of Italy into the war, as previously Malta was the nearest naval base to the Dardanelles and the Adriatic, where the main actions of the naval war were being fought. Italy's declaration opened up the use of Brindisi and Taranto in the south to stop the Austrian fleet from adding its considerable power to enemy operations in the Mediterranean by emerging through the 45-mile wide Straits of Otranto. In the north, Venice provided a base to bottle up the Austrian navy in Pola (Pula), Trieste and Fiume (Rijeka), their main operational ports. U-boats had entered the Adriatic for the first time in June 1915, with five craft based at Pola. They flew the red, white and red ensign of the Austrian navy, until Italy declared war on Germany in August 1916.

In four months the Austrians had upset the balance of naval power by destroying two armoured cruisers, the *Amalfi* and *Giuseppi Garibaldi*, a destroyer, two torpedo boats, three submarines and two airships, all belonging to Italy. They had also put out of action the British cruiser *Dublin*, torpedoed by a submarine, and sunk the French armoured cruiser *Leon Gambetta*. The Italian losses had led to their heavy ships being forbidden to leave port.[1]

'The Austrian fleet has established moral ascendancy in the Adriatic and played the part of a weaker force with conspicuous success,' the British naval attaché in Rome reported to the Admiralty. 'Not only has it succeeded in weakening the Italian fleet, but it has immobilised a force very considerable to itself.'[2]

Admiral Sir Herbert Richmond had castigated the Italians heavily and rudely by informing the Admiralty that 'They had better sell their fleet and take up their organs and monkeys again, for, by heaven, that seems more their profession than sea fighting.' This opinion was backed by Admiral Sir Arthur Limpus, at Malta, who described the Italians as 'children at the game of the sea'.[3]

All the British naval units in Italy were under the control of the country's commander-in-chief, Duke Abruzzi, who used the title Admiral His Royal Highness Luigi di Savoia. Although criticism was directed at him, it was his Minister of Marine who surrendered to public outcry about the shortage of submarines by resigning[4] on the very day that Tomkinson had been given his new appointment. The two happenings were linked because Britain's offer to plug the gap by sending six old B-class submarines to Venice was accepted.

Soon after arriving in Venice, Tomkinson was assured by Hall: 'If you find it is a poor show, or you get them [the submarines] in order and find it developing into the defence of Venice, please let me know and I could probably effect an exchange, but I fancy you will be able to do pretty much as you like.'[5]

Indeed, Tomkinson had to do pretty much as he liked and it was to bring out the best of his organizational powers and prepare him for the biggest build-up of his career three years away. It was also to contradict the lies spread about him after the Invergordon Mutiny that he had never had a lone command. There was virtually nothing arranged for him in Venice – no staff, no stores, no orders, no submarines. His base was the depot ship *Marco Polo*, shared with the Italian navy and moored alongside the Arsenal on the Grand Canal. He found it 'exceedingly dirty' and lacking quarters for the submarine officers and ratings who would be joining him.[6]

Twenty-four hours after his arrival Tomkinson travelled 400 miles by train to Taranto to arrange for stores and a working party to help him set up the base. For his return with a lieutenant, four ratings and an enormous amount of luggage, he commandeered a locomotive and truck, because no other transport would be released by the Italians. It was the first of many difficulties he was to encounter and which were to exasperate him during a year of frustration.[7]

Although admiring the courtesy and social graces of Italian officers, he could not understand their effete indecisiveness. His appointment was made no easier by the state of the B-class submarines, although he knew he could not expect much from them. They were the second models in the development of the original Holland design, bought from the United States in 1901. All were completed in 1906, and even then it was obvious that they were too small for any work, other than harbour defence. They carried a crew of only fifteen and had just two torpedo tubes, whereas the E class, with which Tomkinson had worked in the North Sea, had five torpedo tubes. Admiralty confidence in the effectiveness of the B class had been boosted by the singular feat of Lieutenant Holbrook who, ten months earlier, had slipped B11 through a Dardanelles minefield and torpedoed the old Turkish battleship *Messudieh*. For this he had won the VC. B11 was bound for Venice, which momentarily revived Tomkinson's enthusiasm.

The first submarines due from Malta were B7, B9 and B8, which presaged a catalogue of mishaps and mechanical problems for her sisters by colliding with an Italian tug, damaging her hydroplanes and being unable to dive. When she arrived at Venice on 11 October 1915, she needed dry docking. The other two had defects and were short of crew, with two warrant officers as second in command, to the disappointment of Tomkinson.[8]

Dockyard work was slow because of poor facilities; it was explained by Commander Cappelli, the commanding officer of the *Marco Polo*, that the dockyard was designated as a 'national antiquity' and must not be altered or modernized.[9]

There were also complaints of the indiscipline of the British submarine crews, of which Tomkinson hoped 'we shall not have any recurrence'. To underline his insistence on discipline and respect he assembled all the officers in his cabin for a pep talk and then laid down the rules to petty officers and men on the quarterdeck.[10]

Seven days later B6 and B11 moored alongside the *Marco Polo*. Their arrival caused Tomkinson to go into this paper paroxysm of rage: 'B6 was pushed out of Malta in the usual hurry, for which the admiral there ought to be scrubbed. It is wicked to send a boat away without any reason in such a hurry – a combination of ignorance and obstinacy. The result has been that their speed has been about seven knots, owing to her engine not having been tuned up . . . the ignorance and stupidity still displayed by our senior officers with regard to submarines is extraordinary.'[11]

Yet, a fortnight after his arrival, Tomkinson had managed to get a submarine out on patrol and stay off the Istrian coast, while Italian vessels were forced to return.[12]

He could see how inexperienced his commanding officers were, and tried to exercise at least one submarine every day, but was thwarted in his intentions by lack of interest from the Italian navy. He would arrange for one of their torpedo boats to act as a target ship, only to go out to find it had not arrived because of what they termed bad weather, although Tomkinson called it 'fine'. But there were winter days when fog restricted any movement of submarines for a month.

Coupled with the numerous breakdowns and mishaps, the six British submarines managed only seventy-nine missions in a year. At the end of 1915 Tomkinson wrote: 'All they have sunk is one mine.'[13] They were never to sink anything else. He catalogued every patrol, every mishap, every misadventure, every misdemeanour. It can be summed up thus:

B6. In dry dock for three months. Sixteen patrols in 348 days; little enemy activity reported.

B7. Torpedo-tube, battery and petrol pipe problems; returned to Malta for three months. Fifteen patrols in 365 days.

B8. Under repair for two months; wrecked engine when going astern with clutch in; collided with ferry, exhaust cracked; ran ashore. Nineteen patrols in 365 days.

B9. Batteries half full of water, torpedo-tubes damaged; tried to attack two Austrian seaplanes, but Maxim gun jammed. Nine patrols in 365 days.

B10. In Malta Dockyard for repairs for six months; fired torpedo at small steamer, but missed; fouled mine, which hung on hydroplane until commanding officer managed to dislodge it; ignition trouble after being hunted by seven destroyers. Sunk by enemy aircraft. Nine patrols in 194 days.

B11. Tried to ram and shoot-up ditched Austrian seaplane, which was too fast for it on water; periscope defective; captured broken-down seaplane with two prisoners; battery holed; missed chance of sinking torpedo boat; collided with ferry boat. Eleven patrols in 348 days.

How to stop unruliness, particularly drunkenness, was a constant anxiety for Tomkinson because of the cheap wine available ashore. It was not so much the behaviour of the lower ratings that bothered him, but that of the petty officers. The first signs of an epidemic of them 'returning drunk onboard' came in December, when a chief petty officer was in this category. Tomkinson's answer was to shorten leave 'because it was such a bad example to have these sort of things going on with petty officers'.[14] But it did not improve the situation, and nine days later three petty officers were in cells for insobriety. 'It really is sickening,' Tomkinson lamented. 'One never sees any of the Italian seamen drunk, much less their petty officers. . . . I am disgusted with them and shall stick it into them. I am determined to stop it somehow. It is all due to the entire lack of discipline under which they have worked since the war started.'[15]

Even on Christmas Day, while Tomkinson was drinking champagne provided by the Italians, he refused to relent when four British ratings staggered onboard and were immediately put on charges. 'They have curious ideas of playing the game,' he opined. 'It is, however, confined to a very few and I will ginger them up for it. It is quite inexcusable.'[16]

His 'ginger' did not make the matelots more temperant, mainly because there was no naval headquarters in Venice. One engine-room artificer had four offences of drunkenness and remained onboard, but after a signalman created a disturbance on the *Marco Polo*, Tomkinson committed him to sixty days imprisonment and transportation to Malta to serve his sentence.[17]

The lethargic atmosphere of Venice, with its open-air bars, suggestive signoras and streets of brothels, was having its effect. Tomkinson's steward, a hitherto faithful servant called Bisgrove, invoked his anger by leaving a steam pipe turned on in an adjacent bathroom one night. Tomkinson awoke the next morning to find his sleeping cabin full of steam and his bronchial tubes full of cold. Later he was forced to deprive 'that idiot' Bisgrove of one good-conduct badge for disobeying orders. 'He used to be reliable; now his conduct is unsatisfactory,' he wrote. 'Doesn't seem able to tell the truth about anything.'[18]

Among his officers he found a lack of resilience, or ability to press home attacks, which was not surprising as by now the B-class submarines were regarded as death-traps when submerged, because of their short-life batteries. Although patrols were normally for only forty-eight hours, they were operating in clear waters and could be seen easily by the pilots of seaplanes, which the Austrians were using with devastating efficiency.

Lieutenant Auchterly, the commanding officer of B7, who 'complained about everything and every man in his boat', was one of the first cases of submarine 'shell shock' Tomkinson encountered and he was unable to understand it. During one patrol in June 1916, Auchterly's boat had been bombed by a seaplane, which damaged the scuttles; he had also been forced to go to the seabed after being hunted by destroyers. Eventually, B7 was able to surface and was towed back to Venice. When Tomkinson debriefed him and queried his report, Auchterly began to weep and 'talked a lot of nonsense and begged for the report back, so that he could write out another'. Auchterly was still crying later that day when the base's doctor sent him to bed. 'I cannot make him out at all and am not quite sure what to do about him,' Tomkinson reported. The next month Auchterly was sent back to Britain and replaced by Lieutenant Winn. Within a month Winn was also pronounced unfit to command and went home.[19]

Competent officers were in short supply and at one period during an epidemic of influenza, Tomkinson did not have a single fit commanding officer to send out on patrol.[20]

Morale was low, and to give it uplift officers and ratings were allowed to bring out their wives and families from Britain, if they could afford it. Tomkinson took advantage and sent for Joan, who arrived in the New Year and was ensconced in the Hotel Monaco. She was accompanied by his friend from Keyes' former flotilla, Lieutenant Commander Martin Dunbar Nasmith, VC, who eight months earlier in E11 had entered Turkey's Sea of Marmara to sink four transports and a gunboat.[21]

Both cheered up Tomkinson's flagging spirits. With Joan he was able to explore the antiquities of Venice, while from Nasmith, due back in Malta, he heard of real successes against a real enemy. Nasmith realized there were many targets in the north Adriatic and was keen to join Tomkinson, but not in the B submarines. He agreed that a better class was needed in Venice and that it was 'criminal' to send them out to try to attack the enemy.[22] Tomkinson wrote to Hall, suggesting that more modern craft should be put under his command, but his plea was rejected.[23] He also suggested to the commander-in-chief of the Mediterranean, Admiral de Robeck, with whom Keyes had considerable influence, that Nasmith should be transferred to Venice – a move which would have bolstered the morale of his officers – but this, too, was turned down.[24]

It was when out walking with Joan one afternoon that he discovered a recreational oasis in an English-style garden – a run-down tennis court. It was owned by an Englishman, living in Britain, so Tomkinson wrote to him to obtain permission to renovate it and put down a new surface.[25] By the spring it was ready for use and most afternoons Tomkinson and his off-duty officers played there. But his pleasure paled when the owner refused to pay a bill of restoration of £700. 'I think it rather mean, considering his wealth,' Tomkinson said. 'I suppose I shall have to [settle] as I don't think any of the officers here are inclined to pay.'[26] In spite of the wealth of his upbringing, Tomkinson hated overspending and even insisted on having three lira deducted from his hotel bill each day because the room was unheated and 'like an ice-house'.[27]

Joan's stay ended abruptly after ten weeks when their son Peter's health deteriorated. Her mother, who was looking after the children, wrote to say a doctor was concerned about the boy's anaemia and considered that he might be tubercular. Joan left for Tavistock as soon as she could that week, only to find that his condition had improved when she arrived home.[28]

Although Tomkinson did not have the anxiety of going on patrol, he was always deeply worried when his submarines were late in returning. None was fitted with wireless, and information on their movements only came when the commanding officers released homing pigeons. Many would not fly off; some which winged away became lost, and even when messages got through to the loft in Venice they were often decoded wrongly or incorrectly telephoned to Tomkinson. One message from B9 was deciphered as claiming the capture of an enemy ship; instead it was a weather report.[29]

Within a month of his arrival his old gastric trouble flared under the strain and an

Italian diet, so he went to a Venetian chemist to have Moynihan's stomach prescription made up. His condition was alleviated for three months, then after weeks of dining out with Joan the pains returned. 'I expect I shall have to be careful,' he warned himself.[30]

There was also the worry of air raids, for Venice, although an open city, had more than 700 bombs dropped on it by Austrian planes during the war. In the first raid Tomkinson experienced, nine aircraft strafed the Arsenal, where a storage shed was destroyed, while the *Marco Polo* was spattered with machine-gun bullets and shrapnel. Primarily the attacks were regarded as cinematic interludes and part of the routine of dockyard life, but with every day the accuracy of the enemy pilots improved. On 16 May the *Marco Polo*'s sick-bay on the bridge was wrecked when two bombs fell close to it. A month later a foundry alongside her was hit, while fire raged in a barracks near the Arsenal, lighting up the harbour.[31]

History was made on 9 August during a night attack, when B10, lying alongside the *Marco Polo*, became the first submarine to be sunk by aircraft. A hole 4 ft by 2 ft was torn in her side, but she was salvaged, only to be devastated by a fire in her forward petrol tank, sparked by a dockyard matey drilling into it. The dock had to be flooded to put out the blaze.[32]

Tomkinson never had any faith in the Italian workers, or the Italian navy, whose officers made 'any excuse' for not sending out ships or submarines, refused to help pick up practice torpedoes and were unreliable at rendezvous times. He regarded most of them as 'nice fellows with not much ginger in them' and the 'most impossible people when it comes to making a plan or keeping to any sort of time'.[33]

However, he kept most of this criticism to himself, although he did complain to the *Marco Polo*'s commanding officer that British submarines were 'doing rather a large share of the work'.[34] His tact won him many friends. As he told Keyes in a letter: 'I pride myself that the entente here is very much in evidence and we are very friendly both with the Italians and the French, which is more than can be said at either of the other Italian naval bases. . . . There is perhaps a little jealousy on the part of the younger Italian submarine officers at us having done all their work last winter with these old crocks, because none of theirs would run.'[35]

He was due for promotion to captain and heard in the New Year of 1916 that Willis, ahead of him in the *Navy List* of senior commanders, had not been advanced and this held up his own captaincy. He blamed Hall. 'I see Willis is not promoted and that arch fraud James Moreton is,' he grumbled to himself in his diary. 'It is frightful being saddled with a nonentity like Hall for Commodore S. He either will not, or cannot, look after his own people when it comes to promotion. It is very sickening for Willis, as so many below him have got it. Had Keyes been still Commodore S I am quite certain Willis would not have had Moreton going over his head.'[36]

His hopes of leaving Venice early depended mainly on advancement and they were raised during May when a colleague told him that Keyes was going to command a 'big battle cruiser'.[37] Such was the subterfuge in the navy that when it was suggested that Keyes should captain the *Tiger*, his friend Beatty stopped the appointment by insisting to Jellicoe that although Keyes was a 'good fellow' he had no experience of big ship command and 'has not too many brains'. At the same time, Beatty was assuring Keyes he had recommended him for a new 'galloping ship' – the *Renown* or *Repulse* – rather than the new battleships, which 'are not gallopers'.[38]

When, in June, the first news of the Battle of Jutland reached Venice, Tomkinson feared that officers who had distinguished themselves in it would be promoted ahead of him. 'How I wish I could have been there to take part, instead of doing nothing in this uninteresting spot, which bores me more and more every day,' he jotted down in his diary.[39]

Around this time he wrote to Keyes: 'I need hardly say that I am very keen indeed on joining you, and if as your flag captain, it would be the height of my ambition. It will probably have to be as acting captain at first, as I daresay this big battle [Jutland] will take most of the promotions.' Then he lied: 'My internal complaint seems to have gone and I am now fit to leave here for any job.'[40]

This irksome mood of uselessness disappeared two months later when Rear-Admiral Cecil Thursby, at Taranto, cabled congratulations on Tomkinson's advancement to captain. Even then he considered his friend responsible. 'I expect I have Keyes to thank more than anyone else.'[41]

The same week he heard that Keyes had been made commanding officer of the battle-ship *Centurion* and it appeared that 'it may be some time before I am able to go with him.'[42] Despicable as Hall might have appeared to Tomkinson, he nevertheless got in touch with him just after to ask him what he wanted to do. To Tomkinson's surprise, his relief – a lieutenant commander – was appointed in the next month, only for it to be cancelled within four weeks.[43] For the next six weeks of his Venice command the base was slowly wound down. B8 and B10 were paid off and their crews sent home, leaving B7 as the only submarine available for patrol. Finally, on 10 October all the remaining boats were ordered to pay off and to proceed to Brindisi to be replaced by the *Adamant* and two H class submarines. None of the Bs ever operated as submarines again, or belonged to the Royal Navy. They were handed over to the Italians who, having had five submarines sunk in a year, lost their stomach for underwater attack and converted them into surface patrol vessels.

On the last day of October 1916, Tomkinson said goodbye to the Italian officers, many of whom had become his good friends, and left for home after the most unsuccessful command of his career, yet with an Italian decoration, the Order of St Maurice and St Lazarus.[44]

10
CAUGHT IN THE VORTEX

Joan was eight months pregnant – a condition that appeared to be unknown to Tomkinson until he arrived back in England. His enthusiasm for a new baby was tempered by his own condition, for his stomach troubles kept recurring and four days after his arrival home he saw a specialist in Oxford, who also prescribed medicine.[1] He was given a month's leave until his new appointment was announced and, as usual, took his family to the Tomkinsons' open house at Franche, where he enjoyed four days of shooting.

On 2 December 1916, he heard from the Admiralty that he was to captain the light cruiser *Aurora*, currently refitting at Chatham Dockyard and was to join her three days later. When he arrived he found she was far from ready and it was 'impossible to live onboard',[2] so joyfully he caught the next train back home for another ten days with Joan, who was close to giving birth. Both hoped he would be there when the baby arrived, but on 16 December he was appointed president of a court martial and had to return to Chatham Barracks. Next day Joan gave birth to a daughter, christened Margaret Venetia,[3] and always known by her second name in remembrance of the city in which she was conceived.

The 3,500-ton *Aurora*, first commissioned a month after the outbreak of war, was to join Tyrwhitt's Harwich Force, but then came rumours that she would go north as part of Commodore Le Mesurier's squadron.[4] This upset Tomkinson because it would give him little chance of seeing Joan and their new daughter. It was to open the beginning of a new relationship with Tyrwhitt, who listened sympathetically to Tomkinson's pleas to stay with him.

For the third Christmas of the war Tomkinson was away from home, but his gloom was dispelled when, after a Christmas Day communion service, celebrated in his cabin, he received a note from Tyrwhitt telling him that he had asked for the *Aurora* to remain at Harwich,[5] a recommendation that the Admiralty accepted. The union between the two firmed also when Tyrwhitt entertained Tomkinson for the next two days at his home and on his flagship, the *Centaur*.

The routine for the next seven months was to consist of alternate weeks at Harwich, or Dover, where the *Aurora* was part of the Downs Patrol, an arduous duty of spending every night at sea at action stations, returning at dawn.

During his second night at sea, when a strong southwesterly and a heavy swell was bouncing the *Aurora* around, Tomkinson suffered excruciating stomach pains. Back in harbour he called in the port medical officer, who suggested a different course of medicine to that advised by the Oxford specialist. The next night on patrol his agony had not diminished. Only when the *Aurora* had a complete day and night in harbour did the pain subside.[6]

For the next six months of his captaincy of the *Aurora* stomach problems continued to dog him. During March 1917, he had a particularly bad spell when 'pain became quite bad, so I sent for our doctor, who cleared me out'. Three days later he vomited before dinner and did not 'seem able to eat anything'. It flared again in June after another week of sea duty. Yet during this time when the *Aurora* was in harbour he was constantly involved in all manner of activities from tennis to golf, from shooting to sawing up logs, from birds-nesting to primrosing, from mushrooming to rambling.[7]

The action ashore was more varied than that at sea, although in a confused gunfight off Zeebrugge he came close to making his first kill. An enemy destroyer flotilla was on the way to Germany and two divisions of light cruisers and destroyers were ordered to intercept. At 2.40 a.m., despite blinding spray, which froze as it cascaded over the bows, the *Aurora*'s look-outs sighted three destroyers steaming past the light cruiser *Conquest*, whose commanding officer did not realize that they were hostile. But when their leader was astern of *Aurora*, Tomkinson identified them as 'Huns and let drive with all guns to open the ball'.[8] The shooting was inaccurate and not one hit was scored; however, the enemy fired back just as inaccurately as Tomkinson's gunners and the *Aurora* escaped.

Torpedoes were also let loose at her; they were spotted in the *Centaur*, Tyrwhitt's flagship, and the *Conquest*, but no one saw them in the *Aurora*. 'We were jolly lucky not to be bagged,' Tomkinson reported later.[9] He then turned his attention to the second German destroyer. This time the gunnery was on target and she was hit in the vicinity of the engine-room. She stopped as her companions sped off. The *Aurora, Centaur* and *Conquest* took off at 24 knots in pursuit, leaving the *Penelope* to sink the crippled destroyer. About an hour later Tomkinson saw gun flashes ahead, as a division of British destroyers took on the enemy fleeing towards Zeebrugge. Then a sheet of red flame marked the end of a torpedo run in the forepart of the new British destroyer, the *Simon*. Nothing was left of her from the bows to the forward funnel. The division leader, the *Nimrod*, tried to take her in tow, but realizing it was a hopeless task, Tyrwhitt ordered the remaining destroyers to sink her by gunfire. Fifty of her ship's company were saved.

Tomkinson remarked in his diary: 'It was a sad business and on the whole we are not much up on the deal. . . . We fired 45 rounds altogether of six-inch and four-inch, which was, I should think, a good many more than the other two ships [*Centaur* and *Conquest*] together fired.'[10]

Penelope's commanding officer assured him that an enemy destroyer had definitely been sunk because he had turned his ship round and, although seeing nothing, heard survivors crying for help in the sea. This was confirmed by the captains of the *Cleopatra* and *Undaunted*.[11]

Three days after this action the *Aurora* was forced to go into Chatham Dockyard, when a split was discovered in the steam piping between the boiler-rooms and the forward engine in the bulkhead casting. Although 'sickening' – as Tomkinson, using one of his favourite words, described it – this meant a week's leave at Tavistock to see his new daughter.[12]

When he returned to Chatham he spent all day dealing with seventy leave-breakers, often a problem during his command of the *Aurora*. On another occasion, when fifty defaulters were before him, he recorded: 'It is very bad how little idea they seem to have of playing the game. The more trouble is taken to get them leave, the more they abuse it. It is mostly these youngsters brought in for the war who are a very inferior class to our proper active service men.'[13]

Just as he had settled back at Harwich, with a transference of loyalty and hero worship to Tyrwhitt, the 'call' came from Keyes, newly promoted to rear admiral, and second in command of the Battle Squadron in the old dreadnought *Colossus*. Tomkinson was wanted as flag captain to replace Dudley Pound, later to be both friend and enemy, but it would mean going north to Rosyth. 'It has really put me in an awkward position and I kept awake most of the night,' ran his diary entry for 19 June 1917. 'However, there is no doubt in my own mind what to do. He [Keyes] has done a great deal for me and I promised to go and therefore I shall go . . . it is going from a very nice job, which I like better than anything else I could have, to one that I shall not like so much, except in being with RK [Keyes]. I would not dream of doing it for anyone else.'[14]

Yet he still went to Tyrwhitt for advice the next day. 'I would rather lose anyone than you,' he was told by his senior officer and new patron. But Tyrwhitt agreed to the transfer, so Tomkinson sent off a telegram of acceptance. 'I shall be most awfully sorry to leave him [Tyrwhitt], as I have been looking forward for the last six months to the day when I should get into a scrap with him in command and he has been awfully good to me ever since I came,' he confided to his personal record.[15]

It was a gloomy Tomkinson who left the *Aurora* on 10 July 1917, for the last week had been a sweet one, with Joan and his daughters staying with Commodore Cayley and his wife at nearby Ewarton. They had been cordially entertained by the Tyrwhitts and also onboard the *Aurora*. On his arrival at Rosyth he discovered that the fleet was in mourning for the battleship *Vanguard* which, when lying close to the *Colossus*, had been blown to smithereens as one of her magazines exploded. More than 700 were killed and the only identifiable piece of anyone was the head of a midshipman found miles away.[16]

After a day spent taking over from Pound he wanted to be back in Harwich, but his feeling of being 'out of it' was dispelled when he met Keyes, who was 'in good form and full of energy', and then Beatty, now commander-in-chief, whom he described as a 'great personality and THE MAN'.[17]

At first Tomkinson found it difficult to manoeuvre the awkward 20,000-ton, 540-ft long *Colossus*, which was the only dreadnought to have been at Jutland, but a hippopotamus compared with the raciness of the *Aurora*. In Tomkinson's first attempt to moor her off Charlestown, Beatty signalled his wrath: 'You are very slow.'[18] The next day in a fleet war-game on the way south to Rosyth, Keyes, despite protests by Tomkinson and Bowlby, his flag lieutenant, turned the division of three antiquated ships towards the

'enemy' without orders from the admiral, so that they could get in range. A severe repri-
mand for leaving the line without permission came with a series of 'rude signals' from the
flagship, the *Queen Elizabeth*.[19]

The battle fleet anchored above the Forth Bridge, just 7 miles from Aberdour where the
Keyes' family had rented Whitehill. This new base led to many happy hours there for
Tomkinson. He played with the Keyes' children there, he played tennis, he played golf,
he played cricket – hitting a six off the first ball of the game for the admiral's staff – he
rowed skiffs, he ferreted for rabbits. Socially Tomkinson was now mixing with the upper
echelons of the navy – First Lord Sir Eric Geddes, Admirals Beatty, Wemyss, Sturdee,
Brand, De Robeck and Goodenough, and Captains Chatfield, Boyle and Lambert – and it
was not lost on him that these were the men who could stimulate or destroy his career.
Although he was regarded by many officers as a 'plodder' in comparison with the charismatic Keyes, he nevertheless demanded respect in being able to take a more dispassionate
and calmer appraisal than his superior. However, the renewal of their partnership was
truncated to two months.

On 7 September, a 'much disturbed' Keyes told Tomkinson that he was to become the
right-hand man of the new deputy First Sea Lord, Admiral Sir Rosslyn 'Rosey' Wemyss,
as director of the new department of naval plans at the Admiralty, with Captains Pound
and Cyril Fuller as his assistants. Tomkinson was dismayed that he had given up the captaincy of the *Aurora* to be with Keyes and now found himself stranded in the old
Colossus, while Keyes would have no chance of asking for him to join him at Whitehall
because Pound and Fuller had already been appointed.[20] He immediately wrote to
Tyrwhitt, asking if he could rejoin the Harwich Force. 'Sorry to hear of your misfortune,'
Tyrwhitt replied. 'I'd get you back tomorrow, if I could get you a ship.'[21]

Tomkinson's idyllic summer ended when Keyes said his farewell to the *Colossus* on
24 September. His successor, Rear-Admiral Douglas Nicholson soon fell out with
Tomkinson over a fouled hawse – the crossing of two anchor cables – during a gale.[22] By
now the ship was over complement by 200 men, and sleeping billets were congested, with
sailors slinging their hammocks in every available position. With the poor living conditions came the first whiff of indiscipline, after a Royal Marine lance-corporal had written
a letter of complaint and demanded improved standards, which Tomkinson considered
'mutinous and improper'.

'He wants flogging,' he wrote. 'I believe he is really suffering from cold feet . . . it is a
danger having such individuals about.'[23] Although seemingly a minor incident, he was
careful to make sure that this type of insolence did not spread and warned all officers and
petty officers that discipline must be maintained. Yet as the years went by and the navy
returned to its peacetime activities his hard-line attitude was to weaken.

A welcome interruption to the dreariness of winter at Scapa Flow, where the fleet had
returned, came on 18 November, when a force of German light cruisers was intercepted
by Admiral Alexander Sinclair's and Admiral Walter Cowan's squadrons. Thirty-one
warships, including the *Colossus*, steamed at full speed out of the Flow. 'I don't think
there has ever been such a strong force together since the outbreak of war,' Tomkinson
enthused. 'It was a magnificent sight when we had all met. At about noon we altered to

the south and went to battle stations. I really thought THE DAY had come. We went on south until 2 p.m., when we were 50 degrees east of Horns Reef and then nothing having been sighted we turned right to the north for Scapa.'[24] This was not sheer bravura on Tomkinson's part; most regular naval officers truly believed that one great naval action must be fought, with sheer weight of numbers promising a British victory, leading to command of the seas until the end of the war. Yet this view was not held by Jellicoe, now sitting cautiously in the Admiralty as First Sea Lord.

The indecision of whether Tomkinson would stay or go ended the next day when he was appointed to command a patrol flotilla of yachts and trawlers, equipped with new listening devices, to hunt submarines from Portland, assuming his stomach trouble had cleared up. Somewhat sniffily, due to his disappointment of not being able to return to Harwich, he referred to the job as being connected with 'fish hydrophones', although admitting 'I shall like it all right, if only my inside can stand it.'[25]

He was able to persuade the Admiralty that he was fit, for the responsibility of being given a complete command was more appealing to him now; he was relieved on the *Colossus* on 28 November. The following week was spent between the Admiralty, Portsmouth, Plymouth and Portland, familiarizing himself with his U-boat hunting duties, for which he was to be accommodated in the yacht *Soissa*. Solace in his unsought-after appointment came that Christmas when, for the first time during the war, he was able to spend it with Joan and his family at Franche. But momentous changes at the pinnacle of the Admiralty were about to happen, and Tomkinson, though a small fish, was to be caught in the vortex.

Jellicoe, by this time, had retreated into a cocoon of fatalistic gloom at the Admiralty and considered that it would be impossible to continue the war into 1918 because of a shortage of shipping; he had not welcomed Wemyss's appointment as his deputy and had frowned on the entry of Keyes as an influential Director of Plans. Often an intriguer, one of Keyes' first moves was to criticize Jellicoe's staunchest supporter and later his biographer, Admiral Reginald Bacon, flag officer of the Dover Patrol. Keyes and Wemyss had studied the movements of U-boats and their sinking of merchant shipping – 621,645 tons in one month alone – and decided that Bacon was not doing enough to stop them using the Channel exit, with at least one U-boat getting through each night. Bacon insisted that nets and barriers were fully effective, because no ship had been torpedoed in his immediate area. The theory of Wemyss and Keyes – backed by intelligence reports, which Bacon had knowledge of – was that U-boat captains were not sinking vessels in the Channel because this would give away the fact that they were using it for their egress to and from Germany. Bacon virtually laughed out this 'puerile' perception, so Wemyss, with the approval of First Lord Geddes, decided that someone else must be given the job of stopping the U-boats. Jellicoe, however, insisted that Bacon must stay, which brought Wemyss to the brink of resigning. But before he could do so, Geddes, who for several months had been intent on ridding the Admiralty of Jellicoe, used the controversy to compel the First Sea Lord to resign. Wemyss hesitatingly agreed to take over, and on Christmas Day Geddes went to see the King at Sandringham, with the recommendation for the change at the top. By Boxing Day Jellicoe had gone. Bacon had departed, too, with Keyes, promoted prematurely to vice admiral, taking on the dual job of Director of Plans and Senior Officer, Dover, in command of more than 300 patrol vessels.[26] At the end of his Christmas holiday Tomkinson received orders to abandon his 'fish hydrophone' flotilla appointment and to rejoin Keyes as Captain of Destroyers at Dover.

In a happy hive of activity Tomkinson introduced a new officer to the *Soissa* at Portland 'heartily glad that I shall never have to take up quarters in her',[27] met Keyes at Victoria Station in London, conferred at the Admiralty, drove to Dover to settle himself in at temporary quarters and crossed the Channel for a meeting with Hubert Lynes, commodore of Dunkirk, where the Dover Patrol had an advanced base.

After making arrangements to be billeted ashore with Captain the Honourable Algy Boyle, Keyes' new Chief of Staff and an old friend, Tomkinson reported for duty at Dover on 13 January – only to find that Keyes had a hazardous operation ready for him.

Early the next afternoon Tomkinson boarded the destroyer *Legion* for Dunkirk, where he transferred to the *Lightfoot*, to lead twelve ships on a minelaying operation in the northern approaches to Zeebrugge. Because two destroyers were newly commissioned and their crews had no experience of minelaying, and because the operation was to be carried out on a dark night in shoal water, near a recently laid minefield, Keyes had delayed triggering it until Tomkinson could take charge. Just before nightfall Tomkinson, still in Dunkirk, was told that a strong force of enemy destroyers was at sea, possibly with the intention of attacking patrols. By telephone Keyes impressed on him the importance of laying the mines, even in the worsening weather, for there was a possibility of the returning German ships running into them.

Meanwhile, Keyes hoisted his flag in the *Attentive* and led out from Dover a covering force of one light cruiser, four flotilla leaders and six large destroyers. Later, after Yarmouth and Southwold had been shelled by the German raiders, Tyrwhitt agreed to send the *Conquest* and thirteen destroyers of the Harwich Force. As the weather deteriorated, Keyes was in two minds about recalling Tomkinson; instead he kept him informed of all ships' movements, although by pre-arrangement Tomkinson made no signals of acknowledgement to avoid giving away his position.[28]

Having put his friend in a perilous position, Keyes was determined not to leave him unprotected and arranged for the ponderous 15-in monitors, *Erebus* and *Terror*, with two destroyers to support him at Thornton Ridge, near Zeebrugge.

Tomkinson's diary merely describes that night at sea as: 'Carried out our operation more or less successfully, but didn't see any Huns. Bad weather came on and we didn't get into Dunkirk until noon.'[29] But Keyes later wrote: 'Tomkinson persisted with great determination and much to their credit the *Legion*, *Meteor* and *Ariel* laid their mines, despite the heavy sea, but it was too much for the inexperienced newcomers.'[30]

Within weeks at Dover he had managed to redouble the Channel patrols, and by night illuminated the barrage from end to end 'as bright as Piccadilly'. By early February, U-boat commanders had abandoned the Channel as a safe passage. In three months four U-boats were destroyed, compared with only two from the beginning of the war.[31]

11
THE GREAT PLAN

Tomkinson was now entering the busiest spell of his wartime career, for in addition to ferrying VIPs, such as the King, the Prince of Wales, Premier Lloyd George and Winston Churchill, to France and back in the duty destroyer, and being called out when any of his ships were in an emergency, he worked on the plans for the Zeebrugge raid, which was to become the most momentous three hours of his life.

Credit for the idea of the raid has been claimed by many, so it is worth while tracing its emergence and all involved previously and at the time. Even though the illuminated barrage was most effective, it was obvious to Keyes that U-boats could still steal into the shipping lanes of the Western Approaches by taking the longer Scottish route from their bases at Zeebrugge and Ostend; the only way to stop them was to block both these safe harbours. He knew already that there had been an Admiralty plan for this, and when he suggested that it be revived he was given approval to make preparations for a land, air and sea assault. As early as November 1916 the then Prime Minister, Herbert Asquith, had told General Sir William Robertson, Chief of the Imperial War Staff: 'There is no operation of war to which the War Committee attach greater importance than the deprivation to the enemy of Ostend and Zeebrugge.'[1]

Jellicoe had been asked to invoke a naval bombardment in 1917 and rejected the request, yet later that year he had also pessimistically informed the War Committee that unless the two ports were denied to Germany the Allies would lose the war. In June and July 1917, a combined operation, involving the navy and a division of tanks, supported by artillery, was suggested as soon as General Sir Douglas Haig's armies advanced, but this was jettisoned when the land forces were far short of their objectives.

In a paper written by Beatty and recommended to Jellicoe in August 1917, the idea was dusted off again – except this time it was to be a 'navy only' mission, involving the use of blockships. In effect, it was a revamp of an original plan by Admiral Sir Lewis Bayly and Commodore Tyrwhitt, first unveiled in 1916, which Keyes had known of at the time. Beatty considered that 'the port of Zeebrugge is so narrow that blocking it is practicable. A blockship of concrete, fitted with a crinoline with mine-mooring cutters to take it through the minefields and directed by wireless from aircraft would have many chances in favour of reaching the entrance to the locks.'[2]

It was half of this idea, allied to simultaneous landings at Zeebrugge and Ostend, for which Keyes was given the go-ahead by the Admiralty at the end of February 1918. In the 'O2 scheme', as it became coded, Tomkinson, as captain of destroyers, was responsible for ensuring that every available ship of the Dover Patrol could be at sea. He was also given the day-to-day responsibility of running the patrol in order to leave Keyes a free hand in advance planning and selection of pivotal officers. As Keyes was to comment later about Tomkinson's task: 'This was no easy matter in view of the age of the majority of destroyers and the many demands on the flotilla for escort work – particularly when the enemy's March offensive developed and thousands of extra troops were rushed out to France and the usual transport work was more than doubled.'[3]

It will be remembered that Tomkinson and Keyes had made careful notes of the layout of Zeebrugge, with its mile-long mole and canals, when the *Lurcher* had spent several days there in 1914. Now these were invaluable in the forward planning, when compared with aerial pictures taken by the Royal Naval Air Service of the enemy's main alterations, which included an overhanging U-boat shelter, a seaplane base, and living quarters for a permanent garrison of 1,000. The defences comprised a dozen heavy batteries, anti-aircraft guns and blockhouses, with machine-guns and barbed wire entanglements.[4]

Simplified, the plan formulated by Keyes, Captain Pound and Commander Alfred Carpenter was to sink the old cruisers, *Thetis, Intrepid* and *Iphigenia*, all loaded with cement, against the main lock entrance and the mouth of the 8-mile canal to Bruges, which U-boats used. Two old C class submarines, packed with high explosive, were to be blown up under the railway viaduct. The veteran cruiser *Vindictive*, propped in by two shallow-draught Mersey ferry steamers, the *Iris* and *Daffodil*, was to lay alongside the mole and land bluejackets and marines, whose objective was to put out of action the main batteries, blockhouses and to blow up harbour installations. Most of the operation was to be carried out in the cloak of a thick smokescreen. To complete the blockage of the Zeebrugge–Ostend–Bruges canal-linked triangle, Ostend was to be sealed by sinking the *Sirius* and *Brilliant*, two more old cruisers, at its entrance to the sea.

It was estimated that in the region of 140 craft, including motor launches (MLs) and the faster coastal motor boats (CMBs) for the laying of smokescreens and rescue of the skeleton crews of the blockships would be needed in the two operations.[5]

For Tomkinson, who was to be at Keyes' side in the new destroyer *Warwick* during the assault, it became a nightmare to ensure that at least twenty destroyers were available in a high standard of maintenance, with their crews in constant readiness. His nervousness about his responsibilities, security leaks and his doubts of whether he would survive this suicidal attack, were mirrored in these terse diary entries, which became even shorter as his work in getting out orders increased:

26 February. Had a meeting this afternoon to discuss the GREAT PLAN. It seems not quite certain whether we shall be ready to bring it off in March. Ships are rather behind in fitting out.[6]

18 March. Seems April 11 is earliest possible date. I hope my craft will be ready. Keyes is depending on being able to turn out 18 from here.[7]

5 April. The time draws near for our great operation. I hope we shall not be kept

77

waiting long, or else a good deal is certain to leak out. I should like to get Joan down here early next week. Better that she should be on the spot to welcome us back or otherwise.[8]

10 April. Our enterprise is being altogether too much talked about and I hear it is public property in London.[9]

Other officers, although applauding the boldness of the plan, doubted whether they would return. Commander Henry Halahan, of the *Vindictive*, expected to be killed and when Tomkinson last saw him he was asked: 'Please say goodbye to my brother for me.'[10]

Tomkinson's commitment of keeping the destroyer force intact was undermined by two serious mishaps. First the *Viking*'s centre boiler-room was wrecked after she was run into by a collier. Tomkinson dashed out in the duty destroyer to supervise a delicate salvage operation – 'We had a job getting her back in harbour and got in about 3 a.m.'[11] Then in March, during the expected time for the '02 scheme', the *Botha* was accidentally torpeded by a French destroyer during a confused, smoky action with five German destroyers and two torpedo boats. She was towed into Dunkirk by the *Morris*, obviously too badly damaged to be repaired in time for the big operation ahead.[12]

Because of the effectiveness of the new illuminated barrage, the German navy were making more Channel sorties in attempts to extinguish it. During one raid eight drifters and a trawler were destroyed, with the loss of seventy-five men – and without a British shot being fired in return. Tomkinson had been roused from his bed at 1 a.m. and rushed to the duty destroyer, with the intention of putting to sea to help, but Keyes signalled him 'not to proceed'. An abject Tomkinson recorded: 'We lost a lot of good men . . . without giving them any assistance from our destroyers. A black day for us.'[13]

The success of the Zeebrugge and Ostend adventures depended on the weather, with little wind, so that the smokescreens would not be blown away, and with a calm sea during a moonless night. These conditions were forecast for 11 April, when Keyes and Tomkinson in the *Warwick* rendezvoused with a 'curious collection of old craft'[14] off the North Goodwin. As this odd armada neared the enemy coast at 11 p.m. it split into two forces, the Ostend section being commanded by Commodore Hubert Lynes. By then the plan was working splendidly; the night was dark, the sea calm and the wind zephyr-like, as it blew towards the Belgian coast.

Keyes instructed Tomkinson on the bridge to make the prearranged signal for the operation to proceed to the final rendezvous, a temporary light buoy, where the five blockships were to disembark the surplus steaming crews on to a minelayer. Just as this was going ahead, the wind dropped, then several minutes later it began to blow from the south-west. No longer would the smoke from the CMBs screen the raiders. Anxiously, Keyes conferred with Commander Victor Campbell, commanding officer of the *Warwick*, and Tomkinson, who believed that the wind might settle in the adverse southerly quarter for the remainder of the night. For one of the few times in his life Keyes quelled his impetuosity and took the advice of his friend to turn back. The signal 'N', indicating that the attack must be aborted, was sent out from the *Warwick*.

Now began the difficult manoeuvre of turning the fleet of seventy-four vessels, all without navigation lights. When south of the barrage, in confined waters, another of Tomkinson's destroyers was put out of action when the *Trident* rammed the *Sceptre*. To add to the confusion, the flagship lost touch with the *Sceptre*, which was badly holed; the *Sirius* and *Brilliant*, who were through the barrage, could not find their way back; while a CMB's tow parted and it sank.[15]

The signal for the retreat had to be passed by light to the small craft, which were only 16 miles from their target. It was seen by an enemy battery and a salvo of large shells roared over to plume the sea 200 yards from the *Warwick*. Soon after, the bombing of Zeebrugge by Handley Pages of the RNAS began. All on the *Warwick*'s bridge could hear the clatter of anti-aircraft guns and the dull thud of exploding bombs and see the 'flaming onions' crackling in the darkness. From the direction of Ostend the heavy guns of the navy's monitors boomed out.[16]

It was not until 8 a.m. that Tomkinson, who had transferred to the light cruiser *Attentive* so that Keyes could race back in the *Warwick*, was able to round up the lost and straggling ships and make sure that they were escorted safely home. That night he commiserated: 'It is a great disappointment and very sickening for him [Keyes]. I may have influenced him in abandoning it and he may regret it, but I am sure the decision was right.'[17]

Two nights later, the last of the dark period – the next one was not due until 9 May – with the wind behaving reasonably, it was decided to try again, and a section of the attacking force was signalled to leave the River Swin at Chatham, where it was based. Within two hours the wind strengthened and, with the risk of the sea roughening too much for the small craft, the operation was cancelled again.[18]

The following day, Keyes was informed by Admiral Wemyss that the Admiralty had insisted that the attack should be cancelled because the fleet of odd-looking vessels had undoubtedly been seen by neutral ships and news of it would have reached Germany. The Admiralty decided to pay off all the specially altered ships, disband a battalion of marines and send all Keyes' recruits back to the Grand Fleet. Keyes protested that he wanted to try again in ten days, when there would be a moon. 'I always wanted a full moon, but could not wait for it', he lied. A week went by before he was given permission to mount the raid again.[19]

Tomkinson, who had worked day and night on the plans for the past few weeks, was pessimistic about them succeeding, and commented: 'It is to be a moonlight enterprise this time, so if the smoke doesn't work well, some of us are going to have a warm time.'[20]

This was borne out in his final orders to the captains of the three destroyers to form the eastern guard. He forecast that all of them were certain to be sacrificed – and one of them was his own ship, the *Warwick*![21]

12
St George's Day Raid

The Zeebrugge raid was one of the first audacious commando assaults in modern warfare, and because of this and the bravery of the men of the Royal Navy and Royal Marines it established a special place in maritime semi-mythology.[1] Several books have been written about it; many critics have branded it as foolhardiness, with the sacrifices of human life not being worth the limited nuisance value it brought to Germany. It is not the intention to describe the action in detail or the movements of every unit in a complicated operation; instead this is an attempt to recreate, with the help of Tomkinson's diary and contemporary sources, what he would have seen or been aware of.

Monday 22 April, 1918. Fine and suitable in morning, but wind got up during forenoon and by midday Dunkirk report was wind five to six and it looked unlikely. Neither Boyle [who was to go on the Ostend operation in *Attentive*] or myself, thought it was going to be smooth enough for the small craft, but Keyes thought otherwise and his judgement turned out to be correct.

The Swin force left at 1310, consisting of *Vindictive, Iris, Daffodil, Thetis, Intrepid, Iphigenia. Brilliant, Sirius* and all the destroyers (13), MLs (26), CMBs (18), submarines C1 and C3, one minelayer and one picket-boat formed up at position A at 1700, just north of the Goodwins. Ostend force made up of nine destroyers, 14 MLs, six CMBs, *Attentive*, four monitors. This main force, all for Zeebrugge, except *Brilliant, Sirius, Tempest* and *Tetrarch* and two CMBs . . . about as odd a lot of vessels as ever set out on an expedition. The CMBs, submarines and picket-boat had to be towed at a speed of 11 knots, which allowing for station-keeping meant at times up to 13 knots, none too easy a task. The distance from Dover to Zeebrugge is about 85 miles by the route taken.[2]

All the larger ships except the *Warwick* towed some craft. The *Vindictive* was linked to the ferries *Iris* (captained by Harold Campbell, Tomkinson's former first lieutenant in the *Lurcher*) and *Daffodil*, which in turn each pulled a CMB; the destroyers *Mansfield* and

Trident were responsible for the two old submarines; other destroyers lugged along clusters of CMBs, whose engines needed nursing, but the MLs buzzed along under their own power. Meanwhile sixty other detached ships steamed on independently to their own positions. As Captain (D), Tomkinson was responsible for the destroyers *Myngs, Whirlwind, North Star, Phoebe, Mansfield, Trident, Morris, Velox, Melpomene, Moorson*, and, of course, the flagship *Warwick*.

We were up to time at A position (where the Dover Patrol ships joined the Swin force) and by that time the wind had all gone and the weather reports received from Dunkirk and the Admiralty were favourable. From there on . . . we had the usual anxiety as to whether the wind was going to keep right and it was a relief to pass through the barrage about nine miles from Zeebrugge and to know that we were really at last going to do it.

Just before it got dark, as Keyes and I sat in the *Warwick's* charthouse, he said: 'Well, tomorrow is St George's Day, which is a good omen.' And I said: 'Yes – and my mother's birthday.' So we agreed that it was going to be all right. He then signalled over to Carpenter [in *Vindictive*] 'St George for England.' To which a reply was made: 'May he give the dragon's tail a damned good twist.'[3]

After nightfall the full moon illuminated every ship and gave a visibility of 10 miles, which lessened the chances of Keyes' gamble succeeding. Tomkinson was in no mood to reassure him, as the *Warwick* led the starboard wing. He said dryly: 'But there's one thing about it – even if the enemy expect us, they will never think we could be such fools as to try and pull it off on a night like this.'[4]

After passing through G. position and when the Ostend blockships had parted company, it came on to rain, a sort of fog rain, but the wind still kept in the northeast. Unfortunately, it was not flying weather, so the aerial bombardment had to be cut out of the programme. However, perhaps it was not altogether a misfortune for had it been good flying weather we might possibly have been discovered long before we got there.[5]

At 10 p.m., on arrival at a marker buoy 16 miles from Zeebrugge, the surplus crewmen of the blockships were transferred to a minesweeper for passage back to Dover, but many of them hid away so they could see some action on the other side. The CMBs were also slipped, but the *Iris, Daffodil* and submarines remained in tow. Keyes' force plodded on without opposition, with the *Warwick* and destroyers *North Star, Phoebe, Whirlwind* and *Myngs* scouting a mile ahead. As the remainder of the ships approached Zeebrugge, the motor boats' throttles were opened and they swept in front to lay the smokescreens. On the starboard quarter smoke floats were anchored off Blankenburg to blot out the vision of the enemy's coastal gunners. Another section of CMBs headed towards the harbour entrance in an attempt to torpedo destroyers moored alongside the quay and then to run eastward to lay more smoke to confuse the heavy batteries at the canal entrance.[6]

81

Luckily for the British, by now the moon was obscured by pouring rain and the visibility was down to 200 yards. So far the timetable was working to perfection. The *Vindictive* was scheduled to disgorge her landing-parties at the mole at midnight and at 11.50 p.m. she was less than a mile away. The Germans still seemed unaware of what was out there in the darkness until the roar of the motor launches' engines acted like alarm bells.

When the monitor bombardment started, curiously enough we could occasionally see the flashes of those bombarding Ostend, but our own, who were bombarding (15 inch) from the edge of Dutch territorial waters we could neither see or hear. Owing to the weather conditions we really got quite close in before anything happened and then for a bit it was only star shell and the batteries didn't open up properly until *Vindictive* went alongside the mole. The small craft had by then got well in and were laying the smoke well and this quite defeated the Hun. His star shell was very good, indeed, but were defeated by our smoke and although the fire was heavy it was not accurate. I don't think they realised how close in we were so that most of the stuff went well over us.[7]

Night suddenly turned into man-made morning as dozens of star shells exploded around the *Warwick*, where Keyes and Tomkinson were on the compass platform. This was followed by the screech of shells from the coastal batteries, but the gunners had little to aim at and their salvoes spumed the sea almost a mile away.[8]

The *Vindictive* got under a very heavy fire as she went alongside and her casualties were at that time very heavy. Halahan [Captain H.C. Halahan, leader of the 200–strong bluejacket storming party] and Elliott [Lieutenant-Colonel B.W. Elliott, in charge of 740 Royal Marines] were killed before they actually got alongside.
 Warwick, North Star and *Phoebe* cruised in the vicinity of the mole, waiting to tackle anything in the way of torpedo craft leaving the harbour, but nothing came out at all. One or two of the smoke floats laid by MLs and CMBs were rather far out, with the result that as they were flaming a good deal they showed us up when we passed between them and the mole. This didn't matter when the smoke was thick and the wind still from seaward, but about one o'clock the wind shifted and came away from the south-west and we then got salvoes from guns, four to six-inch, which were very close ahead, astern and on either beam of us, but never hit us. A few signal halliards were shot away and a certain amount of shrapnel bullets on to the upper deck, but nothing more.[9]

The *Warwick* passed dangerously close to the end of the mole, but was cloaked in smoke; not so the *Vindictive*. She emerged dramatically from the smoke to be an open target for the enemy, although unseen from the *Warwick*.[10] From her direction Tomkinson could hear rapid bursts of small-arms fire, and pom-poms, but he could not make out what was happening through the smoke barrier on the seaward side.[11]
 Soon after, Commander Campbell swung the *Warwick* round towards the end of the

mole to protect the blockships *Thetis, Intrepid* and *Iphigenia*, now unveiled from their smokescreen and heading for the canal entrance inside the mole. As they came under fire, the *Warwick* put down more smoke, while her gunners blazed away at the shore batteries. Just as the blockships passed the *Warwick* through the pyrotechnics of flares, Very lights, tracer bullets and the flash of coastal batteries there came a searing flash 200 ft high and nearly as broad at its base.[12]

'There goes a submarine,' Tomkinson cried to Keyes. They had both anticipated a tremendous roar, but the clamour of the guns was so heavy that it masked the explosion of 5 tons of amatol in C3 which had been triggered off exactly on target between two rows of the viaduct piers, to tear a gigantic gap in it. The tow-lines of her sister, C1, had parted several miles out and she had failed to reach her objective under her own power.[13]

The *Warwick* then made a run in towards the *Vindictive*, so Keyes could see how the landing-parties were faring, but the smoke was hindering its layers, too, and instead the flagship scraped alongside the mole beyond the *Iris*,[14] which was out of position and should have been pushing in the *Vindictive*. But this manoeuvre did give the storming bluejackets and marines the morale-boosting, yet bizarre, glimpse of Keyes' long, silk admiral's flag, with the cross of St George above it, appearing like a spectre over the smoke.[15]

From the compass platform Tomkinson could make out all three blockships seemingly scuttled at the entrance to the canals. By now Keyes decided it was time for the recall of the landing-parties, otherwise there would not be a *Vindictive* to take them onboard. Her casualties appeared to be high and her foremost 7.5 howitzer crew had been wiped out. It was impossible to give the order to Carpenter in the *Vindictive*, so he instructed Campbell without delay to put the *Warwick* alongside the old cruiser, which was 300 yards further along the mole than intended in the original plan.

So far Keyes had contained his warrior-like frustration of not being able to get into the fight ashore, but now it seemed to Tomkinson and his staff that he was about to join the assault.[16] However, at 1.10 a.m., when the *Warwick* was going into the mole, the *Vindictive*, with the help of the *Daffodil*, began to pull out, and the helm of the *Warwick* had to be put over hard to avoid a collision.[17]

We saw the *Vindictive* shoving off and she steamed away under a heavy fire at a fine speed with flames coming out of her funnels through the shell-holes in the sides. Most of the time the mole was shut out from us by smoke, but occasionally when the smoke was thin and a good show of star shell in the air we could see pretty clearly and could also see the funnels and upper works of the blockships over the mole.[18]

The *Warwick* followed the *Vindictive* for several minutes, then turned back in a vain attempt to seek out and help the *Iris*,[19] with 77 killed and 105 wounded crammed on her decks. Instead, Keyes could hold himself in check no longer and led the *Warwick, North Star* and *Phoebe* in an ambitious, yet futile, torpedo attack on German destroyers. One missile hit the mole extension and another sank the dredger *Hessen*, but it led to Tomkinson losing touch with one of his destroyers, the *North Star*, which had swerved deeper into the harbour in the same direction as the blockships. As she passed the inner side of the mole all her torpedoes were fired at German destroyers, still moored alongside, but in dashing out she was hit by two salvoes at close range and all her boilers and engine-room were put of action. Lieutenant Hubert Gore-Langton, the commanding officer, raced the *Phoebe* to the rescue, but after two tow-lines had parted – one was shot away – it was decided to abandon the *North Star*, although 75 per cent of the crew were saved.[20]

> At about 1.30 a.m. we were standing in again towards the mole to see if we could pick up any small craft when we came across several MLs, including 282, who looked in the dark as if she had been damaged and was sinking, but in reality it was that she was low in the water owing to having all these men onboard from the [two] blockships. She came alongside us and by this time there was just enough movement to make it awkward for her keeping alongside. We took onboard the *Warwick* under these rather awkward conditions from *Iphigenia*: unwounded – one officer, 36 men; wounded – three officers and 16 men. From *Intrepid* unwounded – two officers, 31 men; wounded – one officer, four men; also two dead. There were two or three dead left in the ML. It was rather a business getting these wounded in with a good deal of movement going on and one couldn't help adding to their sufferings as they had to be hauled in over the side in the dark. They were all simply splendid, even the very badly wounded ones. The boat had come under very heavy machine-gun fire on leaving the harbour.[21]

In the confusion ML282 was nearly torpedoed by an enthusiastic sub-lieutenant on the *Warwick*, who was about to pull the firing-lever on the tubes before he recognized it as a 'friend'.[22] Because of the breakdown of ML128 and the destruction of ML110, Lieutenant Percy Deane, RNVR, in command of ML282, told Tomkinson he had to seek out and take onboard under constant machine-gun fire more than double the number of survivors originally intended. His second in command, Keith Wright, and three deckhands were shot beside him and many of his passengers wounded.[23]

> After getting all those onboard we collected the motor launches and went at eight knots for Thornton Ridge and on arrival there found *Erebus*, *Terror* [monitors], *Daffodil* [in tow of *Trident*] and *Iris*. We got some more doctors and bandages sent onboard *Iris*, who was in a bad way with many killed and wounded onboard, including that gallant captain of theirs [Commander Valentine Gibbs, who had both legs blown off].
>
> Keyes then signalled to *Attentive* to close with her force [the Ostend ships] and sweep to westward from Thornton Ridge, so as to pick up any small craft that might have got out of their reckoning. We in *Warwick* went on at 25 knots in order to get our wounded attended to. The young surgeon probationer [Abercrombie] in *Warwick* did exceedingly well in trying circumstances, but of course there was much more than he could compete with. All the wounded, including those who were dying, were

84

splendid. There was one especially . . . Keith Wright, the second officer of ML282, who was shot through the stomach. He must have been in great pain, but he was thanking everyone for any little thing they did and when the admiral went around the mess-deck, where all the wounded were lying, and said to him 'You did splendidly and nothing could have been better,' he smiled and said 'Well, sir, I had the best job.'[24]

The first man hauled in by Surgeon Probationer George Abercrombie from the ML was dead; two others succumbed later on the deck. There was not a lot he could do for the critically injured. Tomkinson saw that wounds were dressed roughly with septic gauze, wrung out in Izal, and then bandaged; iodine was used for minor wounds. Each man was injected with half a grain of morphia; the worst cases received three-quarters of a grain. Men gassed by toxic fumes were forced to vomit by drinking a mixture of mustard and water. Amid the death cries and the groans of the wounded Keyes and Tomkinson toured the mess-deck, cheering up every casualty and assuring them their deeds had been 'the finest thing in history'.[25]

Lieutenant Deane's survivors included Lieutenant Edward Billyard Leake, the captain of the blockship *Iphigenia*, who, immaculate in leather coat and shrapnel helmet,[26] stiffly saluted Keyes and Tomkinson to report that after colliding with a barge and then the port bow of the *Intrepid* he had sunk his ship across the narrow part of the canal. In disarrayed contrast, bareheaded and wearing a wet, oil-sodden vest and trousers was Lieutenant Stuart Bonham-Carter, in command of the *Intrepid*, which he claimed now filled the fairway across the canal. The lead blockship, the *Thetis* (Commander Ralph Sneyd), which had been unable to ram the lock gates, had run into anti-submarine nets and was hit by a succession of shells before grounding and then scuttling in the dredged channel.[27]

On our way back at about 6 a.m. we steamed past the *Vindictive*. *Warwick* was going at 25 knots and *Vindictive* about 15 and we gave them a good cheer, led by the vice admiral.[28]

The *Vindictive*'s upper works had been pounded into a twisted mass, while flames and smoke poured out of the pepper-pot-like holes in her three funnels. As the *Warwick* whipped by, Keyes signalled: 'Operation successful. Well done, *Vindictive*.'[29] Meanwhile in the *Warwick*'s captain's day cabin a young sub-lieutenant, J.S. Cowie, was dispensing hospitality from two Fortnum and Mason hampers which Keyes' wife had provided before the ship left Dover.[30]

We got alongside the *Liberty* [a hospital ship] just after 7 a.m. and transferred all the wounded and at 11.40 a.m., Keyes having landed, I went out again in *Warwick* to see if I could help with the sweep, but *Attentive* had done it thoroughly and so we returned. I went onboard the *Vindictive* and they had evacuated the wounded and were carrying out the dead. She is a regular shambles onboard and one could see what a bad time they must have had with the wounded as there had not been enough time on the way back even to clear up the human remains. Carpenter met me when I went onboard, wearing the cap he had worn in the early morning – a shrapnel bullet through the peak and another through the crown.[31]

Disregarding the heroism and supreme sacrifices of the raid, Tomkinson's summing up was: 'Although the results of our achievement are now common property and the story is being told everywhere, I shall always consider the passage of the forces as a very great feature of the whole business and it will always appeal to naval officers as a great feat. One has to remember that all these vessels had not any opportunity to practise [together] their different parts and were all of different types.'[32]

When Commodore Lynes phoned from Dunkirk during the morning, Tomkinson was dismayed to hear that the Ostend operation had failed because of ingenious enemy deception. The Germans had moved the Stroombank buoy, a marker at the entrance to the harbour, with the result that the blockships *Sirius* and *Brilliant* both ran aground $1^1/_4$ miles east of the harbour entrance. Their crews were evacuated by MLs after the ships had been blown up.[33]

Meanwhile, that day Keyes was applying himself to another operation – personal public relations. After reporting the Zeebrugge 'success' to the Admiralty, he tried to meet every vessel arriving at Dover. When the *Iris* eventually docked, with rows of dead lying on the poop,[34] he was on the quayside, waving a flimsy piece of paper and shouting to the crew: 'This is the telegram I received from the King, giving me a knighthood. You all did the job and I will never forget you.'[35] He also made a tour of the hospital ship *Liberty*, trying to bolster the spirits of the maimed and diminishing their fears. All the wounded were given a red rose by his wife.[36] It was the beginning of the perpetuation of the Keyes' legend and when the news of the raid was fully released to a war-weary public thirsting for a victory, his name became bracketed with the naval heroes of the past, like Drake, Frobisher and Nelson.

Such was the euphoria at the Admiralty that Keyes was given permission for a second attempt to bottle up Ostend, using the battered, but patched up, *Vindictive*, and another redundant cruiser, the *Sappho*.[37] Not so much strategic importance would have been placed on Ostend, if British Intelligence had carried out its surveillance properly, for at the end of the war it was discovered that the Bruges–Ostend canal was too shallow for U-boats to negotiate and their captains only used harbour facilities at Ostend.[38]

To return to Ostend was regarded as being more suicidal than the original raid. By now the Germans were fully alerted – in fact, their opposition to the first attack at Ostend had been swifter than that of their counterparts at Zeebrugge. Keyes was still keen to bring enemy destroyers to battle, especially as Naval Intelligence reported that a strong force of nine had been sent from Heligoland to Zeebrugge. He hoped that he could tempt them into a night action off Ostend to prove his theory that a unit of four British destroyers could out-manoeuvre them.[39] With this in mind, and with the intention of protecting the left flank of the Ostend raiders, he ordered Tomkinson to select three sound destroyers to accompany the *Warwick* on the mission. Tomkinson picked the *Whirlwind*, *Velox* and *Trident* and kept them in readiness in Dover to await a signal from Keyes. Meanwhile, repair work on the *Vindictive* was being rushed through, while the other blockship, the *Sappho*, was brought up from Southampton. The new operation could have gone ahead within two days, but again adverse weather delayed it.

After the ordeal of battle and the anxiety of waiting for a new zero hour, Tomkinson's health deteriorated just after Joan joined him for a holiday at Dover, where another daughter was conceived. His old stomach trouble flared up and he was often sick. At times he could not eat and went to bed before dinner-time.[40] On 9 May, the day after he had a bout of vomiting, he absented himself from a trip in the *Warwick* with Keyes to lunch with King Albert of the Belgians at La Panne, but in the afternoon, as the wind turned into a gentle breeze from the seaward, he received a signal from Keyes to be ready for the Ostend raid that night.[41]

As Keyes rushed back to Dover to pick up Tomkinson and his staff, the *Vindictive* and *Sappho* were on their way to the enemy coast. There was still time for Tomkinson to try a leisurely dinner at naval headquarters at Fleet House, with Joan, Keyes and his wife. Then at 9 p.m., with Tomkinson 'not feeling up to much' after eating, the two wives walked down the pier to wave off their men.[42] As the *Warwick* pulled away she had an extra observer on board, a naval chaplain, the Revd F.M. Jackson, who had begged to be taken.[43]

Keyes' intentions were clear from the start, because he had put Commodore Lynes in command of the blocking of Ostend, thus leaving himself with the roving role of seeking out the enemy warships and destroying them. His staff had studied the previous mistakes at Ostend and issued new orders which called for a raid by Handley Pages, a bombardment by the monitors – Lynes was not to signal them to go into action until the presence of the raiders was discovered – and an accurately laid calcium light buoy to guide in the blockships.[44]

When the *Warwick* arrived at the centre of her patrol line the approach was incident-free, apart from a few star shells and a powerful searchlight probing from the land. The first augury of plans going awry came when Lynes signalled that one of the *Sappho*'s boilers had blown up and she had dropped out. This made the task of the *Vindictive* disastrously difficult, for German gunners would have only one large ship to concentrate on. At 1.35 a.m. Tomkinson watched enemy searchlights lancing the skies and the approaches to Ostend, for by now the CMBs' engines had been heard as they scurried around laying smokescreens.[45]

Soon after, the clear night echoed to the great guns of the monitors and the whistling and crunching of bombs. Until ten minutes before the *Vindictive* was due to arrive at the canal piers, the sea was calm and the wind pleasantly in the north-west. Suddenly the inshore craft were blanketed by a drenching wet, low sea fog.[46] Then at 2 a.m., which was zero hour for the *Vindictive*, the bellow of heavy guns was heard. The roar was intense and the watchers in the *Warwick* were dazzled by rockets, star shells and 'flaming onions'. Tomkinson waited for a sign of Keyes' 'nine German destroyers from Zeebrugge', but even if they had been out, it would have been impossible to spot them from afar. By now the sea fog was so dense that Tomkinson's destroyers had to switch on their bright, stern lights to prevent collision – and even these were visible only for a few yards.[47]

By 2.45 a.m., fifteen minutes after the planned withdrawal of the light craft, the inactive, yet tense, Keyes realized there was to be little action in his present position, so he ordered Commander Campbell to take the *Warwick* as close as possible to Ostend. When just 1$^1/_2$ miles from the harbour, and minutes before the return to Dover was scheduled, SOS, SOS, SOS flashed from a low, white light.[48]

The *Warwick* headed warily towards it and found it came from ML254, crowded with survivors, the wounded and the dead from the *Vindictive*. As soon as they were alongside Tomkinson helped to get them onboard; as at Zeebrugge it was an irksome operation and it was thirty minutes before nearly fifty men, eighteen wounded and two dead, were on the *Warwick*.[49]

The order to sink the ML with an explosive charge had just been given when Lieutenant F. Trumble, the *Warwick*'s first lieutenant, noticed a Lewis gun on her upper deck. He shouted to a seaman: 'Pass that up. We'll have that as well.' As he caught hold of the muzzle, the gun chattered out. He was shot through the head and died instantly alongside Tomkinson.[50]

By now the tide had dropped so much that it was dangerous to return inside the shoals. With the sun due to rise and the mist lifting, the *Warwick* would be uncovered to German gunners, so the four destroyers retreated at 25 knots through a deep draught gap in the enemy's net defence.[51] In the charthouse Tomkinson was listening to the graphic report of Lieutenant Victor Crutchley, who had escaped from the *Vindictive*.[52] Her captain, Commander Alfred Godsal, had to make four approaches in her before the harbour entrance was spotted. Immediately she loomed out of the fog and smoke, which cut visibility to 300 yards, it seemed as if each of the sixteen heavy shore batteries had concentrated on her. The old cruiser was being steered from the conning tower because shellfire had made the upper position untenable. Just before she grounded Godsal went outside the tower to obtain a clearer view – and was never seen again. At that precise moment a shell burst on him and not a trace of him was found. The navigator, Lieutenant Sir John Alleyn, was seriously wounded and had to be carried aft. The dazed Crutchley found himself in lone command and ordered the port telegraph to full speed astern to try to swing the *Vindictive* across the channel. But she grounded on the eastern pier at an angle of 25 degrees, which meant the canal was not completely sealed. He ordered the crew to abandon ship and then blew the explosives in her bottom. Waiting alongside was ML254, which had careered to the *Vindictive* through a curtain of machine-gun and pom-pom fire.[53]

When the wounded had been transferred to her, Crutchley, still not believing Godsal was dead, searched vainly for him in the shambles that was now the *Vindictive*; then he climbed over the side – only to find that the commanding officer of the ML, Lieutenant-Commander Geoffrey Drummond had collapsed over the wheel from loss of blood. For the second time that night Crutchley took over. With the ML flooding rapidly through a hole in the bows, he sent all spare men aft so their weight would lift the bows and organized a pumping party. Gradually the shattered and unstable ML stuttered along in the fog, with a rating flashing an SOS from Crutchley's torch, until she was seen from the *Warwick*.[54]

Crutchley's story was violently interrupted as Tomkinson felt 'as if the *Warwick* had fallen to pieces'. Her starboard propellor had whirled into a mine, which the Germans had newly laid in anticipation of a second attack on Ostend. The *Warwick* heeled alarmingly 30 degrees to port and from the charthouse it looked to Tomkinson as if she were about to go down stern first. The stern compartment and steering engine were blown clean away and her back was broken 70 ft from the stern. Remarkably, the section near the quarter-deck held on, mainly through the reinforcement of mining rails. The after engine-room bulkhead also held. Engineer Lieutenant-Commander R. Rampling quickly diagnosed her wounds and oil was jettisoned from the port side to right her. She came to rest on an even keel and damage control parties set to work to shore up the bulkhead. The magazines and store-rooms below were flooded, and in the wardroom and officers' cabins water was almost up to the deckheads. There were no casualties, although the wounded in the fore-castle were lucky to escape. When the mine exploded one had cried: 'Oh, my God . . . in the ditch after all.' Another answered: 'That's what comes of shipping a parson. The admiral ought to have known better.'[55]

The redoubtable Crutchley, who had just removed his bloodstained lifejacket, put it on again and immediately began hauling up a cable on the forecastle in preparation for tow-ing.[56]

The captain of the nearby *Velox* was signalled to lash his ship alongside the *Warwick* and take off the wounded; then the *Whirlwind* went ahead and a tow-line was fixed to her, while the *Trident* established a lone guard. In this ungainly and slow fashion, the *Warwick* was coaxed along in broad daylight, but by 7 a.m. she was out of range of Ostend's heavy batteries. At the back of Tomkinson's mind was still the fear that 'Keyes' nine German destroyers' would appear. He had gone looking for them, yet now there was a chance of the quarry becoming the hunters. For one of the rare times in his life Keyes was forced to cry for help and use his radio to signal clearly for reinforcements at the risk of the SOS being picked up by the Germans.[57]

The *Warwick*'s position was made more parlous because, in accordance with Admiralty orders, all signal books and ciphers had been destroyed on entering hostile waters. Eventually, ships were contacted by naming their captains and ordering them to concentrate on Z position, one of the temporary buoys laid for the raid. A great collection, including monitors and destroyers, answered and the *Warwick* was enclosed in a protective ring of warships. The *Velox* was unlashed and sped back to Dover with the wounded and the 'unlucky' Mr Jackson, who had been tending them, bidding farewell with: 'Is this what you call a quiet night?' Keyes could not be persuaded to leave the *Warwick*, although it was argued that he should not put himself at risk. At one stage, when taking in huge quantities of water, it looked as if she would have to be abandoned. Then salvage tugs with pumps arrived from Dover and her position improved. But the tedious passage home did not end until 4.30 p.m. – and there on the quay waiting for Tomkinson was Joan, accompanied by Keyes' wife, who had been told of the mining that morning. Tomkinson quietly slipped away with his wife, for outside Keyes' office at Fleet House were forty reporters waiting for news of the admiral's latest adventure.[58]

Rewarding times were ahead. Loyalty deserved to be recognized, and through the new

Sir Roger's patronage Tomkinson was made a Companion of the Order of the Bath. He also received this mention in dispatches from his friend:

> I was able to devote more personal attention and time to working out the plan of operations and the preparation of personnel and materials than would otherwise have been possible because Rear-Admiral Cecil F. Dampier, admiral superintendent and second in command of the Dover Flotilla, Commodore the Hon. Algernon Boyle, chief of staff, and Captain Wilfred Tomkinson, commander of the 6th Dover Flotilla of Destroyers, practically relieved me of all routine work of the Dover base and patrol . . . in order to bring together the number of destroyers required for the operation, while maintaining the work of the patrol it was necessary to have the entire available force in running order. This called for high organisation on Captain Tomkinson's part.[59]

Tomkinson never gave any written indication of whether the three operations were worthwhile in strategic attainment, balanced against the loss of life. The canal from Zeebrugge to Bruges was reopened through German diligence within a month, by the removal of two piers on the western bank and the dredging out of silt. Ostend was never bottled up, and it is doubtful whether it was necessary, anyway. Psychologically and for propaganda reasons,[60] it was at the time an impressive British victory, although in succeeding years historians denigrated the wisdom of the raids. More than 200 men had died and over 400 had been wounded in the three attacks. The Zeebrugge operation accounted for most casualties, with 215 dying and 385 being wounded. The Royal Marines bore the brunt of the enemy's resistance and, out of a total of 740, around 300 became casualties. The second Ostend attempt, although running into heavier fire, got away with ten dead and thirty-one wounded.[61]

Beatty's reaction was diluted after the initial acclamation. 'I have lost some magnificent officers and men,' he wailed privately. 'Nearly all came from us [the Grand Fleet] and we gave of our best, which could be ill spared.'[62]

Keyes has rightly been castigated for being a self-publicist, yet he was always prepared to battle for those who gave him their unflinching loyalty. When his recommendations for decorations were about to be published in the *London Gazette*, he received a printers' proof of the announcement and discovered that several names had been omitted. He immediately sent for Tomkinson and Boyle and told them to take over because he was going to the Admiralty and would not return to Dover unless the names were restored. His determination succeeded. The *Gazette*, although already issued to the Press, was stopped and Keyes inserted every name that had been missed out, plus three more for devilment![63]

The final list for Zeebrugge and Ostend included 11 Victoria Crosses – Crutchley and Drummond among them; 24 Distinguished Service Orders, or bars; 41 Distinguished Service Crosses, 18 Conspicuous Gallantry Medals, 210 Distinguished Service Medals and 424 names mentioned in dispatches.[64]

Tomkinson's health was now at its nadir and the news that the Admiralty had agreed to

Keyes' suggestion that a third attack should be mounted on Ostend – later to be over-turned[65] – did not help his nervous condition. In the immediate days after the *Warwick*'s escape he also had the sorrowful and onerous duty of commiserating with the relatives of the dead, or wounded, who went to Dover. It was an indication of the softness in his character that he entertained them all and treated them all with tenderness and humility.

On the day after the return from Ostend he had a 'rather bad go' of his stomach disorder, just before he and Joan went to the birthday party of Keyes' daughter Elizabeth. Two days later, on acidulous, yet sympathetic, orders from Keyes, he relinquished command as Captain of Destroyers and was admitted to Chatham Royal Naval Hospital for examination. He felt something of a malingerer, or a fake, for among the patients were the many wounded from the Zeebrugge raid.[66]

But he was in a serious condition himself and underwent a long operation by Sir Wilson Cheyne for adhesion of the intestines, a duodenal ulcer of 'several years' standing' and the removal of his appendix.[67] He was confined to bed for twenty days and remained in hospital for another month, before he was allowed to go on a month's leave until 30 July. The following day he was invested with his CB by the King at Buckingham Palace. Typically, and modestly, he did not elaborate on the occasion in his diary.

13
LAST 'BIG PUSH'

After such serious surgery – for those times – Tomkinson could have applied for, and been given, a shore-based appointment. Instead, he insisted on taking over again as Captain D at Dover, alongside Keyes, and rejoined him on 1 August 1918, two days after his investiture, just as plans were made for the 'big push' along the Belgian coast. As he waited for inevitable action, Tomkinson pushed himself to full fitness by going on long walks and managing several games of tennis.

Whenever King George V wanted to make a visit to France it was Keyes who escorted him and it became the accepted pattern for Tomkinson to go, too. On 5 August, the King and his entourage, personal secretary Lord Stamfordham, Derek Keppel and Lord Cromer were passengers in the destroyer *Whirlwind*. They disembarked at Calais and six days later Tomkinson picked them up for the return to Dover, escorted by five destroyers, several CMBs, and an assortment of aircraft. These were contacts that would be of value to him in the future.[1]

The niceties of Royal occasions were thrust aside nine days later when Tomkinson was selected by Keyes for a more dangerous escort duty – a minelaying operation in the approaches to Zeebrugge. The *Abdiel* and five destroyers were to put down new magnetic mines, while Tomkinson, in the *Velox*, in charge of five other ships of the 6th Flotilla and supported by two monitors, were to deal with any counter-attack, either from land or sea. The morale of the *Abdiel*'s captain, Berwick Curtis, was at a low point because a few days earlier two of his minelayers were blown up, with the loss of many lives, when caught in an enemy minefield in the Heligoland Bight. The new operation was completed without casualties, or a sight of the enemy, but Tomkinson did not have a great deal of faith in the magnetic weapons, for he reported: 'All the mines were successfully laid, but unfortunately they don't seem to have got these new machines right yet and about half of them had gone off when we left.' However, there came a quick 'kill', for Naval Intelligence indicated that an enemy destroyer had been sunk by a magnetic mine the next day.[2]

As if to prove that he was definitely sea-fit again, Tomkinson spent three successive nights out with the Dover Patrol. He returned without any misgivings about his health; in fact, never again did his diary have any mention of his stomach problems. Instead, he became worried for the health of his eighteen-month-old daughter, Venetia, and his fear for another death in his family was stressed in this entry of 10 September: 'Have been feeling very sad ever since getting Joan's letter this afternoon saying Venetia is still bad and today she talks of it as if it might be that awful meningitis, which I have dreaded since we lost our little Rachel. I can't bear to think of it and to think of dear Joan having to bear it all by herself.'[3]

Keyes felt for him, too, and gave him special leave to go to Mortehoe, in North Devon, where the family were on holiday. By the time he got there Venetia had recovered. He returned to find Dover in mourning for the death of nearly 100 sailors. During his absence there had been an explosion in the shell-room of the *Glatton*, one of his destroyers, which was in harbour, and she caught fire. With his inimitable *élan*, Keyes took charge and ordered her to be torpedoed in case the blaze caused a larger explosion, with possible danger to the town. It took three close-range torpedoes to sink her. Later he sought permission from the Admiralty to do it![4]

During the last September of the war Keyes made frequent visits to France, as he planned with Field Marshal Sir Douglas Haig the navy's cooperation in a bombardment of the Belgian coast. The Dover Patrol were given the task of supporting the heavy monitors and to make fake threats of a naval invasion, in order to pin down German coastal garrisons, which otherwise might be rushed as reinforcements to the main front. Keyes was also told that he should be prepared to land an army brigade at Ostend.[5]

It began at 2.30 a.m. on 28 September. Tomkinson, in the *Velox* and in company with the *Morris, Matchless* and *Phoebe*, newly repaired after a collision, was protecting the 12-in monitors, *Erebus* and *Terror*, in an hour-long bombardment of the stretch of coast from Zeebrugge to Ostend. German coastal batteries quickly got their range and 'some big stuff' dropped around the British, but not one ship was hit.[6] At 3.30 a.m. Keyes, who had transferred his flag to the monitor *Princess Eugene*, had a more nerve-wracking mission for Tomkinson. He ordered the four destroyers to make a 'demonstration' against the coast towards Ostend. The division turned through the centre of an area, which was marked on Tomkinson's chart as an enemy minefield, to within 5 miles and well within range of the coastal guns. When nearly across the minefield, Tomkinson gave the word for a bombardment of high explosive and star shells. 'The Huns must have thought something was coming as they put on a tremendous display of fireworks and fire shells,' he wrote, 'and fired on us with other stuff.'

At daylight the destroyers rejoined the monitors and another bombardment began. It lasted from 6.30 a.m. to noon; by then most ships were short of shells, so a general recall to Dunkirk was given to re-ammunition. Tomkinson went ashore to see Keyes and was immediately instructed to repeat the performance. In just over two hours he was at sea again in the *Velox* for a successful encore.[7]

Yet the expected land advance was not fully achieved, although at one stage of the offensive it appeared that the enemy was in headlong retreat. Inside the week the Germans had recovered and regrouped, and by October the 'big push' was called off for a reassessment of the situation.[8]

After a respite of nine days it was on again, and Tomkinson, in the *Douglas*, with the *Termagant, Mansfield* and *Morris*, returned to the scene for similar missions with a larger force of eight monitors. The targets were in areas between Nieuport and Ostend and included bridges, crossroads and rail installations, and were to be attacked in cooperation with siege guns roaring out in the offensive from the coast to Ypres. All opened fire at 5.30 a.m. and put in an hour's concentrated bombardment, followed by another hour of 'resting', with every ship getting off one round every six minutes. There was no reply, so after two hours, Tomkinson's division switched towards Zeebrugge to encourage the shore batteries to reveal themselves. He ordered the *Douglas* to put six broadsides into the coast, but again there was no answer.[9]

By breakfast he was back in Dunkirk for a hasty meal and then off by car with Keyes to La Panne, the Belgian army headquarters, where they asked King Albert and General Degouette how they could help. They were told that their efforts were keeping the enemy pinned down, but General Degouette was anxious to know which German coastal batteries remained. Another sortie was devised to draw the Germans out. This time the force of destroyers and monitors steamed closer to the shore between Nieuport and Ostend. The German gunners held their fire, then opened up. The monitor *Gorgon* was straddled and fortunate not to be hit. Quickly Tomkinson, now in the *Termagant*, ordered a smoke-screen to be laid and the warships retired, followed by salvo after salvo. Spray fountained higher than their mastheads. 'In fact we nearly caught a Tartar,' Keyes wrote.[10]

No further risks were to be taken immediately; not until three days later, when reports reached Dunkirk that there was 'no life on the coast between Nieuport and Ostend', did Keyes allow another reconnaissance. With Tomkinson in the *Termagant*, accompanied by the *Morris* and *Mansfield*, and with aircraft overhead, progress was made warily through the West Deep and Nieuport Roads, without a shot being fired. No British vessel bigger than a CMB had been in the area for four years.[11]

Off Middleknocke the destroyers did several turns to attract attention – but again there was no response. On the way to Ostend the division approached closer to the coast. Then all could see British aircraft looping the loop over the town. In landing on the beach, one plane crashed against a groyne. Abreast of the harbour Tomkinson saw on the sands hundreds of people waving flags; and then into sight came the upper part of the wrecked *Vindictive* and, beyond, the remains of the *Sirius* and *Brilliant*.

As the *Termagant* headed towards the harbour entrance fishermen came out in a boat to warn that the Germans had mined the waters. Keyes had the whaler lowered and with schoolboy enthusiasm he, Tomkinson, marine staff officer Major R. Godfrey and a yeoman of signals, rowed themselves ashore. Keyes was first up a ladder on to the packed pier, followed by Tomkinson, with the yeoman carrying a white ensign. According to Tomkinson: 'The people all fell on us, some trying to embrace us and others to lift us on their shoulders, making any chance of progress quite impossible. Fortunately, at this stage, there fell within 20 or 30 yards a shell, without causing casualties.' He used the word 'fortunately' because although the Germans had suddenly taken an interest and opened fire they had dispersed the throngs. Before the people ran off 'some of the crowd told us that there were a fair number of Huns in the town and we were warned it was not advisable to proceed.'[12]

After a hurried row back to the *Termagant*, the would-be 'liberators' ran into accurate shell-fire and steamed into one splash, which drenched them all on the bridge. Before landing, the ardent Keyes had signalled King Albert and Queen Elisabeth an invitation to make a triumphant entry into Ostend, but now this was too hazardous. However, when Keyes and Tomkinson arrived at Dunkirk they found the royal couple waiting; both were advised to postpone the trip, but they would not hear of it. Keyes, bathing in the glory of royal favours, foolishly relented and led them into a bizarre, though humorous, adventure.

As the king, queen and their aide-de-camp embarked on the *Termagant* a hastily made Belgian flag was hoisted at the masthead. Because it was low tide off Middleknocke, the party transferred to a ML, which towed the *Termagant*'s whaler. Outside the harbour they moved into the whaler, with the king, queen and vice admiral in the stern and the energetic Tomkinson pulling away at stroke oar. Tomkinson wrote:

> The king got up the [pier] ladder well. The queen was splendid and managed most successfully. The ADC tried to go up behind her to help, but fell in the water and we had to drag him out, so I went up to assist the queen, not that she really wanted any, but to keep her tidy. It being quite dark by now there were not many people about and we got along for 200 or 300 yards without any trouble, but as soon as people saw who it was they at once began shouting: '*Vive le roi; Vive la reine*' and a great crowd gathered. The king, being tall, was all right, but the admiral and I had great difficulty to keep the queen in touch and she was continually being embraced, sometimes by people who were desirable; at others, I fear, by those who were not entirely so.[13]

The party struggled through the masses in the dark – the Germans had destroyed the power station – to the Hotel de Ville and walked in on a candlelit town council meeting, celebrating with champagne. All were astounded to see the king, who made a short speech in reply to that of the deputy burgomaster. Although Keyes thought it 'very moving and exciting', he was still worried about the town being shelled, so suggested that the king and queen leave after twenty minutes. Tomkinson was glad to hear them agree because there was an alderman 'who was drunk and making a nuisance of himself . . . he continued outside to be rather affectionate and when we got out into the dark I disposed of him!'

To protect their royal charges through the crowds again Tomkinson 'took station behind the queen' and linked arms to form a square with Keyes, Godfrey and Commander Ian Hamilton Benn, RNVR who, although a Member of Parliament, was commanding officer of a ML flotilla.

After the return to the *Termagant*, the royals and Keyes were moved into a CMB for a speedier trip at 40 knots to Dunkirk. Once again the ADC fell into the sea between boats and was nearly squashed before being lugged inboard.

When Tomkinson arrived at Dunkirk in the *Termagant* he was alarmed to find Keyes' car still waiting on the quay and no sign of the CMB, which should have brought the king and queen back. He waited an hour without there being any sighting of the boat, then ordered out 'everything that could move' to search the sea for them. Meanwhile, to his increased anxiety, the enemy had reopened their shelling in the Ostend area. Just as he was about to join the hunt himself in the *Termagant*, a CMB was spotted, and as it came closer Tomkinson could see the king, queen and Keyes on the torpedo platform. By now even Keyes was horrified at the risk he had taken that night as he explained to Tomkinson that the boat had broken down off course and had lost touch with an escorting CMB; for an hour they had drifted, firing Very lights before another CMB rescued them – with the ADC tumbling into the sea for a third time.[14]

Now that Ostend was in allied hands, Keyes planned for the Dover Patrol to liberate its other old target – Zeebrugge. Because German mines had sunk several unwary British vessels, he decided with Tomkinson to make a close-in reconnaissance in a shallow-draught CMB. Off Blankenburg they saw the first sign of a German evacuation, with crowds waving flags again on the beach; yet closer to Zeebrugge it was ominously quieter. They went outside the viaduct, to find C3's conning-tower sticking up with an enormous 'break in it', then ran down the outside of the mole, for which scores of men had died, and manoeuvred off the lighthouse. In the silence Tomkinson feared they could be heading into an ambush, but as the CMB went into the harbour, past the many wrecks, he noticed two French MLs already moored. 'They had forestalled us by an hour or two,' he grumbled. 'It seems that the Belgians were in here this morning and the French were told about it, but we were not.'[15]

Keyes had his triumphant entry a week later, however, when King Albert insisted he should join him in a victory horseback ride into Bruges at the head of the Belgian army.[16]

The work of the Dover Patrol diminished as the German front crumbled, like the entries in Tomkinson's diary. Most of his time was spent on land now and he took the chance of visiting the old battlefields to lay crosses and wreaths on the graves of navy comrades and army friends. At the end of October, with the shooting war virtually over, he took Keyes and his wife Eva on a shooting expedition to Franche, where they bagged more than 100 pheasants in two days.

Among the last words in his war diary were:

9 November 1918. In this evening's paper the Kaiser has abdicated and little Willie has renounced his claim to the throne – very good of him, isn't it?
10 November. The armistice was signed this morning and hostilities ceased at 11 a.m. Tremendous jubilation in Dover, everyone letting themselves go.[17]

The Tomkinsons had emerged from the war without a death – unusual for so large a family – and with many honours. Martin, thirty-five years old and a lieutenant colonel, who had fought on the Western and Italian fronts, won the DSO and bar, the Legion of Honour and the Italian Croce di Guerra, and was mentioned in dispatches six times; Geoffrey, now aged thirty-seven, who also finished the war as a colonel – in the Royal Engineers – had left Brazil to fight, been wounded twice in France and won the MC and OBE. Herbert, aged forty-seven, who was on General Allenby's staff in Egypt, received the OBE and the Order of the Nile. Charles, at twenty-five the youngest in the services, fought in Kenya with the Eastern Africa Rifles and was mentioned in dispatches. Dora, aged thirty-two, chief personnel officer at the Ministry of Munitions, received the OBE and MBE. Marion, aged forty, had set up her own VAD emergency hospital in Kidderminster, for which she was awarded the OBE; while Christine won the Florence Nightingale Medal as a state registered nurse. To add to this list was Wilfred's CB, MVO, which he did not get until 1919, Croix de Guerre, Order of St Maurice and St Lazarus (Italy) and Order of Leopold (Belgium). Of the men, only Raymond, aged thirty-eight, who was unfit because of a knee injury, father Michael, aged sixty-seven, and Gerald, aged forty-two, who had switched from carpet manufacturing to blanket-making for the forces, stayed at home. To celebrate the end of the war, Gerald fired all the cannon outside the front door at Franche, before lighting a monster bonfire, while Michael preached two sermons in one day at separate churches because of the shortage of priests.[18]

At the Victory Parade through tumultuous throngs in London, Tomkinson was near the head of the Royal Navy contingent. Although behind Keyes, he was in speaking distance at his shoulder. It was a position he would enjoy until one of them died.

14
HOOD AND THE MEDITERRANEAN

In the last months of the war, Tomkinson was let into a secret – that Keyes was on the threshold of being appointed to the most responsible position so far in his career, the command of the Battle Cruiser Squadron, and that Tomkinson would go with him as chief staff officer.

The speed and power of these glamorous, yet controversial, warships had fascinated both men, and they remembered their lost chance at the opening of the war when their appointment to the new *Tiger* had been cancelled and they had remained on smaller craft. The staff work for Tomkinson would have been massive, for the force was made up of two battle cruiser squadrons, a cruiser squadron and a destroyer flotilla. However, the end of the war found the navy overmanned, with too many ships, so when Tomkinson was appointed as CSO to Keyes in March 1919, the force had been decimated to one squadron of battle cruisers, comprising the flagship *Lion*, the *Renown, Princess Royal* and *Tiger*. To add to Keyes' disappointment, when taking over from Vice Admiral Sir Henry Oliver at Rosyth he was forced to revert from acting vice admiral to rear admiral for two years. He had supreme consolation, however, in the heap of honours bestowed on him. He was created a baron, given a war service award of £10,000 and received honorary degrees from the universities of Oxford, Cambridge, Aberdeen, Bristol and St Andrews.[1]

Tomkinson was still a captain and foresaw many years in this rank before being able to fly his own flag; nevertheless, he was rapidly climbing the seniority list and this was his most prestigious appointment so far.

After a spell of leave at Whitchurch Villas, Tavistock, where Joan had given birth to a fourth daughter, Joyce, at the end of January, he took command of the *Lion* on 16 March 1919 at Scapa Flow, where the Battle Cruiser Squadron were acting as guard ships to seventy units of the surrendered German fleet. With the euphoria of peace fading fast, it was a gloomy place to be. In the *Lion* alone there were 200 disgruntled stokers, who should have returned to civilian life. 'They seem to have demobilised most of the seamen, who were due,' Tomkinson immediately wrote to Keyes, who had yet to arrive. 'But they still have 240 stoker ratings due for dispersal, who cannot be spared without relief and there seems to be no chance of any reliefs until June. It seems rather absurd that there should be such a hang-up – a good many of them are 1914–15 men and time expired men and it seems rather bad luck on them.'[2]

This was the first written evidence from Tomkinson that he had the men's welfare at heart and it denoted a complete change in his attitude towards the deprived lower deck. On his first morning aboard it was reported to him that the engineer commander had seen a deputation of disgruntled stokers, which 'may lead to trouble'. There were more than 800 engine-room ratings in the squadron wanting to go home, and although they had put up with cramped quarters in wartime, they were not prepared to go on doing it in peacetime. Additionally, many had voluntarily enlisted for 'hostilities only', yet were kept in the navy, while conscripts who had joined in 1917–18 were demobilized. The same morning, dockyard draughtsmen were onboard drawing up plans to remedy the men's accommodation complaints – at the expense of Keyes' and Tomkinson's quarters.[3]

When Keyes transferred his flag to the *Lion* a fortnight later he was briefed by Tomkinson about the problem and soon suggested to Admiral Sir Charles Madden, the commander-in-chief of the newly named Atlantic Fleet, that with the arrival of a few regular replacements and the 'surrender' of a few knots speed, the engine-room complements could be reduced. He warned: 'We cannot settle down with 200 disgruntled men onboard. They provide fertile soil for Bolshevik propaganda, which I don't believe would have a following of any sort in a ship manned by active service ratings under the new conditions of pay and leave arrangements . . . the lower deck are agreed that they would rather be shorthanded than continue under the present conditions.'[4]

However, the Admiralty pig-headedly opposed, and Keyes was admonished in this letter from Madden which, if released, would have inflamed the situation:

So long as there is a chance of a renewal of hostilities in the form of a rigid blockade of the German Baltic and North Sea ports, I cannot consider a reduction in speed, or other sacrifice of efficiency. The temporary rejection of peace terms is quite possible and we will then be required to *act*. The case of the HO [hostilities only] men was badly handled by your predecessor and captains. I was seriously informed that the men would refuse to leave the home ports and that the Battle Cruiser Squadron must remain in them until all HOs were relieved; thus stopping the leave of the 5th and 1st Battle Squadron crews. Considerable pressure was also brought on the Admiralty to relieve the crews of the Battle Cruiser Squadron ships because they had burned more coal and fought more actions than others etc.

I refused to consider the Battle Cruiser Squadron for preferential treatment, for although they were fortunate enough to meet the enemy more frequently and certainly did more work than battleships, they, on the other hand, had many advantages, not the least being that the Battle Cruiser Squadron were based for four years on Rosyth, which as compared with Scapa, was a heaven, and so little did they find Scapa to their taste that it was difficult to keep a Rosyth squadron there for more than a sufficient time to carry out gunnery practice. The men were well aware of the efforts made to secure preferential treatment for them and their failure naturally produced unrest.

I (when commanding the 1st Battle Squadron) saw all the ships' companies and explained that none could be relieved until June, gave reasons and although the men were disappointed nothing that could be termed unrest resulted . . . and if the men are then plainly told what is expected of them I think they will settle down, not contentedly, but with resignation.[5]

This letter is given in full, as an example of high-ranking officers' attitudes towards the 'fortunate' – Madden's description – of the war-weary lower deck, which was nowhere near parallel to the feelings of Tomkinson or Keyes. But the two did tour all the ships in the squadron, with Keyes reassuring the 'time expired' men that he would do all in his power to hasten their release and improve conditions.[6] It was a gesture which Tomkinson should have filed away in his memory for the future and brought out to his advantage.

The other problem for them was the German fleet, in which there were many crews ready to join the Bolsheviks. The Royal Navy had no jurisdiction over them, but the unpopular routine of ensuring that they were immobile and that their crews remained onboard fell to Keyes. He had heard rumours that the Germans secretly hoped that the fleet, commanded by Admiral Ludwig von Reuter, would be returned to them under the terms of the peace treaty, but knew that this was not British policy. He warned the Admiralty that the ships would probably be scuttled and, with Tomkinson, drew up plans for a *coup de main* for the British to seize them before this could happen.[7] Early in May, however, the Battle Cruiser Squadron's turn as guard ships ended and, although Keyes and Tomkinson's ideas were handed over to their reliefs, when the peace terms were decided there was an interval of forty-eight hours before the announcement and signing. Reuter took the opportunity of ordering the scuttling, and before Keyes' coup could be activated fifty-three warships were self-sunk.

Within a year the war-torn *Lion* was paid off after routine Atlantic Fleet duties. Tomkinson was now on the brink of taking command of the *Hood*, the last yet, at more than £6 million, the most expensive British battle cruiser. On 22 August 1918, four years after originally being planned and with much alteration, as the longest ship in the navy, she had rattled down the slipway of John Brown's yard at Clydebank. As the world's largest warship, her 860 ft hull of steel and iron, weighing 21,920 tons, dwarfed everything surrounding her. Not until 9 January, 1920 was she to take to the water under her own power.

Tomkinson had already begun familiarizing himself with the great and gracious-looking vessel, as advanced parties from the *Lion* began to join her. Like the matelots, he was amazed at the roominess of this clean ship, in which one could become lost. She was so massive that he arranged to have notices posted, giving directions to the upper deck. There was a barber's shop, cinema, canteen, bookshop, chapel and a soda bar.[8]

Tomkinson was on the bridge at 12.45 p.m. as the *Hood* left the fitting-out basin. It was still frosty, with heavy sleet and a driving cold wind. There was no ceremony, although the dual directors of Browns, Sir Thomas Bell and Sir William Ellis, were alongside Tomkinson. As four tugs shunted her into position, a desultory gleam of sunshine relieved the steely drabness. Suddenly, like the crack of a whip, her heaviness snapped a stern rope to the tug *Dalmuir*, but she behaved properly after a new hawser was fixed and she was eased along the Clyde until the tugs slipped her at Greenock.

100

On the way to Rosyth came the first indication to Tomkinson that she would be a 'wet' ship. With waves of 15 ft and a force eight wind, water continually rushed over the forecastle, deluged over her first breakwater and cascaded spray on the foremost turrets. Yet she was not fully laden and more than 3 ft short of her mean draught. Tomkinson soon realized, too, that she was not going to be the easy ride her designers had predicted. He was also worried about fierce vibration in the spotting-top above him, a fault that was never remedied.[9]

Until 29 March, her commissioning date, more of the 967 ship's company joined. The first batch again came from the *Lion*, then they arrived thick and fast from all the bases, although her home port was to be Devonport, fortuitously close to Tomkinson's home at Tavistock and to Sparkwell on the edge of Dartmoor, where Keyes had rented Beechwood House.

The *Hood* needed a great deal of working up, practice in gunnery and torpedo firing. Tomkinson was lucky in having for his commander Lachlan McKinnon, who was just the officer to inspire the crew and encourage them. As a young lieutenant he was an instructor to the Turkish navy and had been dubbed 'McKinnon Bey'. At Jutland he was the gunnery officer of the *Indomitable* and in later years he was to become Rear Admiral Commanding the Second Battle Squadron. After he and Tomkinson had put both ship and crew through their paces, the *Hood* went into Rosyth Docks. For a month experts probed every section of her structure. They found nothing to undermine their confidence and on 15 May 1920 Tomkinson was ready to show not only the mighty *Hood* to the world, but also a happy, spirited crew. Most were thankful to have survived the war and to be in the cleanest and most luxurious ship of any fleet.[10]

The nucleus from the *Lion* had already established comradeship and brought loyalty and pride. As she was to be a show ship the sportsminded Tomkinson instructed his divisional officers to select promising athletes who could be relied on to make her the top dog in the fleet, with exemplary behaviour ashore.

On her first passage south, athletes were singled out for soccer, rugby, running, boxing, hockey and regatta training. The cutter crew, however, needed little coaching to lift the fleet's Rodman Cup on her first stop at Portland. The *Lion*'s oarsmen, who had won it in 1918, had been transferred complete to the *Hood*, together with their cutter, *Dipping Lug*, and by stroking at the rate of thirty trounced the *Tiger*'s crew by three lengths. It was the ship's first victory in a long line of successes, which were to make her the navy's sporting palace.

She still had to visit Devonport, her home base, but steamed past the mouth of Plymouth Sound and anchored off nearby Cawsand on 17 May 1920. The next day Keyes joined her and at last Tomkinson showed her to Devonport, where she moored alongside two wharves, which were too small to handle her efficiently.[11]

Unknown to the crew, Keyes had passed Admiralty orders to Tomkinson to prepare the *Hood* for a mission to Reval (now Tallin) in Estonia, where, with the *Tiger* and nine of the newest destroyers, she was to act as a 'frightener' to the Bolshevik fleet. The men were told that the squadron was going on an official visit to Scandinavia, but in fact it was planned to be the forerunner of a more serious Baltic mission.

Tomkinson's first overseas voyage in the *Hood* was meant not only as a show of power to the Soviets, but also as a goodwill trip to Sweden, Denmark and Norway. Unfortunately it was badly planned, not taking into account the *Hood*'s size. It was only when she arrived at Kioge Bay, near Christiania (now Oslo) that it was realized she could not steam close inshore because of her draught. Nevertheless, anchored several miles away from the port, she was visited by King Haakon and Queen Maud, the sister of George V. At the same time Tomkinson encountered his first meeting with thousands of visitors, who were to set the pattern of 'open ship' for the rest of the cruise.

The next stop was Kalmar, 200 miles from Stockholm. Among the busiest of the ship's company were the seamen who manned the 3-lb Hotchkiss saluting cannon. They were firing twenty-one-gun salutes for kings and admirals and seven–gun salutes for consuls more than twice a day for a week.

Tomkinson ordered smoke of a different nature on 13 June, when Keyes exercised the squadron in hide-and-seek manoeuvres. More festivities were celebrated at Apenrade two days later when the area was handed back to Denmark by Germany. At Copenhagen the now familiar routine was gone through again, with comings and goings of consuls, mayors and senior civics and the crash of cannon. Finally, Tomkinson escorted the King and Queen of Denmark on a two-hour inspection. The throngs of visitors continued unabated during the *Hood*'s stay. It was at Copenhagen that Keyes was told by the Admiralty that the squadron's aggressive stance was to be called off. The Government decided that as the Baltic states had agreed to live at peace with the new Soviet regime, Britain should not take any more offensive action against Russian ships. Instead, the squadron were ordered to Christiania again for another visit by King Haakon, before sailing home.

Tomkinson had obtained complete elitism in the ship's company, who on 5 August, off Rosyth, were proud to be called in to provide search parties and armed guards to board the surrendering German ships, *Helgoland*, *Westphalen* and *Rugen*. Six days later he looked on proudly as the *Hood* won the Battle Cruiser Squadron Regatta at Lamlash, off the Isle of Aran.

Throughout that autumn he kept his men hard at work, with gunnery and torpedo trials off Portland. With the help of his executive officers he moulded them into a team, ready to protect the reputation of their ship and the cap-bands that they wore. Yet all this was undermined by the Admiralty, who announced that by the end of 1920 the navy would revert to the peacetime system of manning by crews from one depot.

The final cruise for Tomkinson and the united men of Chatham, Portsmouth and Devonport, came in January 1921 – the improperly named spring cruise – to Vigo, Arosa Bay and Gibraltar. It was overshadowed by tragedy from the start after a gale confined the Atlantic Fleet – the Battle Cruiser Squadron with them – in Torbay until 20 January. Then, on the first day out, the submarine K5, which was exercising with the *Hood*, failed to surface 120 miles south-west of the Scillies. All that was found of her were two pieces of timber, a ditty box and an oil slick. But the sixty-five officers and men were not forgotten. On the return passage, Keyes ordered a church service to be held over the spot where the submarine disappeared. The squadron assembled in a rough circle, engines were stopped and wreaths dropped on the sea. It was a sad end to what was Tomkinson's happiest commission in a magnificent new warship, whose name was to be synonymous with Britain's naval power worldwide.[12]

That June, Tomkinson paid homage as a pallbearer, with five of his brothers at the funeral of his eighty-year-old father, fifteen months after the death of his mother at seventy. Both, however, had lived long enough to celebrate the fiftieth anniversary of the Tomkinson carpet empire.[13]

With the infamous Geddes axe cutting great swathes in the ranks of regular officers, and with Keyes' tour of duty with the battle cruisers coming to an end, there was no suitable appointment of flag rank. He was told by the Admiralty that he would be 'on the beach' for the next year on half pay, but was promised an important position in Whitehall afterwards.[14]

For the next six years Tomkinson was also on shore, serving the type of 'apprentice-ship' that normally presaged elevation to sea lord. His first appointment was as Chief of Staff and Maintenance Captain to the Commander-in-Chief Chatham, Admiral Sir Hugh Evan-Thomas. In this type of 'office job' he was able to resume a normal family life, and moved Joan and his daughters, Betty, now twelve, Venetia, five, and Joyce, two, into The Grange, a house in Gillingham, and it was here a year later that his wife gave birth to their sixth and last child, Susan. Meanwhile, their son Peter was about to follow his father by joining Britannia Royal Naval College, Dartmouth.[15]

Around the same time, Keyes' direction changed dramatically within six months. The Deputy Chief of Naval Staff, Vice Admiral Sir Osmond de Brock, was taken ill and Beatty, the First Sea Lord, called on his old colleague Keyes to take over on 1 November 1921. Keyes now controlled the intelligence, plans, operations, local defence, training and trade divisions and was in the middle of the majority of important naval issues. The direct result for Tomkinson was that at the end of two years at Chatham his faithful colleague, who was also a lord commissioner, gave him the post of Director of the Operations Division in Whitehall.[16]

When two uneventful years at the Admiralty had passed Tomkinson was able to move his family back to Devon, where he took over as acting commodore of the Royal Naval Barracks, Devonport. His course to seagoing flag rank was now clearly defined. During 1926 he went on a senior officers' technical course and finally, on 2 August 1927, was promoted to rear admiral.

Keyes' career was also about to reach its peak. He had been earmarked as Commander-in-Chief, Mediterranean, after three-and-a-half years at the Admiralty, and by May of 1925 he was ensconced in the position at Malta, with the substantive rank of admiral. He was still only fifty-two, and because of his early promotion after the Boxer Rebellion was four years ahead of his age-group in the admirals' list.[17]

For one of the few times in their long friendship Keyes was unable to ask for Tomkinson to join him immediately. The Mediterranean Fleet was Britain's biggest and required a chief of staff of flag rank to run it. Keyes arrived in Malta in June 1925, and it would be at least two years before Tomkinson was promoted to rear admiral, having still to go through his technical course. He was keen to join Keyes, because not only would he have been able to take Joan and his four daughters, but they would all have been together, as his son Peter was a midshipman on the battleship *Barham*, based at Malta.[18]

Instead, Keyes was able to obtain as his chief of staff another old friend in Rear-Admiral Dudley Pound, who had been his number two in the *Opossum*, in 1898, his first chief of staff on the *Colossus* and his assistant at the Admiralty.[19] In fact, Tomkinson had been following Pound around since he started at Britannia a year behind him. The pattern was not to change. After twenty months as Keyes' confidante and adviser, Pound was called home to the Admiralty, as Assistant Chief of Naval Staff. It was a valuable move also for Keyes, as for the next fifteen months Pound kept him fully informed of the intrigues going on in Whitehall. It also gave Keyes the opportunity to have Tomkinson brought out as chief of staff.

His appointment began on 1 December 1927, four months after his promotion to rear-admiral. Few officers on newly achieving flag rank could have been plunged into organizing and running one of the largest British fleets ever assembled, which filled the anchorages at Valletta's Grand Harbour and cluttered the surrounding creeks with small craft. Through Keyes, he was responsible for eight battleships, which formed two battle squadrons, ten cruisers in two squadrons, the aircraft-carriers, *Eagle* and *Courageous*, thirty-six destroyers in four flotillas, sixteen submarines, and gaggles of other craft, including seaplane carriers, sloops, minesweepers, minelayers and depot ships.[20]

The Mediterranean, because of its mild climate and high number of seagoing days, was considered an ideal naval training area. Outwardly Tomkinson found the fleet in good heart and sport, although there were rumbles of discontent later. Keyes and Pound had improved training and efficiency and they had been most successful in the yearly war-games against the Atlantic Fleet. This was a necessary point to prove because the Admiralty looked on the Mediterranean Fleet as Britain's main naval force and, if there had been war in the Far East, it would have been the commander-in-chief who would have led it through the Suez Canal, Red Sea and Indian Ocean to Singapore.

Tomkinson also discovered that Keyes had matured a great deal as he approached what appeared to be the final phase of a career leading to the office of First Sea Lord. Many of his cruises were diplomatic missions, in fact, and included visits to Italy, flexing her muscles with Mussolini newly in control, Yugoslavia, Greece, France and Egypt.

A new world of big ships in big numbers, big parties and even bigger contacts opened up for Tomkinson. From the greyness of a wintry Britain, immobilized by strikes, unemployment and the depression, he became immersed in a world of social graces. Cocktail parties, seasonal balls, horse-racing and polo were all part of the life ashore, which whirled around Keyes, his menage and entourage. Yet Tomkinson never became caught up in it entirely at the expense of service efficiency. He brought out his family to live at Floriana, where his eldest daughter, Betty, and a French governess taught the younger girls.[21]

In particular, he kept himself out of Keyes' polo activities, which were eventually to play a part in preventing his reaching the pinnacle at the Admiralty. Keyes so encouraged polo, which he played on his appropriately named ponies, Fame, Lurcher and Warwick, that he brought down the price of it to 5*s* a game for officers above the rank of lieutenant and half a crown for midshipmen, although, of course, it was still expensive for them to buy and stable strings of horses. It got to the extent of his wife forming a women's team –

consisting of herself, her two daughters and a girl friend – who would play midshipmen before 8 a.m., with the sides later breakfasting at Admiralty House, Keyes' headquarters. Indeed, Admiralty House became the fleet meeting-place, for every new officer joining was invited there for drinks with the commander-in-chief.[22]

At a more rarified altitude, Keyes met the Duke and Duchess of York (later King George VI and Queen Elizabeth), Winston Churchill, the future Lord Louis Mountbatten, then the assistant fleet wireless officer, and his ally Lord Beatty.

Keyes' kaleidoscopic style of command and way of life brought the first tinge of criticism, however. Many considered that the command was overstaffed – his entourage in the flagship *Queen Elizabeth*, was a heavy thirty-one.[23] The issuing of orders was Tomkinson's responsibility and it was claimed that individual captains were not given the chance of showing their solo initiative at sea. Keyes was also despotic enough to ensure that his family enjoyed his power. They regularly cruised in his 700-ton dispatch vessel, the *Bryony*, an unarmed sloop, and his sons Geoffrey, then nine and Roger, seven, were allowed to go to sea in the flagship.[24]

Polo, which was a fetish with him, also brought scurrilous 'buzzes' through the fleet wardrooms that officers who played the game were favoured and stayed in much sought-after appointments, while on the mess-decks there were moans that the commander-in-chief was commandeering the men's soccer pitches for polo. All these smears were vastly exaggerated instances of isolated occurrences; nevertheless, they tarnished Keyes' image and also that of Tomkinson, as the conveyor of his orders.

Lieutenant-Commander Charles Lambe (later to become an admiral and a knight), who, although a polo player himself, still thought Keyes' passion serious enough to write home: 'People are very bitter out here about polo – and rightly so. Keyes has done a great deal of harm by such iniquitous favouritism as recalling a cruiser in the middle of a day's exercising and sending the barge for one of his team. The polo players in the flagship are never allowed to be prevented by duty from playing and their work falls on the shoulders of others (who would probably play if they had the money). It is a great pity.'[25]

The headiness of his command also swayed Keyes' judgement. Beatty, who was nearing the end of his tenure as First Sea Lord, and who was convalescing from an operation, went to the Mediterranean in the yacht *Sheelah* and intimated that he wanted Keyes to succeed him. But it meant terminating his appointment as commander-in-chief a year in advance of its scheduled length. Keyes, still only fifty-three, was savouring his life at Malta, and did not relish an immediate return to the dullness of Admiralty routine, so he suggested that Admiral Madden, fourteen years his senior, should be appointed as a form of 'caretaker'. This diplomatic suggestion was accepted – with later regrets for Keyes – particularly as Madden was Jellicoe's brother-in-law and his appointment might heal the breach that existed between the Beatty and Jellicoe factions after the Battle of Jutland controversy.[26]

So Beatty stayed at the Admiralty until the late summer of 1927 and Keyes, now with Tomkinson at his side and Beatty's son in his flagship,[27] lingered on in the Mediterranean, only to run into childish conflict and career-breaking publicity.

15
ROYAL OAK FARCE

The farcical *Royal Oak* affair, which was to show up the puerility that existed among senior officers, broke on a sleepy, sunny morning in Malta on Saturday, 10 March 1928. It was the eve of the Mediterranean Fleet's sailing for a combined exercise with the Atlantic Fleet off Gibraltar, when Admiral John Kelly, in command of the 1st Battle Squadron, walked into Tomkinson's office at Admiralty House, Valletta, to report that there was unprecedented friction between his recently appointed second in command, Rear-Admiral Bernard St George Collard, in the battleship *Royal Oak*, with his flag captain, Kenneth Dewar, and Commander Henry Daniel.

After Kelly and Tomkinson had conferred with Keyes, it was decided to postpone the sailing for fifteen hours to enable a board of inquiry to meet that afternoon.[1]

In order to comprehend the subsequent proceedings it is necessary to understand the characters of the three officers involved in a wrangle that Tomkinson was to commit hurriedly to paper within the next forenoon.

Both personally and through an infamous reputation, he was acquainted with Collard, who joined the Mediterranean Fleet a month before him. Collard, short both in stature and temper, but not in courage, had commanded the monitor *Lord Clive* during Tomkinson's days with the Dover Patrol, but was also known throughout the service for being responsible for the Portsmouth Barracks riots more than twenty years earlier.[2]

He had been in charge of the last parade of the day at the barracks when a rainstorm swept the square. A few ratings ran for shelter and the remainder followed, mistakenly thinking Collard had ordered the dismissal. He called them all back, lined them up again and then formally gave the order to 'double off'. But one group of stokers was heard to grumble. Collard recalled them a second time to lecture them and shouted 'on the knee' – an old custom used by gunnery officers to ensure that they could see every man they were speaking to. The stokers, many new to the navy, refused to obey. He ordered it again and this time only one refused to kneel. He dismissed the rest and then berated the disobedient stoker.

That night a drunken rating gave the order 'on the knee' as a joke in the barracks' canteen. It acted like a call to arms, for 300 stokers wrecked the building and then rushed to the officers' quarters, but the gates were locked in time and armed guards stopped them from going in. They then rampaged through the barracks, smashing windows and furniture. The following evening there was another disturbance. Collard took the blame for both incidents and at a court martial was reprimanded for giving an unauthorized punishment, but cleared of swearing at a stoker and making improper use of 'on the knee'.[3]

It hardly affected his career, however, for officers of his ilk were needed in wartime. As an assistant beachmaster in the Gallipoli campaign, where he first met Keyes, he won the DSO after being wounded, and by June 1915 he was one of the youngest captains in the navy at that time. This was two years ahead of Tomkinson, yet both were made rear admirals at approximately the same time. There were few 'blood and guts' admirals like Collard left, and it was inappropriate that when he went to the *Royal Oak* at Malta he should have as his two right-hand officers Captain Dewar and Commander Daniel.[4]

It underlined the tempestuous reputation of Collard that he could not find a flag captain willing to join him, and in the end accepted Dewar, who was loath to serve under him.[5]

Fifty-year-old Dewar had the superior air of an intellectual, which was borne out by his towering over Collard. Already he had been marked down for the highest command, being one of the new wave of officers not prepared to drop into the mould of old-fashioned admirals, such as Collard. Even as a junior officer he was invited to lecture commanders and captains at the War College, which he was later to join at the age of thirty-one after serving in eleven ships in eleven years. Later he was assistant to Pound, when Keyes was at the Admiralty, and although he argued with the admiral that Gallipoli should never have happened, Keyes still recommended him for promotion; at thirty-nine he, too, became one of the youngest captains. From then on most of his career was centred on Whitehall, and after two years as Deputy Director of Naval Intelligence – a position to which he was well suited – he was appointed to the *Royal Oak*.[6]

Daniel, like Collard, was the son of a country clergyman and had also won the DSO, but the resemblance ended there. Like Dewar, he was tall and an intellectual who wrote plays and technical manuals. He had been on the Mediterranean station since 1925, serving in the *Iron Duke* and *Barham*. He was popular ashore, where he organized dances, treasure hunts and fancy dress parades.[7] Daniel boarded the *Royal Oak* for the first time on Christmas Eve 1927, but was not to find peace and goodwill.

Even before those junior to him had time to settle in, Collard was criticizing them. Tomkinson was told that the first minor clash – later to become a major one in the light of publicity – came on 2 January at a dance on the *Royal Oak*. After dining with Keyes and his wife and the Tomkinsons, Collard and his guests went on the quarterdeck and found several women, who had been invited as officers' partners, sitting out dances. Collard called over Dewar, complained to him and insisted that Daniel should arrange partners for the 'wallflowers', even though many officers were committed to entertain their own parties, which they had invited. Soon after, Collard did not like the music selected by Bandmaster Percy Barnacle and played by the Marine band. He ordered Daniel to tell the musicians to pack up their instruments, so that the ship's volunteer jazz band could take over. He also sent for Barnacle, made insulting remarks about the music and the bandmaster's professionalism and threatened to send him back to Britain.[8]

The controversy flared the next day when the rankled Barnacle, a popular figure onboard, put it around the ship that he would ask to leave the service at the expense of surrendering his pension. He also broke down in tears to the chaplain, the Revd Harry Goulding, who, in an attempt to clear an atmosphere of disunity, went to Collard as an intermediary. A night's sleep had not sedated the admiral's temper, however, and he told the chaplain not to intrude into matters that did not concern him, or he would be court-martialled.[9]

Keyes and Tomkinson had noticed already that in static war-games Dewar, who was normally at ease on these occasions, was far from happy in the presence of Collard. Within a month the situation deteriorated further.[10]

The next flare-up on the *Royal Oak* occurred on 5 March, when Collard complained that a disembarking ladder had not been lowered quickly enough for him. Although in earshot of several ratings he grumbled to Dewar that seldom could he get an order obeyed; that he was fed up with the ship and threatened to have his flag transferred. Again the admiral did not calm down the next day and snubbed Dewar by not returning his salute.[11]

That was the trivial background of the affair. But Daniel objected to the innuendo that was directed at him as the ship's 'manager'. He wrote a letter to Dewar, insisting that a protest should be made against Collard and alleged that the crew were afraid that his forthcoming admiral's inspection of the ship would turn into a tirade of fault-finding. Dewar concurred with Daniel's recriminations, for instead of asking him to have second thoughts he bypassed Collard and sent the letter to Kelly.[12]

And so this trite clash of personalities first landed in Tomkinson's lap when Kelly arrived at his office that Saturday morning. After consulting with Tomkinson and his staff about the wrangle, Keyes, probably reacting too peremptorily, but without taking sides, postponed the fleet's sailing until midnight because it was important that this prickly trio must not go to sea together until the position was investigated. He instructed Kelly and Tomkinson to rush through the orders for a board of inquiry that afternoon at 1.30 p.m. This in itself added fuel to the farrago, for not until ten minutes before board members were due to convene at the Castille was Dewar informed. With only minutes to get there he dashed off, but told Daniel to pick up as many witnesses as he could from the *Royal Oak*. Daniel compounded his indiscretion by reading a copy of his letter of complaint to officers in the wardroom behind locked doors and then taking volunteers, who backed him, to the inquiry.[13]

Because of the imminent sailing of the fleet, the board, headed by Kelly, had to be swift in reaching a conclusion. Their verdict was that all three officers were gravely at fault, but Keyes and Tomkinson were not able to peruse the evidence until the following morning.[14]

Keyes quickly concurred with the findings and also thought it undesirable that the three should stay in the *Royal Oak*. Tomkinson signalled Dewar and Daniel to 'repair onboard fleet flagship forthwith', then went to his cabin to change into his full rear admiral's trappings of cocked hat, frock coat with gold epaulettes, white gloves, belt and sword, and all his medals and ribbons. After he had dressed, he went to the admiral's day cabin, where Keyes, with a foot-long bar of medals on his left breast, and Kelly were similarly attired.

When Daniel entered, all three stood up, with Keyes, stern faced and hard jawed, in the middle, Kelly, also tense looking, on the right and Tomkinson, with a 'rather unhappy expression', on the left. Keyes cleared his throat and announced in monotone: 'You are dismissed your ship and will return to England.' Daniel saluted and answered smartly 'Aye, aye, sir,' swivelled round and left the cabin.

Dewar was not as easily disposed of a few minutes later when he was told that he, too, was to be dismissed the ship. He wanted to know why he deserved such harsh treatment. Keyes stared back at him, but remained silent. 'May I ask of what charge I am guilty?' Dewar persevered. Still Keyes refused to reply. 'I shall ask for a court martial, sir,' Dewar warned. Keyes replied coldly: 'Then it will have to be on this station.' To prevent any further discussion, he held up his hand in a halt sign and nodded: 'You may go.'[15]

Later Dewar was to write in his book, *The Navy from Within*: 'No doubt this ceremonial dismissal was meant to impress me, but to my mind it merely accentuated the stupidity of the whole affair.'[16]

In fact, the summary removal of a flag captain without formulation of a charge, or choice of a court martial, was without precedent in the modern navy and contravened King's Regulations. Keyes had arrogated powers that could be invested only in a court martial.[17]

As a rear-admiral, Collard could not be dealt with so summarily. In a private discussion with him Keyes said he intended to transfer Collard's flag to the *Resolution*. Although agreeing that he should leave the *Royal Oak* at once, Collard refused to shift his flag, preferring instead to resign his appointment. This would have been an easier way out, but instead Keyes ordered him to strike his flag.[18]

Thinking he had rid himself of a problem, Keyes signalled the Admiralty of his actions and advised: 'I am strongly of opinion, however, that it is not in the interests of the service to give these matters the publicity that a court martial would involve and I trust that after reading the evidence Their Lordships will concur.'[19]

That evening Tomkinson collated all the minutes of the inquiry and arranged for an officer to take them to London. But if he, too, thought that it was the end of the affair he underestimated the resoluteness of Dewar and Daniel.

Keyes' hopes of stifling publicity were short-lived. As soon as the officers arrived home, the press were handed the story – probably by Daniel, who was to join the *Daily Mail* – and there were lurid accounts of 'mutiny' in the *Royal Oak*.[20] There was even the suggestion by some hapless scribe, who might have linked Dewar with the distilling family of the same name, that he had attempted to get Collard into trouble by planting a bottle of whisky in his luggage!

Dewar, however, had political friends and his case was raised in the House of Commons by Commander Carlyon Bellairs, MP. Admiral Madden had originally approved Keyes' actions, but in the face of a gathering political storm he fell in line with the views of Lord Bridgeman, the First Lord, and it was decided on 19 March that Dewar and Daniel should be court-martialled, as they had requested. Collard's resignation was accepted and he was never to hoist his flag in a ship again.[21]

Their Lordships took heed of Keyes' warning about adverse publicity and endorsed his suggestion that the court martial should be held at Tetuan Bay, a lonely anchorage on the

Moroccan coast,[22] which national newspaper correspondents would find almost impossible to reach without expensive chartering of boats or seaplanes. But this subterfuge triggered another outcry in the press and finally the Admiralty ordered Keyes to convene the trial at Gibraltar on the aircraft-carrier *Eagle*.

When Daniel's trial opened in the ship's hangar on 31 March, there was a 'gallery' of 200, mainly officers, while a special section of the deck had been built as a press-box for world-wide correspondents, who had gone to write reports which would ridicule the navy. All the squabbling was revealed in the first court martial, which ended with Daniel being severely reprimanded and dismissed his ship, something that Keyes had already achieved.

Tomkinson was a member of the court for Dewar's hearing and was assembled in all his ceremonial dress with his fellow 'judges', waiting for it to start, when the dapper, monocled Rear-Admiral W.H.D. Boyle, who was defending Dewar, with a King's Counsel, objected to his presence, because he had played a major part in preparing the papers for both the board of inquiry and court martial. There was also an objection to Rear-Admiral Meade, who had been a member of the inquiry board. The court was cleared while the judge advocat considered the arguments, and when it was resumed both Tomkinson and Meade were ordered to stand down.[23]

All the wrangling and animosities between Dewar and Collard were repeated and at the end of the third day Dewar was found guilty and suffered a similar fate to Daniel. He was to say later: 'Officers convicted of drunkenness on duty, losing their ship by negligence and wilful disobedience of orders have received lighter sentences, but the action of the commander-in-chief had to be justified at all costs.'[24]

Justification or not, it had given newspapers columns of scurrilous accusations, spread over five days. But it did not satisfy the navy lobby in the House of Commons and the Admiralty had to make it clear that the sentences would not prevent Dewar and Daniel being given other appointments.

On 17 April, when questions were asked about why it was necessary for the Government to put a veil around the affair when questions were originally asked but not answered satisfactorily, the reply was that Keyes had failed to send enough information – a statement that was far from the truth.[25] In the event, Dewar continued his naval career, while Daniel resigned his commission and turned to journalism. Collard was put on the retired list immediately.[26]

In June 1928, Keyes' term as commander-in-chief came to an end and he and Tomkinson returned to England, knowing that there were no posts available for them and that they would probably be unemployed for a year on half pay. Within six months, however, Tomkinson had been elevated to Acting Chief of Naval Staff (ACNS) at the Admiralty and was to remain there working closely with his friend Pound for the next two years. Although at the very seat of naval power, he appears to have disentangled himself from the intrigues centred around Keyes, who relied mainly on Pound to keep him informed.[27]

The *Royal Oak* fiasco was yet to blight Keyes' prospects of becoming First Sea Lord, for now King George, to whom Collard had once been an aide-de-camp, entered the controversy and sent for him to explain.[28] Keyes was surprised to find that the king did not know all the facts, so he took the final draft of his report with him. It placated the king, but he still considered Keyes had 'made a mess of things' by ordering a flag officer to haul down his flag. The contentious subject of Keyes taking more interest 'in polo than the conduct of the fleet' was also raised.

Meanwhile, Madden, who had failed to realize that he had been appointed First Sea Lord mainly because Keyes stood aside,[29] was making secret overtures for his successor to be Admiral Sir Frederick Field, who had relieved Keyes in the Mediterranean. Beatty, under whom both Keyes and Field had held the post of Deputy Chief of Naval Staff, was still pressing for Keyes to be the First Sea Lord. Just as Tomkinson was about to move into Whitehall, Keyes accepted the appointment of Commander-in-Chief Portsmouth, which was to become available in May 1929. He was promised by Madden and Lord Bridgeman that it would not lessen his chances of becoming First Sea Lord, although Admiral de Brock, from whom he was taking over at Portsmouth, was also in line.[30] There was also the assurance that a junior would not be promoted over Keyes' head. The promise was insincere; Madden had already warned Field that he should be ready to take control by the spring of 1929, before the appointment of a new civil First Lord after the General Election – when, of course, Keyes would be safely sidelined in Portsmouth.

These secret bargainings never reached Tomkinson's, or Pound's, desk. It was Beatty who, in January 1929, informed Keyes about the back-door negotiations with Field. The intriguers won, however, and although he waited longer than expected, Field became First Sea Lord in the spring of 1930.[31] The consolation for Keyes was that he was promoted to Admiral of the Fleet, at the age of fifty-seven in May 1930, and created a GCB in the king's birthday honours list.

Tomkinson continued as ACNS, with the knowledge that after another spell at sea he was almost certain to become a sea lord. That seagoing appointment arrived in the spring of 1931, when he became Rear-Admiral Commanding the Battle Cruiser Squadron, flying his flag in one of the happiest ships he had captained – HMS *Hood*.

For two years the *Hood* had been in Portsmouth Dockyard for a refit costing nearly £900,000 – a sizeable sum in those days of Admiralty austerity. It was due to end in March 1931, in time for trials off Portsmouth, where she was expected to be recommissioned in the May. By the beginning of the year there seemed no chance of this schedule being met. For the next four months train-loads of scrap and dirt were taken from her, and not until 12 May was she recommissioned at Portsmouth. Previously she was Westhoe- or Devonport-based, but facilities there were not ideal to handle her. From 15 June she 'worked up' for a month, off the south coast, which necessitated Tomkinson temporarily hoisting his flag, for the first time in lone seagoing command, in the battle cruiser *Renown*.[32]

He had initially set foot in the *Hood* as her first captain – and a popular one – in 1920, so the ship's company were expecting a warm welcome when she rejoined the battle cruisers in Torbay on 10 July 1931. But Tomkinson, who was on the *Renown*'s bridge, did not like what he saw as the *Hood* took station astern of the squadron. He signalled 'Manoeuvre badly executed' to her commanding officer, Captain J.F.C. Patterson, who was expecting something like 'Glad to see you back.'

Worse followed; after Tomkinson's flag had fluttered to the *Hood*'s masthead at 8 a.m. the next day, he walked around Sunday divisions and again did not like what he saw of the untidy mess-decks. The men were dismissed and then came the pipe 'Clear lower deck. All hands aft.' Standing on the capstan, an angry Tomkinson told them: 'I was the first captain of this ship and until you reach something like the standard in which I left her, I shall not be satisfied and until then I have not much use for you.'

This 'insult', meant mainly to drive the crew towards better things, had the reverse effect, and did not endear him to the lower deck. Later Vice Admiral E.W.L. Longly-Cook, then a lieutenant-commander in the *Hood*, was to say: 'The men had worked hard to get her from dockyard condition to fleet condition.'[33]

Within two months Tomkinson would have cause to regret his maiden speech, for soon the *Hood* would be steaming to Invergordon, where his career was to be wrecked in the maelstrom of mutiny.

HMS *Fame*, the little ship that took Tomkinson to high adventure in China, 'dressed overall' on Christmas Day at Hong Kong in 1899

The ship's company of the *Fame*, with Tomkinson (front row, fourth from right) alongside (to his right) Keyes, Chief Engineer Ham and Gunner Mascull

Wei-Hai-Wei during the Boxer Rebellion, with the *Fame* (centre), the *Iphigenia* (left), which saw action with Tomkinson as a block-ship at Zeebrugge eighteen years later, and the *Centurion* (right), the commander-in-chief's flagship

Admiral Sir Roger Keyes' impression of the 'cutting out' of Chinese destroyers at Tongku by the *Fame* and the *Whiting* in June 1900

The captured Chinese destroyer *Hai Loong*, with the *Hai Hse*, alongside Tongku wharf. Tomkinson was given command of the *Hai Loong*, renamed HMS *Taku*, for his part in taking the prizes. The stern of HMS *Fame* is to the right of the picture

The *Fame*, decks crowded with Royal Welch Fusiliers, on the way to Tongku (above), and embarking troops from HMS *Terrible* (below)

Keyes with Chief of Staff Admiral Frederick Sturdee (left), one of his main critics, who objected to his 'barging about' in the Bight (*Imperial War Museum*)

The destroyer, HMS *Lurcher*, Tomkinson in command, going full speed astern after rescuing more than two hundred men from the stricken German cruiser *Mainz* during the Battle of Heligoland on 28 August 1914

A British seaplane taken in tow by the *Lurcher* after the Christmas Day air raid on Cuxhaven, 1914

A German aerial view of British block-ships in the canal at Zeebrugge, 23 April 1918

HMS *Warwick*, flying Keyes' flag, leads the way to the Zeebrugge raid, April 1918 (from the painting by Bernard Gribble)

The *Warwick* being towed into Dover after hitting a mine on the way back from the Ostend raid, 10 May 1918

Sir Roger Keyes, with Tomkinson behind, at a victory parade in London at the end of the
First World War

Tomkinson, proud captain of HMS *Hood,* during a visit by King Haakon and Queen Maud of Norway (centre), at Kioge Bay, near Oslo, in 1920

HMS *Royal Oak* departing from Grand Harbour, Malta, on 13 March 1928

Above Left
Rear-Admiral Bernard Collard, short in stature and temper, whose petty demands led to the *Royal Oak* affair

Above
Captain Kenneth Dewar, 'severely reprimanded' and dismissed from command of the *Royal Oak* by a Navy court martial

Left
Commander Henry Daniel suffered a similar fate to Dewar for his part in the *Royal Oak* farce

DAILY HERALD, September 16, 1931.

Daily Herald

Holbrook's Worcestershire **Sauce**
the Sauce of appetite

No. 4863   WEDNESDAY, SEPTEMBER 16, 1931.   ONE PENNY.

ATLANTIC FLEET RECALLED—*Official*

UNREST FOLLOWS PAY CUTS AMONG LOWER RATINGS

Exercises Suspended Pending Admiralty Inquiry

REAR-ADMIRAL TOMKINSON

Premier's Talks With Crew of Warship at Portsmouth

CLEANING THE DECKS under the guns of H.M.S. Warspite, one of the big ships now lying at Invergordon.

TRUTH ABOUT MISS SLADE

LIFE DEVOTED TO INDIA

LUXURY RENOUNCED

MISS SLADE

£500 A WEEK FILM ACTOR

RECORD SALARY FOR MR. LESLIE HOWARD

SNOWDEN HINTS AT ELECTION

SUGGESTS IT MAY COME ABOUT IN FEW WEEKS

MR. SNOWDEN, in the House of Commons last night, hinted at the possibility of a General Election within the next few weeks.

"During the last few days," he said, "I have been able for the first time to study in the House the faces of my late associates. I have admired the way they have cheered to keep their spirits up.

"I have admired those who have done that, knowing that only a few weeks possibly remain before the place which now knows them will know them no more."

THE only motion on the House of Lords' paper for Thursday is for the adjournment.

To-day Lord Melchett will put down a motion to the effect that "This House approves the action of the Government with setting up a Committee of the Cabinet to inquire into the question of methods of balancing the exchange trade."

His real purpose in putting down this motion is to get a house before which he can demand that there shall be no immediate election—no election in fact until after the Budget of 1932 has been passed.

The "Daily Herald's" disclosure yesterday of the Tory scheme to force a snap General Election on October 8 created a sensation at Westminster.

Tories who had hoped to catch the Labour Party napping were angered at the disclosure, which put Labour on its guard throughout the constituencies.

A very prominent Tory M.P. closely in the confidence of the Cabinet when asked yesterday if the General Election would take place in November, replied: "It must be earlier than that—sometime in October."

During the day Lord Stonehaven, Chairman of the Conservative Party Organisation, met London M.P.s and warned them to get ready for a General Election at early date after the new register comes in force on October 11.

There is strong opposition in the City and especially on the part of the Bank of England to the proposals of the Tory Party organisers for an early election (writes our City Editor).

All the influence of the Bank of England will be used to obtain an agreement to keep the present Government in office till next year.

CONVERSION LOAN PROSPECTS

The City considers it especially necessary that there should not be an election before the end of October; as plans will be ready for launching the Five per Cent. War Loan Conversion scheme by the middle of that month.

Accompanying the conversion offer there will probably be an issue of a new loan offering interest of either four or 4½ per cent. sent issued at a slight discount, to raise funds for repaying foreign holders of five per cent. War Loan who are not prepared to convert into new stock.

The banks and the big insurance companies are holding funds ready to subscribe for this new loan.

An immediate election would upset all of

RATHER WARM

(SEE PAGE THREE)

	Page
Women's World	8
Letters to the Editor	4
We Are Not Alone in the Universe	8
—By Sir Francis Younghusband	
Serial Story	11
Radio Thoughts from Abroad—	10
—By Sydney Moseley	
Radio Programmes	10

the plan for war loan conversion and might also, in the opinion of the Bank of England, lead to another crisis in sterling.

POLICE RESENTMENT

Mr. J. H. Hayes, M.P. yesterday said there was considerable feeling and resentment in the police force concerning the proposed cuts.

"Not only," said Mr. Hayes, "is their opposition to the amount of the cut, but to the methods employed to bring them about.

"Although put forward as emergency measures, the Government proposals have about them the atmosphere of permanency."

"The wholesale revision of expressed and implied standards—some even laid down by Statute—has done much to destroy the belief that the Government would honour its contractual obligation to its employees."

"This has been made perfectly clear by members of the Force at the many meetings which have been held all around London and in the provinces where the machinery of negotiation has been roughly and ruthlessly swept about.

HOOVER'S NEW DEBT MOVE

President Hoover has been recommended to extend immediately the one-year moratorium on war debts and reparations to three or five years.

It is believed, cables the New York correspondent of the "Daily Herald," that the suggestion of a further war debts moratorium was put to Mr. Hoover at a dinner at the White House attended by Governor Eugene Meyer and twelve business men and bankers who compose the Federal Reserve Board's Advisory Council.

The invitation to them was interpreted as eagerness on Mr. Hoover's part to stimulate business developments and to obtain ideas to relieve the crisis.

He sounded the bankers on the necessity of liberalising credits for the benefit of both domestic and foreign interests.

Mr. Snowden stated in the Commons yesterday that he was inquiring into the Lord Nelson pension and similar payments.

Premier Talks to Lower Deck Men

THE "Daily Herald" learns that the Prime Minister was among the men of the Navy at the week-end when he visited Portsmouth to see the Schneider Trophy race.

He embarked with the First Lord of the Admiralty, Sir A. Chamberlain, on the destroyer Winchester, and at Spithead transferred to the aircraft carrier

SAILORS HOLD MASS MEETING ON SHORE

THE Admiralty issued the following statement last evening:

"The Senior Officer, Atlantic Fleet, has reported that the promulgation of the reduced rates of naval pay has led to unrest amongst a proportion of the lower ratings.

"In consequence of this he has deemed it desirable to suspend the programme of exercises of the Fleet, and to recall the ships to harbour while investigations are being made into representations of the hardship occasioned by certain of the cuts in pay in order that these may be reported for the consideration of the Board of Admiralty."

Later, the Board of Admiralty issued another statement, as follows:

"Their lordships have approved of the exercises of the Atlantic Fleet being temporarily suspended whilst certain representations of hardship under new rates of pay are being investigated for the consideration of their lordships."

Rear-Admiral Wilfred Tomkinson, C.B., M.V.O., is the senior officer mentioned. He commands in the absence on sick leave of Admiral Sir Michael Hodges, K.C.B., C.M.G., M.V.O.

AIR DASH TO LONDON

At Invergordon, where ten ships of the Atlantic Fleet are lying, the men to-day await the return of an officer who flew to London yesterday.

He bore with him to the Admiralty full news of resolutions protesting against pay cuts passed at mass meetings of the Lower Deck held ashore.

At the famous Rosyth dockyard 375 men of the battleship Iron Duke presented a protest petition to their commander.

From Our Special Correspondent

ABERDEEN, Tuesday.

INVERGORDON to-night is as quiet as a village on the shore of a South Sea island.

All the ships of the fleet are lying peacefully at anchor in the bay, and there is no sign of trouble or disturbances.

Members of the local town council and municipal officials assure me that for two days there has been no difficulty with members of the crews.

PROTEST RESOLUTIONS

Meetings of the lower ratings were held ashore on Saturday and Sunday, at which resolutions were passed protesting against the cuts in pay and seeking their withdrawal.

The Saturday meeting was very well boisterous, for most of the sailors had been in Invergordon games, and all ended the gathering in a lively mood.

Extra pickets were brought on shore to prevent disturbance.

The Sunday meeting was an orderly and serious affair, at which speeches were delivered and questions asked and answered. There was no trouble with pickets or police.

Resolutions passed at the meeting were presented to the commanding officer with the request that they should be communicated to the Admiralty.

I learn to-night that a high officer travelled by air to London to-day. The lower deck hopes that he will re-

tura to-morrow with a reply to their representations.

All shore leave was stopped yesterday and to-day, when Invergordon was surprised to find the Fleet had not sailed, nor a single bluejacket landed.

Meanwhile no bluejacket passed between the men and the bulk of the officers, and the ships seem absolutely at peace.

Yesterday spectators on the shore observed crowds of men meeting on board various ships, from which sounds of cheering could be heard, followed by the singing of popular choruses.

On one ship sailors were collected in groups on deck. A party gathered round a plane and held an informal concert.

Another crowd indulged in an acrobatic performance, and this indicated that they were having time off from their usual duty.

Where the Ships Are

UNITS of the Atlantic Fleet, now at Invergordon, Cromarty Firth, comprise the battleships

Nelson,   Valiant,
Rodney,   Malaya,
Warspite,

the battle-cruisers
Nelson and Rodney,

and the cruisers
Norfolk,   Dorsetshire,
York,

Destroyers and submarine flotillas, also belonging to the Atlantic Fleet, are at Rosyth, Firth of Forth.

375 SIGN PETITION

PROTEST BY IRON DUKE'S SEAMEN

From Our Special Correspondent

DUNFERMLINE, Tuesday.

Dissatisfaction has also arisen among the lower naval ratings at the Rosyth naval base on the Firth of Forth.

A petition against the pay reductions signed to-day by 375 seamen of the battleships Iron Duke, and presented to the Commander, Captain E. O. Boyle, V.C.

He explained that the cuts had been made at the direct command of the Admiralty, but in accordance with the Government's economy policy.

Rear-Admiral Tomkinson, who took command in his stead, flies his flag in Hood, which is the largest man-of-war in the world.

From Our Film Correspondent

Mr. Leslie Howard, the young English actor, who played Lesie in Tallulah Bankhead's "Her Cardboard Lover," has come over from Hollywood to play in a British film at a salary of £500 per week.

This is a record salary for a film actor in this country.

Mr. Howard has the leading part in the Paramount Company's new picture "The Head Waiter," now starting at their Elstree studios, under the Austrian director, Mr. Alexander Korda.

Another American company, Warner Brothers, have engaged Mr. John Longden, Mr. Ben Field, Miss Joyce Bland, and Miss Pat Paterson, for "Murder on the Second Floor," their first British film, now started at the Teddington studios.

Two leading young West-End actresses, Miss Gillian Lind and Miss Joan Maude, will play with her brother Quentin Quentin McMaster and her Arthur Wontner, in "Jack o' Lantern," at the Twickenham studios.   P. L. M.

£425,000 SCHEME SHELVED

Norwich City Council yesterday decided by 30 votes to 26 to postpone the proposed construction of a north-south road through the city at a cost of £425,000. The scheme was sanctioned two months ago.

By Our Special Representative

A TALL, slight woman, wearing Indian costume but unmistakably British, who is now to be seen sometimes moving among the ci-devant managers' barrows and entering the little shops in the slums of Bow, is the centre of so much interest and curiosity almost, as Mahatma Gandhi himself.

She is Miss Madeline Slade, daughter of the late Admiral Sir Edmond Slade.

She renounced a life of ease and elegance in London to become a disciple of the Mahatma, and she has followed him through good and evil report for the past six years.

Women write to her, begging for admission.

Poor people like their blessings.

"A common occurrence brings the doors of Kingsley Hall asking for a message from her to the United States.

She, meanwhile, has probably slipped out by a side door, to buy a cabbage or some fruit for the frugal meals of Mr. Gandhi's suite.

Your people at Kingsley Hall have constituted themselves into a personal suite for the Mahatma.

They are his own (Mr. Devidas Gandhi, his secretary (Mr. Desai) M.)

(Continued on Page Two, Col. One.)

SAVING ON SHELLS

ECONOMY MANŒUVRES PLANNED

The training period of the Atlantic Fleet exercises is considered the most important event of the naval year.

Economy, however, was to be enforced throughout this year's exercises.

Every effort was being made to strike at speeds most economical for all consumption, and gunnery practice was to be curtailed to save on the enormous expense incurred each time a shell is fired.

The Mersey Firth, where these sea "battles" with gunfire, smoke screens

and all the elaborate and expensive paraphernalia of modern war, takes place, is ideal for the purpose.

Decisive and wide, it is hardly used by normal shipping.

Admiral Sir Michael Hodges, the Commander-in-Chief of the Atlantic Fleet, who flies his flag in Nelson, is in hospital at Gosport, recovering from a severe attack of pleurisy.

The prices of **OVALTINE** are reduced

from 1/3, 2/- and 3/9 to

1/1, 1/10

and per **3/3** tin

These prices apply to Gt. Britain and N. Ireland.

DAILY HERALD, September 17, 1931.

Daily Herald

No. 4864 • THURSDAY, SEPTEMBER 17, 1931 ONE PENNY

FLEET OBEYS "MIDNIGHT" ORDER

Sailing for Home Ports After Admiralty Promise

CREWS STATE THEIR GRIEVANCES AGAINST PAY CUTS

Cheers For The King And Flag

Commands Of Officers Not Obeyed

DESTROYERS LEAD WAY DOWN FIRTH

SIR AUSTEN CHAMBERLAIN, First Lord of the Admiralty, entering the Admiralty by his private door to attend a conference of Navy chiefs.

AFTER receiving a promise that their representations would be earnestly considered by the Admiralty, the crews of the Atlantic Fleet agreed yesterday evening to obey the order to take the ships to their home ports.

They also asked for and received assurances that the ships really would go home, and that they would not, when once at sea, be ordered to some other destination.

The ships sailed from Invergordon at midnight.

During the day perfect order was observed, and the men demonstrated their loyalty by a ceremonial cheering of the flag and the King.

But no orders were obeyed, and except for the essential services of the ships no work was done.

The Government's decision was announced by the First Lord (Sir Austen Chamberlain) in the House of Commons yesterday.

"The Government has authorised the Board of Admiralty to make proposals for alleviating hardships in those classes—[especially hard hit by Navy pay cuts]—as soon as the facts have been ascertained by the contemplated investigation," he said.

Replying to Mr. W. G. Hall, Labour M.P. for Portsmouth Central, Sir Austen had previously remarked:—

"The Board of Admiralty have had under their earnest consideration representations received from the Officer Commanding the Atlantic Fleet as to the hardships involved in certain classes of ratings by the reductions ordered by H.M. Government in naval rates of pay.

"Their Lordships have directed the ships of the Atlantic Fleet to proceed to their home ports forthwith.

"Investigations will then be made by the Commander-in-Chief and representatives of the Admiralty in those classes of cases in which it is alleged that the reductions pressed exceptionally on those concerned."

A special meeting—the second during the day—of the Cabinet was held in the Prime Minister's room at the House of Commons yesterday evening. All ten Ministers were present, to discuss the situation at Invergordon, and at other naval stations. Facts were also brought to their attention concerning unrest both in the Army and Police Forces.

From Our Special Correspondent
INVERGORDON, Wednesday.

AFTER a good deal of persuasion the men of the Atlantic Fleet who have been on "strike" all day, decided this evening to obey the Admiralty order to take the ships to their home ports.

The Government's promise to "make proposals for alleviating hardships" was conveyed to the men during the afternoon.

It was discussed at length by the crews, who then decided to ask for assurances that they would in fact be taken to their home ports.

Men Reassured

There seems to have been suspicion that once at sea the order to go home would be cancelled, and the ships sent to some distant station.

I understand that the men required a great deal of persuasion to agree to man the ships. In some cases more than two hours were spent debating the question.

The men were finally reassured that they would be taken to their home port, and that cases of the greatest hardship would be investigated.

Valiant, which had taken the initiative in the "strike," was one of the last ships to agree to the order, and word was passed round that the men had decided to man the vessel.

REAR-ADMIRAL R. M. COLVIN, Chief of Staff of the Atlantic Fleet, who flew from Invergordon to London yesterday to attend Conferences at the Admiralty.

About half-past ten to-night the first of the Fleet, one or two destroyers, steamed down the Firth.

The men are now confident that their representations will be investigated.

"We have not been beaten," was the declaration of one of the leaders.

They have sent the following letter to the Admiralty.

"We, the loyal subjects of His Majesty the King, do hereby present to our Lords the Commissioners of the Admiralty our representation and implore them to amend the drastic cuts in pay which have been inflicted on the lowest-paid men of the lower deck.

"It is evident to all concerned that these cuts are a fore-runner of tragedy, misery and immorality among the families of the lower deck and unless a guaranteed written agreement is received from the Admiralty, confirmed by Parliament, stating that our pay will be revised, we are still to remain as one unit, refusing to serve under the new rates of pay.

"The men are quite agreeable to accept a cut which they consider within reason."

[A description by our Special Correspondent of the extraordinary scenes on board the ships yesterday before the Admiralty assurance was received will be found on Page Two.]

WOMEN BOWLERS' "OPEN"

The world's first open bowling tournament for women began at Eastbourne yesterday.

There were 224 entries from all over Southern England and South Wales.

The tournament was started by the Deputy Mayor, Alderman Miss Alice Hudson.

BRITAIN USES £16,000,000 U.S. MONEY

£65,000,000 DRAWN TO SAVE POUND

NEW YORK, Wednesday.

IT is circumstantially reported on Wall-street that £16,000,000 of the recent credit of £40,000,000 to the British Treasury has already been used for the support of sterling (says the New York "Evening Post").

The British Treasury is reported to have drawn £8,000,000 of the new credit immediately after it had been granted, and it is alleged that a further £8,000,000 was used last Thursday.

These heavy drafts on United States credits are explained here by the fact that the French credits will not be available till Monday, when £30,000,000, which has been subscribed by the French public, will be transferred to the British Treasury.

No further drafts will be made upon the United States credits until the French credits have been drawn upon to an equivalent amount.

It is thus estimated that Great Britain has used about £65,000,000 of the £130,000,000 of credits granted by the Federal Reserve Board, the Bank of France and United States bankers, including the first credits of £50,000,000 advanced by the Federal Reserve Bank and the Bank of France.—Reuter.

U.S. INDUSTRY MUST INSURE WORKERS

BIG BUSINESS LEADER'S BOMBSHELL

NEW YORK, Wednesday.

A bombshell for big business men is contained in the proposal by Mr. Gerald Swope, the president of the General Electric Company, when addressing the National Manufacturers' Association, that industry should bear the burden of social insurance.

Mr. Swope said industry must act to forestall legislation threatening the "fundamental structure of American business society."

His plan provides for compulsory pensions, unemployment, and disability payments, life insurance, and workmen's compensation, the costs to be borne equally by employers.

Fear must be removed, he declared, and this cannot be done unless workers have reasonable protection for their families in the case of the breadwinner's death, old age and unemployment.—Reuter.

ANOTHER TITHE SALE SCENE

BIDDER ESCORTED AWAY AND JEERED

From Our Special Correspondent
ASHFORD (Kent), Wednesday.

A peaceful Kentish field, Shottenden Farm, Westwell, near here, threatened to become a battle ground this morning when a man asked permission to make a bid of £5 at a distraint auction sale for recovery of unpaid dues under the Queen Anne Tithe Act.

"Will you act as men?" he asked the crowd. "Yes," answered the assembled farmers and farm labourers with emphasis. Eventually the man was escorted from the field by the police, followed by a jeering crowd.

At the beginning of the sale the Rev. R. M. Kedward, M.P. for Ashford, who also figured in yesterday's sale scenes, asked Mr. Joy, the County Court auctioneer, if there was any reserve price.

Mr. Joy having replied "No," Mr. Kedward offered 5s. for a load of hay belonging to Mr. Richards, owner of the farm, whose tithe debt was assessed at £21 8s. 9d.

"That is no bid," replied the auctioneer. "I declare no sale."

To this Mr. Kedward replied, "Your action is illegal. We will take proceedings to recover expenses for loss of time and attending this sale."

BREMEN "LOST" IN FOG

So thick was the fog in Southampton Roads yesterday that the Norddeutscher Lloyd liner, Bremen, was "lost" for six hours.

ON OTHER PAGES

GOVERNMENT EXPLAINS TO M.P.s

After Conference With Flying Admiral

THE First Lord's statement in the House of Commons yesterday followed long and anxious conferences at the Admiralty, which were attended by Rear-Admiral R. M. Colvin, Chief of Staff of the Atlantic Fleet.

Rear-Admiral Colvin had flown from Invergordon with full news of the Lower Deck protests.

In the Commons, Major Elliot, Financial Secretary to the Treasury, replied to Commander Kenworthy, Labour M.P. for Central Hull, that the total savings proposed on the three fighting services were:—

Navy	£2,942,000
Army	£3,897,000
Air Force	£954,000
Total	£8,388,000

Savings on pay and pensions, continued Major Elliot, would be:—

Navy	£1,612,000
Army	£1,960,000
and Air Force	£194,000

Sir Austen Chamberlain then made a statement in which he said the Admiralty had been authorised to make proposals for alleviating hardships.

"MOST FOOLISH DOCUMENT"

MR. J. M. KEYNES ON THE MAY REPORT

From Our Lobby Correspondent

"The most foolish document I have ever had the misfortune to read."

This was how Mr. J. M. Keynes, the noted Economist, described the May Economy Report at a meeting of the Parliamentary Currency Group held last night in one of the House of Commons Committee rooms.

Sir Norman Angell occupied the chair and was supported by Mr. Winston Churchill on his right and Miss Eleanor Rathbone on his left.

Asked what he would do if he were Prime Minister, in this crisis, Mr. Keynes replied:—

"Scrap the Economy Bill.

"Abolish the Sinking Fund.

"Summon an International Conference to promote the free regulation of gold.

"Return to the Civil servants and other people the salaries which have been unjustly taken from them.

"And I think," said Mr. Keynes, "that's enough for one night."

The home ports of the ships of the Atlantic Fleet are—

CHATHAM—(Repulse, Valiant, and York).

DEVONPORT—(Rodney, Malaya, Dorsetshire, Norfolk, and Exeter).

PORTSMOUTH—(Nelson, Hood and Warspite).

SMITHY'S £1,670 INCOME

GRETNA GREEN ASSESSMENT RAISED TO £500

The revenue last year at the Gretna Green "smithy," famous for its marriages, was £1,670, it was stated at the Dumfries Valuation Appeal Court yesterday.

The Court fixed the valuation at £500.

The assessor had asked that it should be £990. Previously it had been £38.

PACIFIC FLYERS FOUND

MESSAGE TO GIRL WHO HOPED ALONE

AFTER being missing for more than a week, the trans-Pacific flyers, Don Moyle and Cecil Allen, who left Tokyo for Seattle, Washington, on September 5, have been found safe on an uninhabited island in the Gulf of Oliutorski, off the coast of Kamchatka, according to a report from the Soviet steamer Buriatee.

A message relayed to Moyle's fiancée, Miss Frances Brisson, said:

"Landed uninhabited island. Everything all right. Will be at Seattle on September [illegible]. Love.—Don."

When she received the message, Miss Brisson, who is a typist at Riverside, California, remained silent for several minutes, and then burst into tears, followed by exclamations of joy.

WAITING

Miss Brisson flew to Seattle to meet her fiancé on September 9, and has been waiting there ever since.

Others gave up hope six days ago, but Miss Brisson remained firm in her belief that the airmen were alive.

Moyle and Allen were trying to win a £5,000 prize offered for the first non-stop Tokyo-Seattle flight.

An hour after they left Sabishiro, Japan, they were seen passing Cape Erimo, and no further news was received of them until last night.

COAST SEARCH

A ship's captain reported that he had heard the noise of aero engines off the coast of Alaska on September 10.

When the scheduled time of their arrival had passed, coastguards began a detailed search [illegible]

The airmen appear to have been driven many miles north of their route.

AILING BISHOP'S PILGRIMAGE

The Catholic Bishop of Northampton, the Right Rev. Dudley Charles Cary-Elwes, was so ill when he arrived at Victoria station yesterday, after a pilgrimage to Lourdes, that he was taken by ambulance to a nursing home. His condition is serious.

H.M.S. NELSON

Gandhi in the Commons

Mr. Gandhi sitting cross-legged at prayers in a committee room of the House of Commons was the spectacle seen by many M.P.s last night.

This took place at the end of a crowded meeting of Labour M.P.s, at which Mr. Gandhi expounded his policy.

After he had spoken there was a great rush for his autograph, and it was while he was signing his name dozens of times that the [illegible] arrived.

"I can write no more," he said, laying down his pen. "It is the hour for prayer."

As Big Ben chimed the hour, Mr. Gandhi squatted with one of his sons and Mira Bai (Miss Slade), his English disciple.

For the next 10 minutes their chanting of Hindu prayers was the only sound in the big room.

(Round-Table Conference—Page 4.)

Admiral Sir Frederic Dreyer, a friend, then later a critic of Tomkinson, revealed that some Cabinet ministers wanted the rebellious fleet to be fired on

First Sea Lord Admiral Sir Frederick Field, who at first congratulated Tomkinson on the way he handled the Invergordon Mutiny.

Admiral Sir Reginald Tyrwhitt, who thought his old colleague, Tomkinson, had 'made a balls of it through sheer inactivity' at Invergordon (from a painting by Glyn Philpot)

Admiral of the Fleet David Earl Beatty, warned Keyes about the accusations being made in his defence of Tomkinson (from a drawing by Francis Dodd)

Admiral of the Fleet Sir Roger Keyes (later Lord Keyes), a lifelong friend and admirer of Tomkinson from the time they met in China, during 1899, to the time he died in 1945

Tomkinson pictured just after being promoted to captain in 1916

Joan Bittleston, who met Tomkinson in Simonstown, South Africa, and married him in Kensington, London in June 1907

A family photograph of the Tomkinsons on a shooting expedition during his retirement

16
MUTINY OR
DISAFFECTION

The Invergordon Mutiny – a label much deplored by the navy at the time and since, and often replaced by the word disaffection – has been well documented, discussed, argued over and written about for more than sixty years. The situation was complex then and, despite the release of many official and private papers, remains that way today. This is not an attempt to absolve Tomkinson for his part in it; instead the aim again is to reconstruct the happenings through his eyes both at the time and in hindsight.

Twenty-four hours before the Atlantic Fleet were due to sail for large-scale manoeuvres on Tuesday 8 September 1931, Tomkinson was in a high fever of activity on being suddenly thrust into leadership. The fleet commander-in-chief, Admiral Sir Michael Hodges, had returned ill from leave that day and, after being examined by a surgeon commander on the flagship *Nelson*, was taken to the Royal Naval Hospital at Haslar. The first diagnosis was pleurisy; later he had thrombosis.

As the most senior officer, Tomkinson was instructed by the Admiralty to take over, although he had only a few hours to familiarize himself with the concept of Hodges' plans for the second largest fleet operation of that year. Through attending the war-games conference earlier he knew what was expected of his battle cruisers, but to understand the complete scenario he had to confer at Hodges' bedside. The talk was all of tactics and no mention was made of the now notorious warning signal about imminent naval pay cuts, sent to all nine commanders-in-chief.[1]

The reason for this became evident when later Tomkinson was briefed by Rear-Admiral Reginald Colvin, Hodges' chief of staff. In handing over the relevant documents of the command, Colvin explained that the warning signal had been received in Hodges' absence, and when he returned he was too ill to consider its implications. Colvin had written a draft reply and locked it in the confidential safe.[2] Tomkinson was then shown the Admiralty warning, originated on 3 September, which read:

For your confidential guidance. The financial crisis obliges H.M. Government to take immediate and stringent measures to balance the budget. These measures will involve sacrifices for all classes of the community and reductions of pay in public services. H.M. Government have decided that they are obliged to call upon the Fighting Services to make this contribution to the common end. For the Navy the sacrifice involves the acceptances of the recommendations of the report of the Committee on National Expenditure and these include placing all officers and men at present in receipt of pay on 1919 scales on the revised scale introduced in October 1925 and reducing all standard rates of pay of officers by 11, instead of 8 per cent, as previously decided to come into force in July last. The new regulations are to come into force from 1st October next.

Reductions in kit upkeep allowance or grog money are under consideration. Apart from emoluments, the Admiralty are required to make further drastic economies in expenditure. Their Lordships' view is that in order to interfere as little as possible with the new construction programme, or Fleet numbers, it is better to make economies in such directions as reduced fuel expenditure (say to 10 per cent) of main fleets, ammunition practices and fleet exercises also in diminution of standard of training.

Their Lordships will be grateful for any early suggestions that you wish to make.[3]

Tomkinson was then shown Colvin's draft reply, which made no reference to the pay cuts. Because the Admiralty message did not emphasize that these were the prime causes of their warning, he agreed that it should be sent. He was unaware, however, that the Admiralty considered that the 20 per cent cut, proposed hurriedly by Ramsay Mac-Donald's National Government after only a week's life, would have a 'deplorable effect on the navy'. Neither did Colvin inform him that he had originally drafted a reply suggesting that the pay reduction bore too heavily on ratings and junior officers and that the board should try to get it altered. Colvin had re-read the warning telegram, however, and tore up his original draft and then written the second, which Tomkinson approved.[4]

Although Tomkinson must have known of the climate in which the cuts were agreed, there was a great deal he did not know. He knew that in April 1931 the May Committee on National Expenditure (headed by Sir George May, the former president of the Prudential Assurance Company) had asked the Admiralty to report on naval pay since 1919 and on 'the vested rights of the 1919 scales'. He knew that in the Labour Government's budget there had been a deficit of more than £23 million, with a threatened rise of more than 50 per cent. He knew that during the July run on the Bank of England £33 million in gold had been wiped out in two weeks.

But he did not know that, before a National Government came into power, the May Committee report on 24 July had recommended a 10 per cent reduction in the armed services' expenditure, together with cuts in dole money and the pay of teachers and police.[5] Even then, the saving of £97 million against a budget deficit of £120 million was still underestimated by £50 million. Rumours, of which Tomkinson must have heard, were already about that a cut in pay was hanging over the lower deck. The Admiralty board, decimated by leave and sickness, had reluctantly approved the May Committee's proposals and instigated the warning signal.[6]

There were whispers throughout the Admiralty that a campaign of disobedience was possible in the wake of the economic crisis. As early as June, Sir Vernon Kelly, the head of security and intelligence, and Sea Lord, Vice Admiral Frederic Dreyer, had been warned of a possible mutiny by a source described in official records as a 'distinguished Spaniard'. The day after the Atlantic Fleet sailed for Invergordon, Mr W.A. Appleton, secretary of the General Federation of the Trade Union Congress, told Admiral of the Fleet Lord Wemyss: 'I want to give you a word of warning – watch the fleet.' This was reported to the Admiralty two days later, just forty-eight hours before trouble began, but was not passed on to Tomkinson, who by then was the senior officer of the Atlantic Fleet. There were also attempts by the Communist Party to unsettle ratings during a public meeting at Chatham's Navy Week, when a naval patrol cleared uniformed men from the rally as Harry Pollitt, the party secretary, was speaking.

But Tomkinson's mind was on a more imminent event – the sailing next day of the fleet, particularly as it was decided that the administrative staff should remain in the *Nelson*, which was to stay in Portsmouth for at least a day in the forlorn hope that Hodges – then not known to have thrombosis – would recover and rejoin his flagship. Tomkinson had noted that the pay reductions would not come into force until 1 October; in itself this was an administrative matter, which he, too, was optimistic enough to hope that Hodges would be back to deal with.[7]

His designation as SOAF (Senior Officer Atlantic Fleet) by the Admiralty did not help him; it would have been to his advantage to have been given the rank of acting vice admiral, for with him in the fleet were two officers almost with the same seniority – Rear-Admiral E.A. Astley-Rushton, commanding the 2nd Cruiser Squadron, and Rear-Admiral French, a former captain of the *Hood*, in charge of the Second Division of the 2nd Battle Squadron.

Yet there was pride in Tomkinson's heart as the *Hood* steamed from Portsmouth on the afternoon of Tuesday 8 September to lead the fleet to Invergordon. The Devonport Division joined him off the Isle of Wight, while ships of the Nore Command met him off the Outer Gabbard, at the approach to the Thames. Now he was in control of the most powerful fleet that was to manoeuvre together in these waters for a decade.

The two-day run to the north took the form of a convoy problem, with attacks from the Blue Fleet. The ship's company of the *Hood*, which spearheaded the raid, were at action stations for long spells, while the squadron flag officers were struggling to adjust to fleet duties which had been thrust on them by the absence of the *Nelson* and her staff.[8]

More momentous moves were being made ashore, however. On Thursday 10 September, while the ships were still engaged in mock battle, Phillip Snowden, the Chancellor of the Exchequer, unveiled his emergency budget to the House of Commons and announced the expected deficit of £170 million. To counterbalance this, 6*d* was put on income tax, 2*d* on petrol and 1*d* on beer.

The pay economies were published in a White Paper. Six days earlier the Admiralty had the foresight to print a Fleet Order, which again warned of the sacrifices the navy were about to make. But this was regarded as a 'leak' by the Treasury and was cancelled at their behest.[9] As a substitute, after the budget speech, the Admiralty issued another warning of the forthcoming cuts. This was sent by signal to all the fleets, except the Atlantic, still exercising at sea. Instead, it was duplicated and dispatched through normal land postal channels. The *Nelson*, still officially the flagship, although dockbound at Portsmouth, received the first letter. It was put in the pigeon-hole of Admiral Hodges, who was still in hospital, to await delivery to him.[10]

Admiralty records state that there were illegal meetings among the Atlantic Fleet to discuss the sacrifices the lower ratings would be asked to make.[11] There is little doubt that most crews knew of the pay docking, which would have been heard on BBC news broadcasts, but there was nothing definite, although it was believed to be as high as 25 per cent. There might have been individual discussion, but no organized meetings were reported to Tomkinson.

The *Hood* arrived at Invergordon during the afternoon of Friday 11 September, the day after the budget. As the flagship buoy opposite the pier was reserved for the *Nelson*, the *Hood* anchored a mile away, to form part of a northern line, which included the *Rodney, Centurion, Dorsetshire, Norfolk, Warspite, Valiant* and *Malaya*. The southern line consisted of the *Tetrarch, Snapdragon, York* and *Adventure*.[12]

Soon the waters of the Cromarty Firth were dotted with drifters and motor-boats collecting mail, newspapers and provisions. During the lunch hour the papers were on sale in the ships' canteens. The *Daily Express* and *Scottish Daily Record* revealed that the lower 1925 pay rates would apply to everyone, with pensions restricted to the 1930 grades, while the *Daily Mirror* confused readers by quoting the reduction as from 10 to 20 per cent.[13]

Ratings were already abuzz with the news; to many an able seaman it meant his pay being slashed from 4s to 3s a day, with less than three weeks' warning. Officers and petty officers had no answer to the questions that were being asked, so a communications barrier between the leaders and the led was set up.

Tomkinson was oblivious of the enmity that was being bred in his new command. His copy of the second warning signal was still in the *Nelson*, so he had no indication that the Admiralty was worried about the effect of the revised pay structure. But a new Admiralty Fleet Order was on the way; it did not arrive in the *Hood* until the next day, when Tomkinson's office was closed, as was normal on a Saturday.[14] Because there was no preliminary signal about it, the AFO was pigeon-holed until after the weekend, but there were not sufficient copies anyway to put on the *Hood*'s many notice-boards. Not until the Sunday was distribution completed throughout the remainder of the fleet.[15] Across the water from the *Hood*, Astley-Rushton, French, Captain Roger Bellairs, of the *Rodney*, and Captain A.D.H. Dibben, of the *Adventure*, had copies of the Admiralty's second warning as soon as the fleet arrived. Tomkinson had yet to study it; his personal copy had been wrongly addressed to the *Renown*, which he had left two months earlier![16]

Saturday afternoon passed pleasantly, with the off-duty watches going to the Invergordon Highland Games, where the *Hood*'s marine band played.[17] In the early evening it was the custom for most men to drink in the fleet canteen. Although there was an unusually high number there, the shore patrols were not called on to put down any indiscipline;[18] yet it is certain that on this evening arrangements were made for a bigger meeting to be held the next day to discuss what action, if any, would be taken about the pay stringencies.

116

Midshipmen in charge of liberty boats reported that there was rowdiness and singing on the way back to ships, but officers-of-the-watch put it down to normal 'first night ashore' behaviour and did not pass on the information.

The next day there were more disturbing revelations about the cuts in the Sunday newspapers, brought onboard ships by men returning from a church service ashore. After reading one paper, Lieutenant Commander Harry Pursey, who had been promoted from the lower deck and who was to become the Labour MP for East Hull for twenty-five years, went to his executive officer in the *Hood*, Commander C.B. McCrum, and warned: 'If the cuts are not reduced there will be trouble. And if there is trouble it will be on Tuesday at 8 a.m.' Pursey based this forecast on the fact that it would be 'tailor made' for a mass protest at the end of breakfast hour, just before the big ships sailed for exercises.[19]

McCrum thought Pursey was being overdramatic and did not tell anyone. Yet two hours later McCrum was called to Captain Patterson's cabin to discuss a private note from Captain Baldwin Wake, of the *Warspite*, who claimed that he had heard through his master-at-arms that there was to be a mass meeting in the canteen ashore that afternoon among Devonport ships' companies. There is no indication in Patterson's report of proceedings that he bothered Tomkinson with the rumour, neither is it mentioned in the SOAF's report. Surprisingly, Patterson did warn Captain Bellairs, of the *Rodney*, 'for information' because the *Rodney* was a Devonport ship and the *Hood* was not![20]

However, the two *Hood* officers went ashore in the afternoon to make sure nothing untoward was happening and found the canteen orderly and quiet.

The first serious indication Tomkinson received of the gathering storm came when Astley-Rushton made a hurried visit to him that night. He told him that he had passed the canteen during the evening and was worried by the tone of speeches made to more than 600 ratings packed inside. He had contacted Commander W. Fallowfield, of *Warspite*'s shore patrol, and suggested that he should send for reinforcements to break up the meeting.[21] When Tomkinson later interviewed Fallowfield – who was wrongly rumoured to have been knocked out – he was told that glasses had been thrown in the canteen, but then the men had quietened. When the second patrol arrived at 8 p.m. the bar was closed without fuss.[22]

Confirmation of a growing air of disobedience came to Tomkinson's ears when men from the *Hood*, who had been at the meeting, returning singing and shouting in the drifter *Horizon*. He talked the situation through with Astley-Rushton and Captain Patterson and concluded that no action was necessary at that moment.[23]

At 9.15 p.m. the *Nelson*, which had left Hodges in hospital, anchored at Invergordon. Only then was the Admiralty's warning letter passed over to Tomkinson. 'On arrival of *Nelson*, I first became aware of the issue of the Admiralty letter . . . stating the principles on which the reduction in pay had been based and explaining the views of Their Lordships,' he wrote later,[24] although, strangely, Astley-Rushton and French had ample chance of making him aware of it from their copies. It underlined, on their part, either a hesitancy to tell Tomkinson his business or a lack of realization of the effect of the cuts.

Tomkinson decided not to signal the Admiralty that night about the initial glimmers of unrest. He wanted to wait for a 'sign' the next day when the *Warspite*, the flagship of the

2nd Battle Squadron, under French, and the *Malaya* were due to sail for sub-calibre exercises in the Moray Firth.

He was on the admiral's bridge at 8 a.m. the next day to watch their going and was not disappointed, for their sea-duty men were drawn up in perfect order on the forecastle and quarterdeck. He also focused his binoculars on the rest of the fleet and noted their crews were carrying out normal harbour drill. Next he saw Rear-Admiral Colvin, who came over from the *Nelson*. Together they studied the three foolscap sheets of the Admiralty letter, which read in part:

> I am commanded by My Lords Commissioners of the Admiralty to inform you that Fleet Orders will shortly be issued intimating that owing to the imperative need of economy in national expenditure, H.M. Government have found it necessary as from 1st October next –
> (a) to reduce the pay of junior serving officers and of men to the revised scales introduced in 1925;
> (b) to apply a cost of living reduction of 11 per cent, instead of 8 per cent, as at present, to the standard rates of pay of officers below the rank or relative rank of vice admiral, this reduction to be subject to variation at 6–monthly intervals in accordance with further changes in the cost of living;
> (c) to apply a special cut of 10 per cent until further notice to the current rates of pay of officers of and above the rank, or relative rank, of vice admiral (ie to their standard rates of pay, less 8 per cent).
> The revised rates of pay introduced in 1925 for ratings and junior officers were the result of a report of the Committee on Pay of State Servants in 1923, which expressed the opinions –
> (a) that none of the fighting services err on the side of paying officers of the highest ranks too much;
> (b) that the pay of officers of middle rank is not excessive, subject to such adjustment on cost of living grounds as is already provided for in regulations;
> (c) that the pay of junior officers is more than is necessary, or even fair to the rest of the community; and
> (d) that the pay of the men is too high and should be reduced in correspondence with the wages paid in civil employment.
> In 1925, as you are aware, junior officers and men already in the service were, nevertheless, allowed to retain the advantage of the existing higher rates of pay. At the present time, however, when the need for reducing the national expenditure is urgent and the community as a whole is being called upon to make heavy sacrifices, it is found to be impossible to permit this concession to continue.

Colvin and Tomkinson agreed that these sections should be explained to the men by junior officers. But then came the problem of not having enough copies. Extra ones had to be typed and, although most ships received copies that evening, they were not delivered to some vessels until the next day.

118

Tomkinson's WT office then began transmitting a series of signals, with raised urgency levels, during the next three days. At 10.02 a.m. a message was sent to all ships that the pay cuts were to be 'explained without delay', as soon as the copies of the letter were received.

Because there were no more reports of rowdyism or unruliness, let alone insubordination, Tomkinson composed, just over twenty minutes later, this signal, designated 'Important', to the Admiralty: 'There was a slight disturbance in the Royal Naval Canteen, Invergordon, yesterday, Sunday evening, caused by one or two ratings endeavouring to address those present on the subject of reduction in pay. I attach no importance to the incident from a general disciplinary point of view, but it is possible it may be reported in an exaggerated form by the press. Matter is still being investigated.'[25]

Indeed, the matter was still being investigated, because the *Warspite* had sailed and Tomkinson had yet to receive Commander Fallowfield's considered written report of the 'slight disturbance'. Signals labelled 'Important' normally received a reply. This one should have been read by the first lord, the first, second, third and fourth sea lords, the deputy chief of naval staff, the acting chief of naval staff, the Parliamentary secretary, the permanent secretary, the naval secretary, naval law and the director of naval intelligence. Tomkinson did not receive an answer and none of those listed attempted to initiate one. All he had achieved was to cover himself if newspapers did get hold of the story.

Captain Patterson cleared the lower deck at 11.45 a.m. to explain the cuts to the *Hood*'s crew. Because of the financial structure, based on the dates when a man received his full rating, it was difficult to analyse individual cases, but one example was that an able seaman on a 1919 rate would have his basic pay reduced by 1s a day to 3s. Patterson ended by warning the ship's company that they would not improve their chances of any revision of the new rates by irregular concerted action; instead he advised them to make their representations through him.[26] Similar assurances were given by other captains, but they did little to cool the feelings of the men, who gathered again in the Invergordon canteen that evening. Many carried copies of the *Daily Worker*, which was endeavouring to inflame the crisis by publishing on its front page a spurious scale of pay cuts that put able seamen at 25 per cent, petty officers at 12 per cent and officers at only 9 per cent.

Tomkinson must have been satisfied that he had done as much as was required of him, for if he had any doubts about another outbreak of rowdiness he would surely have cancelled the dinner party that night which he held in his quarters for the admirals and captains of the fleet, in an effort to get to know them.

As they were eating they discussed the disturbances; many of them agreed with Captain F. Burges-Watson, of the *Nelson*, that the lower ratings were being treated harshly and unjustly in the pay reductions and that many were facing ruin of their 'carefully and thriftily built-up homes'.[27] But, at around 8.45 p.m., their meal was interrupted by cheering, singing and shouting of men who had just returned to the *Hood* from shore leave. Half an hour later Patterson told Tomkinson that there was trouble onboard.[28]

When the *Hood*'s drifter had approached the gangway, the noise was so great that officer-of-the-watch Lieutenant J.S. Gabbett had ordered the midshipman in charge of the boat to lay off until there was silence. The men quietened and were allowed onboard, but some attempted to go to their mess-decks without having their names ticked off by the duty quartermaster. After Lieutenant-Commander J.F. Mudford had reported that there was a 'large gathering in the eyes of the ship', Commander McCrum went there with the master-at-arms and saw a rating inciting more than 100 men to take action about the pay cuts. McCrum deduced that it 'was not the beer speaking', and as the master-at-arms and a regulating petty officer cleared them from the forecastle they heard remarks that work would stop next morning.

Meanwhile from the *Rodney*, Tomkinson's guests could hear cheering and 'continual noise' from men on the forecastle. As the dinner party broke up, Lieutenant Robert Elkins, who was in charge of the *Valiant*'s shore patrol, arrived onboard, convinced that the entire fleet was about to rebel. He was ordered to go to the admiral's cabin, where Tomkinson, Colvin, Captain of the Fleet Alfred Evans, Patterson and Captain C.A. Scott, of the *Valiant*, listened intently to what he had to say.[29]

Elkins had been given instructions to arrest the ringleaders, if there was any subversive talk in the canteen. It was all quiet there soon after he landed at 5 p.m. but fifteen minutes later he was warned that a meeting had begun there, that the doors were locked and the chief petty officer of his patrol could not get in. Elkins watched through a window of the canteen as a 'three-badge man with red hair' spoke to the meeting in an 'inflammatory nature'. Elkins was able to persuade a man inside to open the door. As he walked in, with the patrol, there were shouts of 'Get out, get out.' When he could make himself heard he told the meeting that he would stay there until he was satisfied that the discussion did not prejudice discipline. The jeers continued; then Elkins went over to talk to two civilians, who had no right being there. As he did so, he was hit in the back by a beer mug. Then a group of sailors and marines crossed hands, bent down in 'the shape of a rugger scrum' and pushed him out of the door, which was locked behind him.

He was unable to get back in until the chief petty officer of the patrol, who was still inside, unbolted it for him, but the men were streaming out on to the nearby soccer pitch to continue their meeting.[30]

Elkins sent a messenger to the patrol office for reinforcements and then joined the outside gathering. It was being addressed by a marine and he assumed that the sailors intended to mutiny after breakfast the next day. *Hood*'s reinforcing patrol of thirty, under Lieutenant-Commander G.N. Robinson, aided by Lieutenant T.A. Pack-Beresford, now joined up with Elkins and together they got into the canteen through the petty officers' room at the rear. There were still about three hundred men inside, many drunk, and several making mutinous speeches.

The ringleaders chorused 'Are we going to take our pay cuts lying down? Is the fleet going to sea tomorrow?' and received the resounding answer 'No.'[31]

Robinson jumped up on the bar and blasted his whistle to obtain silence. Gradually he was given a hearing as he advised them to make their complaints in a 'service-like manner'. Meanwhile, Pack-Beresford and Elkins were reassuring and calming other ratings. After Robinson announced there were to be no more speeches and the canteen would be closed, the men filed off into the night.

More than thirty years later, Elkins, who became an admiral and was knighted, was to reveal that although Tomkinson asked him a lot of questions, he already knew a good deal about it and considered 'it was not so bad as it sounded'.[32] When Elkins returned to the *Valiant* to tell his fellow officers that he had been 'chucked out of the canteen', they had laughed at him.

At this stage Tomkinson seemed inclined to believe that the reports from ashore were exaggerated and that it was just a case of a 'lot of drunken sailors shouting their mouths off'. Nevertheless, after turning it over continually in his mind until 11.15 p.m., and discussing the evening's events with Astley-Rushton, Colvin, Patterson and Evans, he considered the outbreak serious enough to signal the Admiralty: 'Further disturbances took place among libertymen landed at Invergordon this evening. Libertymen have all returned onboard, but there is considerable unrest among a proportion of the lower ratings. The cause of the complaints appears to be the drastic reduction in pay of rates below petty officers who were on pre-1925 scales of pay. Further telegram follows.'[33]

Captain Scott later reported to Tomkinson that on the way back to the *Valiant* he noticed someone on the *Rodney* flashing a searchlight into the sky. When he boarded his own ship he found that men had tried to get on to the bridge to signal the *Rodney*.[34] Through his commander and master-at-arms he had discovered that the *Rodney* and *Valiant* would not sail next day and his men had managed to get an 'OK signal' to the *Rodney*. Tomkinson was told that 'the leader is someone in *Rodney*, who is a great speaker', and that the feeling was being whipped up by him and two civilians ashore.[35]

Some commanding officers failed to realize the extent of the unrest. Captain Wilfred Custance, of the *York*, reported to Tomkinson that everything seemed normal[36] and apparently failed to know that men were circulating around his ship giving orders about who was to 'down tools' the next day and who was to carry on as normal. His lack of foresight was probably due to the fact that hours earlier Commander Coppinger had dived fully clothed into the sea to rescue Stoker Eric Clegg,[37] who had toppled overboard when returning from shore leave. He considered that this had strengthened the affection of the crew.

Captain Dibben, of the *Adventure*, also reported conditions 'normal'.[38] Yet the men were meeting secretly in their messes, after closing all scuttles and watertight doors so they could not be overheard. A similar tactic was adopted in the *Norfolk*, but in *Repulse* and *Valiant* there were large gatherings on the open forecastles.

On the *Valiant*, Captain Scott met his senior officers and warned them that trouble was looming.[39] The captain of marines wanted to parade his men fully armed at 6 a.m. – but this was countermanded. Nevertheless, Elkins locked away his target pistols before going to sleep.

In the *Nelson*'s recreation space there was wild talk of the sailors taking over a train and driving it to London to protest to Parliament. In the *Rodney* a band of stokers woke up boys on their mess-deck and told them not to get up the next morning when the pipe to 'rise and shine' was made at 5.15.

Astley-Rushton returned to the *Hood* before midnight for more consultations with Tomkinson, who by now had received reports of disturbances from several captains that night. For the first time he realized that the dissension was widespread and at 1 a.m. he sent an 'Immediate' signal to the Admiralty, which stressed his fears. 'Having received reports from flag and commanding officers, I am of the opinion that it may be difficult to get ships to sea for practice this morning, Tuesday. I have made the following general signal to the Atlantic Fleet in company. Begins: "The Senior Officer, Atlantic Fleet, is aware that cases of hardship will result in consequence of the new rates of pay. Commanding officers are to make a thorough investigation and report to me typical cases without delay in order that I may bring the matter at once to the notice of the Admiralty." '[40]

A reply could not be expected for at least eight hours, so Tomkinson went to bed, wondering about the correctness of his decision in allowing Astley-Rushton to persuade him, against his judgement, to bring the discontent out into the open by not abandoning the exercises. He had wanted to keep all the ships in harbour, so he could investigate the complaints. The fiery leader of the cruiser squadron was not the best of advisers, however, because none of his ships was due to go to sea next day, while the battleships were not his responsibility, but that of French, who was already at sea.

At dawn Tomkinson was up, hoping that certain ships' companies would obey orders to leave and that the others would follow. In some vessels Tomkinson's signal about investigation of hardship cases was being broadcast as early at 5.45 a.m.

The schedule was for the *Repulse*, which was lying further down the Firth of Cromarty, to sail at 6.30 a.m., with the *Valiant* leaving ninety minutes later, to be followed at 10 a.m. by the *Nelson*, *Hood* and *Rodney*, in that order. The cruisers were not to raise steam, but were to exercise in harbour.

The morning dawned golden bright and clear, with the waters of the Firth calm and unruffled. It was a perfect day for exercising – and also for a mutiny. The turmoil in Tomkinson's mind eased when he was told that the hands had fallen in for work on the *Hood*'s forecastle as normal at 6 a.m. and that the decks were being scrubbed. Unfortunately for him he was unaware that the previous night the word had been passed round to stop work at 8 a.m. His spirits rose when the *Repulse* weighed anchor half an hour later and left. But unknown to him mutiny had already begun in other ships.

In the *Rodney* only seventy-five men out of a complement of 1,200 reported for duty, while in the *Dorsetshire* nearly a hundred were absent. But in the *Adventure* all the men 'fell in', although reluctantly. All was correct in the *Norfolk* and the *Exeter*, which had arrived later. In the *York* the men worked for two hours, then stopped.[41]

From the *Hood*, Tomkinson could see that work was not being carried out on the deck of the nearby *Rodney* and that men were massing on the forecastle. Yet at 7.31 the *Valiant* had unmoored in record time, mainly through the efforts of midshipmen and petty officers, and was ready to sail. Soon a boat drew up at the *Hood*'s quarterdeck gangway, with a scribbled message from Captain Scott, of the *Valiant*. Tomkinson read that the battleship could not proceed as the stokers had refused to work.[42] Scott had to write his message because he could not rely on his signalmen. There was no movement of the *Nelson*, either, because a group of men had gathered around the port bower cable to prevent the anchor being weighed. Their captain, Burges-Watson, had addressed them just before 7 a.m. and had advised the men to send their women to work if there was hardship. Then he turned to Commander Lake and said: 'I'm going to my cabin. The men are yours.' He was not seen by them for the remainder of the mutiny. Meanwhile, stokers went to the seamen's mess-deck to persuade the occupants to stay there or assemble on the forecastle – but not to work. The anchor cables were lashed so they could not be moved, while piles of stanchion bolts were placed on deck to stop any bid to free the cables by force. The overworked and overworried Lake also had wardroom trouble. One officer wanted to call out armed marines, but Lake had him confined to his cabin. Marines could not be found anyway, because they skulked away in the locker compartments.

Similar advice to that of Burges-Watson was given by Captain Scott in the *Valiant*, where he was greeted with a roar of protest. On the ship's notice-board someone had daubed 'Cancelled' across the daily orders.

Dibben, in the *Adventure*, could not believe it when his hands refused to fall in. He took the unusual course of trying to cajole them back to work by talking to them in the recreation room, but he was close to tears when they refused.

In the *Rodney* the boys had stayed in their hammocks as advised by their seniors, while seamen had battened down the hatches to the engine-room to stop stokers reporting for duty. Boilers had been ordered to be lit at 5.30, but the engineer commander could not find his duty watch, who were in their recreation space. Some officers attempted to slip the cable mooring her to a buoy, but gave up when men sat on the links with their arms and legs through them. Surprisingly, the cooks joined in the disobedience, but after a discussion with the mutineers the galley ratings agreed to carry on so that their shipmates did not go hungry.

In the *York* the crew turned their back on Captain Custance when he tried to talk to them on the forecastle. He warned that he would have the hoses turned on them, but could not bring himself to give the order. Loyal marines with fixed bayonets guarded strategic points and a unit of them advanced along one side of the ship, allowing the mutineers to escape along the other side.

Norfolk's marines knew that they would be called out, so they barricaded themselves into their quarters. Brawling broke out with men who did not want to strike.

Around Tomkinson in the *Hood*, there was mutiny now, too. At 7.45 'clear lower deck' was piped. Most of the duty crew assembled on the forecastle, but Commander McCrum realized from the grumbling that they were 'obviously determined not to go to sea'. He advised them to 'turn to' but they were unresponsive. Then he reported to Patterson and Tomkinson that the men were being stubborn and advised: 'No good purpose will be served by your addressing them, sir.' Patterson heeded the advice.[43]

Some ratings were working on the *Hood*'s upper deck, and this brought a storm of jeers from mutineers on the *Rodney*. Soon after, 200 of the *Hood*'s seamen ignored the order to clean guns. Preparations were made to get her to sea at 8.30 and 'both watches for exercise' was sounded. About a third of the crew reported; some were told to hoist in boats, others were ordered to haul in the lower boom. Both commands were obeyed, as Tomkinson from the bridge watched anxiously. But the cable party did not arrive. When Lieutenant-Commander Mudford and volunteers went to the forecastle they found demonstrators sitting, or standing, on the cables and refusing to budge. A messenger was sent to the captain, who ordered Mudford to 'leave things as they are and make no further attempt to unshackle'.[44] A 4 $\frac{1}{2}$-in wire hawser was wrapped around sections of the cable by the mutineers to make sure that the *Hood* could not be slipped easily.

It now seemed certain to Tomkinson that there would be a 'sit down' in other sections of the ship, but he was surprised to find that normal work continued and divisional drills went ahead, although throughout there was cheering from the *Hood*, as other crews refused to put to sea.

Most of the time he was able to rely on loyalty from operators in his signal office, through which came a stream of messages now . . . mutiny in the *Rodney*, mutiny in the *Nelson*, the *Dorsetshire* and the *Norfolk*. *Rodney* had set the style, which was taken up by the largest ships, and once the lead had been given the cruisers joined the 'sit down'. The cheering from the upper decks was echoing around the Firth, as at 9.16 a.m. Tomkinson reported to the Admiralty in an 'Immediate' signal: 'Situation at 0900 today – *Repulse* has proceeded to sea for exercises, other ships have not proceeded and considerable portions of ships' companies have absented themselves from duty. Attitude of all ratings towards their officers is at present correct. I have recalled the ships not exercising and stopped leave of officers and men. Chief of Staff leaving here today, arriving Admiralty early tomorrow evening.'[45]

Tomkinson had instructed Colvin, who was taking hardship statements from men in the *Hood, Nelson, Dorsetshire* and *York*, to try to persuade the board to send at least two sea lords to Invergordon for an on-the-spot investigation. Colvin and Paymaster Captain E. Goldsmith, the commander-in-chief's secretary, left at 2 p.m. to fly in an RAF aircraft to London, but fog forced it down in the Midlands and they had to complete the journey by train.

Only in the *Dorsetshire* had the crew been 'talked back' to duty. They were wary of the promises of Rear-Admiral Astley-Rushton that hardship cases would be investigated, but later listened to the pleadings of their captain and the chaplain and returned to work.

Meanwhile, Tomkinson waited patiently for another three hours before he received a reply to his 9.16 a.m. message. Around him the mutiny was polarizing in the fleet, with the cruiser *Norfolk* becoming its epicentre. The mutineers there had drafted this manifesto, which was to become infamous world-wide:

> We, the loyal subjects of His Majesty the King, do hereby present to My Lords Commissioners of the Admiralty our representations to implore them to amend the drastic cuts in pay that have been inflicted upon the lowest paid man of the lower deck.
>
> It is evident to all concerned that this cut is the forerunner of tragedy, misery and immorality amongst the families of the lower deck, and unless we can be guaranteed a written agreement from the Admiralty, confirmed by Parliament, stating that our pay will be revised, we are still to remain as one unit, refusing to serve under the new rate of pay.
>
> Men are quite willing to accept a cut, which they, the men, consider in reason.[46]

This demand was left in an officer's cabin and taken to the *Norfolk*'s captain. It was claimed to have been smuggled to mutineers in other ships by normal boat traffic. There is no record of Tomkinson having received a copy, nor, indeed, any sign of one being handed around the *Hood*. News of it reached the outside world through a *Daily Herald* journalist, who was given a copy at Invergordon, passed it on to his London editor, who in turn sent it to Captain W.E. Hall, the Labour MP for Portsmouth North.

Now Tomkinson considered whether he should visit individual ships to make a personal appeal to the men to relent and allow the fleet to sail. Later he revealed that he rejected this approach because he was 'practically unknown' outside his own comparatively small command and was therefore unable to rely on his personality to influence the men, unless he had a definite assurance from the Admiralty that their grievances would be redressed.

As that fateful morning continued, he discovered the mutineers were using a system of signalling by cheering hourly from each ship – a ploy he knew was used by the German High Seas Fleet mutineers in 1918. Messages of assurance were also passed by the lowering of the jack on the forecastle staff, secret signs came from boats – folded arms indicated a ship was not working – and even through the telephone exchanges. He could hear men singing 'The More We Are Together', while on the *Rodney* a piano was hoisted on to a turret and its player tinkled out the latest music hall hits, old war songs and sea shanties.

Their Lordships, who met at 10 a.m., were disunited about what action to take. Tomkinson would have despaired if he had heard of a suggestion by some Cabinet members that guns should be turned on the mutineers.[47] He had discarded this idea almost as soon as it entered his thoughts.

The Admiralty's message to him at 12.05 p.m., agreed with his handling of the situation so far, but was still indefinite. It ran:

> Their Lordships entirely approve of the action which you have taken. Any representations which you think it right to make, as a result of your investigations, will be carefully considered by the board. Meanwhile officers should also take every opportunity of laying stress on the fact that great sacrifices are being required from all classes of the community and that unless these are cheerfully accepted by all concerned, the financial recovery of the country will be impossible. Similar changes of pay have been made in the Army and RAF.[48]

Already Tomkinson had instructed officers to explain the situation, and knew that this had been done in all ships. As the quiet mutiny became quieter in the afternoon, with little communication with the men, the officers preferred to let it remain that way. Yet in the *Hood*'s wardroom they were surprised that Tomkinson had not ordered them to take a firmer line. No doubt he believed his methods were effective, for he noticed the men remained polite, saluted and stood to attention for colours, or similar minor ceremonies. He feared the petty officers would join the mutiny, but they continued with their duties, although they made little attempt to persuade the junior ratings to work.

His other concern was about the *Repulse, Warspite* and *Malaya*, whose return he had ordered, joining the fleet that afternoon. Would their crews obey at sea? As they steamed in, however, he could see them lined up properly fore and aft. But within hours the

Warspite and the *Repulse* were embroiled in the mutiny; only the *Malaya* remained loyal for a few hours.

He had drafted a reply to the Admiralty, which analysed the men's dissatisfaction. This he sent at 3.40 that afternoon:

It seems clear that the chief causes of complaint are –
(a) the extent of the cuts of pay of leading rates and below, who were on old scale;
(b) the short interval before reductions take effect;
(c) alleged affirmation by Government on several occasions that ratings on old scale would continue to receive it during the whole period of their continuous service.

As regards (a) the 10 per cent reduction of unemployment benefits is compared with an approximate 20 per cent cut in an able seaman's pay and allowances and the principle of equal sacrifice is appealed to.

As regards (b) the short interval is insufficient to allow married men to readjust their standard of living.

Apart from this, so many men have commitments in the shape of life assurances, house mortgages, hire purchase of furniture etc., that no mere postponement would save them and their families from heavy losses and, in some cases, from actual want. I do not consider that the men will feel they have received justice unless reductions are more in proportion to their pay – e.g. the pay of an able seaman to be reduced by 6d instead of 1s.

Then came this caveat, to stress the explosiveness of his situation: 'I would urge a very early decision should be communicated by Their Lordships. Until this is received I regret that in my opinion discipline in the Atlantic Fleet will not be restored and may still further deteriorate.'[49]

Discipline in the *Hood* had not deteriorated further, in fact. At Rosyth the crews of the fleet submarines had remained loyal and had proceeded to sea for exercises.[50]

To let the men understand that he was trying to end the hiatus he allowed it to be announced that he had sent Colvin to London to confer with the Admiralty board. It had little effect and he was told that 'the men just remained silent'.[51] The men at the Admiralty were also remaining silent. For six hours Tomkinson waited for advice, then it came at 7.10 p.m. with the caustic opener that he 'had failed to convey to Their Lordships a true picture of the situation'.

It continued: 'The board of Admiralty will give their earnest and immediate consideration to representations of hardship. Meanwhile you should impress on ships' companies that existing rates of pay remain in force until 1st October and Their Lordships confidently expect that the men of the Atlantic Fleet will uphold the tradition of the service by loyally carrying out their duty.'[52]

The normally placid Tomkinson boiled. All this had been explained to ratings. He was seeking clarity. His chagrin increased thirty-five minutes later when he read this mutilated, unnecessarily complicated (through lack of punctuation) and involved signal from Whitehall, which was repeated to all commanders-in-chief:

It is important that programme of exercises should be resumed as soon as your investigations are complete. As regards comparisons mentioned, it must be remembered that naval cut is not on total emoluments but on pay only. For instance, in a typical case of an AB of over six years' service, holding non substantive ratings of gunlayer 2nd class and seaman gunner with wife and two young children present weekly emolument is as follows –
pay 31s 6d, non substantive pay 5s 3d, badge pay 1s 9d, standard rates and messing allowance of 8s 9d, kit upkeep allowance 2s 1d marriage allowance 15s total 64s 4d. After October 1 the value will be pay 25s 8d and all other emoluments unchanged except standard ration and messing allowance 8s 10d. Total 57s 8d percentage reduction is therefore 10 per cent. If unmarried comparison would be present emoluments 49s 4d after 1st October 42s 7d percentage reduction 13 per cent. It is impossible to contend that these reductions are out of proportion to reduction of 10 per cent in unemployment benefits. Reductions on precisely similar basis are to be put into effect in army and air force.[53]

Before Tomkinson could reply, the dilemma of Their Lordships was evident, for within an hour there was another 'Immediate' signal at 8.35 p.m., which countermanded the previous orders. It said: 'Pending investigations and subsequent consideration by the Admiralty of representations as to hardship caused by new rates of pay, the board have approved the temporary suspension of Atlantic Fleet programme.'[54] For the first time it was signed by a friend of Tomkinson since his cadet days at Dartmouth – Admiral Dreyer, the Deputy Chief of Naval Staff. Tomkinson noted on the message: 'Received much mutilated at about 2030 Tuesday, 15th.'

Dreyer, too, was in a quandary for, having agreed to suspend the fleet's programme, he followed the message with another, inside half an hour, which ordered: 'It is desirable that practices should be continued as soon as you have had time to complete your investigations.'[55]

By now Tomkinson's patience left him, because it was obvious to him that he was not making himself properly understood. He mulled over his desperate plight, gave himself time to cool and at 1 a.m. sent this signal of semi-admonishment: 'I must emphasise that the situation at Invergordon will not be met until definite decisions have been communicated. A continuation of the exercise programme is out of the question in the present state of mind of a considerable proportion of the crews.'[56]

He also informed the fleet that his chief of staff would arrive at the Admiralty next morning, that no decision could be made for a day or two and that no indication of its nature could be given. 'I confidently expect you to carry out normal duties,' he added.

Early next morning the silent and polite deadlock continued in the *Hood*, with routine work until 'stand easy' at 10 a.m. The contents of the newspapers that had arrived inflamed the men because in them was an Admiralty statement which merely indicated that the 'reduced rates of pay has led to unrest among a proportion of the lower ratings'.[57] During this break the tide turned and the *Hood* and *Rodney* swung parallel to each other. Tomkinson heard the shouts of 'blacklegs' and 'yellow' from the *Rodney*, which stopped all work on the *Hood*'s upper deck.

127

The *Malaya, Warspite* and *Repulse* had lowered stages over their sides ready to paint ship, but again the catcalls from the *Rodney*, backed by the *Valiant*, were so vehement that these three crews also refused to obey orders. No work was being done on the *Norfolk* and *Adventure*, either. As soon as the *Hood* caught the fever, she passed it on to the men of the nearby *Dorsetshire*, who had been carrying on normally.

To Tomkinson it seemed that the mutiny was raging into full momentum again, like an epidemic. He had arranged for Astley-Rushton and French to meet him in the *Hood* to report on their efforts to talk to the men of the *Norfolk, Adventure* and *Valiant*; they had failed abysmally. As they were discussing the latest flare-ups, the Admiralty signalled that the board had been deliberating since early morning on the points raised by Colvin, who had arrived in London overnight. The message said that Admiral Field, the First Sea Lord, was still in discussion with the Cabinet. 'You will receive earliest possible announcement of their decision,' it ended.[58]

It was obvious to the three admirals from the shouting they could hear rolling around the fleet again that the mutiny was closer to flashpoint. They talked about forming a committee of senior officers to interview lower-deck delegates and to seek the feelings of ratings. But Tomkinson could see the difficulties. How could they select representatives from the men? How could they inform the fleet, because intership signalling had become unreliable? How could a committee begin their business before the afternoon, when action was expected immediately by the Admiralty? And, after all these considerations, perhaps the men might reject the plan and refuse to nominate spokesmen. The whole idea of amelioration was dropped in the face of these obstacles and at 11.48 a.m. Tomkinson was forced to compose this 'Most Immediate' signal – the highest possible priority – to Whitehall: 'I am of the opinion that the situation will get entirely out of control unless an immediate concession is made. Suggest (a) that percentage in pay (without allowance) for ratings below petty officer be proportionately that of higher ratings; (b) that marriage allowance be applied to those ratings under 25, who have married on old scale of pay. Further I recommend representative of board visit me to discuss matters on the spot.'[59]

Resistance hardened on the *Hood*'s mess-decks when the rum issue was ladled out, just before the lunch hour. It was rumoured that the Admiralty intended harsh punishment for the fleet; that they would be isolated at Scapa Flow, or separated and sailed to Spithead, where marines would take over, or put under close arrest in the home ports. It was reported to Tomkinson that mess-deck feeling was growing stronger and there would be a complete stoppage. Violence also seemed possible, with the lives of ratings against the mutiny 'being made difficult'.[60]

The stokers rekindled the insubordination by refusing to go below after their lunch. At the suggestion of Pursey, the captain ordered a 'make and mend', or half holiday, to be piped.[61] The men were surprised by it and many went to sleep, instead of joining in the cheering on the forecastle. Captain Patterson passed the idea on to commanding officers of the *Repulse, Malaya* and *Dorsetshire*, where it was also a success.

Still attempting to press the Admiralty into a decision, Tomkinson had this signal transmitted at 2.06 p.m.: 'Situation 1400 – fleet informed Cabinet meeting at noon. More ships have ceased ordinary harbour work and men are massing on forecastles at intervals.

Adjacent ships cheering each other. Interference with running machinery and forced inter-ship communication may be the next step.'[62]

He did not mention that he was afraid some crews might break out of their ships, probably holding back the information as a final, more serious cry for help to the Admiralty.[63]

The message stirred Their Lordships, who, for the first time, attached a 'Most Immediate' label to their reply, which directed the fleet to sail to home ports. In full it stated:

> The board of Admiralty is fully alive to the fact that amongst certain classes of ratings special hardship will result from the reduction of pay ordered by H.M. Government. It is therefore directed that ships of the Atlantic Fleet are to proceed to their home ports forthwith to enable personal investigation by commanders-in-chief and representatives of Admiralty with view to necessary alleviation being made. Any further refusal of individuals to carry out orders will be dealt with under the Naval Discipline Act. This signal is to be promulgated to the fleet forthwith.[64]

Several admirals wanted to take a harder line. As Dreyer was to note later, 'lesser lights' than Field among the sea lords were suggesting that the fleet should be bombarded by heavy land artillery from beyond the hills around the Cromarty Firth.[65] After Tomkinson's telegrams were discussed some members of the Cabinet were also ready to approve an assault on the mutineers, but Austen Chamberlain, now First Lord, persuaded them to reject the proposal, and preferred to leave the order to Field. Dreyer later insisted that after the meeting there were still ministers who were adamant that no concession should be made about pay and that the only way out was to open fire on the fleet. Even J.H. Thomas, Minister for Unemployment, and Secretary for the Dominions, who had been leader of the Railwaymen's Union for many years, advocated 'making an example' of the mutineers, instead of allowing them to 'sovietize the British Navy'.[66]

The House of Commons, in fact, had been informed of the 'proceed to home ports' decision by Chamberlain, before Tomkinson had been given the opportunity of digesting its contents. It had taken Tomkinson by surprise because he had just sent another of his staff to London with a second portfolio of hardship cases and was anticipating a definite offer from the Admiralty.

After the message had been decoded Tomkinson, through Patterson, allowed some of it to be filtered into the *Hood* as a 'mess-deck buzz'. At 4.45 p.m. the men were piped to assemble on the forecastle. Tomkinson watched, as from the top of one of the gun turrets Patterson explained they were returning to Portsmouth, where their grievances would be considered. 'I can guarantee that any rumours as to this being a ruse to divide the fleet are entirely unfounded and that any further refusal on your part would do still further harm to your cause,' he said.[67] This short speech was received silently, but after he had gone aft there were shouts of 'no, no, no' in a short demonstration of solidarity. At 6 p.m. there was another gathering on the forecastle and the yelling was repeated. Tomkinson now despaired whether anyone could persuade the fleet to sail. After receiving the Admiralty's last signal, he had asked Astley-Rushton and French to meet him to draw up sailing orders. Four hours were needed to raise steam; the capital ships required slack water to leave and that would not be until later in the evening.[68] The three admirals agreed that squadrons should sail independently, with the cruisers in the van at 9.30 p.m., although Astley-Rushton did not think the *Norfolk* would be in a fit disciplinary state to move.

He had obtained first-hand information by visiting the ship earlier that day. The men had ambled to the quarterdeck, where he lambasted them in a paroxysm of abuse and curses. But as he yelled at them they turned their backs and returned to the forecastle. Captain Prickett followed them and found they were listening to gramophone music. He put his arm around the shoulders of one man and with a trickle of tears on his cheek pleaded with them all to end the mutiny. They took no notice. Astley-Rushton had also attempted to visit the *Adventure*, but a human barrier refused to let him board.

From the *Hood* the new orders were dispatched to individual captains by boat, but Captain J.B. Watson, of the *Nelson*, asked to discuss the departure with Tomkinson and Patterson personally in the *Hood*. He was worried that the mooring parties would not go to their stations, and that the men would sit on the cables. It was decided that if this happened the massive anchor hawsers of the capital ships would be unlinked at a suitable point below; combined with the weight and power of their engines this would unleash a lethal whiplash to anyone sitting on the cables.[69]

From his quarters Tomkinson, still ominously pessimistic, could see cars lining the length of the coastal road from Invergordon to Saltburn, their drivers and passengers waiting to watch the navy's 'unrest'. Suddenly the mood of the mutineers seemed to have changed in the *Hood*, for around 5 p.m. a complete engine-room watch fell in. But Tomkinson's mood did not change. At 7.17 p.m., still doubtful, he signalled the Admiralty: 'I am not sure that all ships will leave as ordered, but some will go.'[70]

Stringent measures were being considered in the *Valiant*, where Captain Scott found that only 200 men had reported and were being addressed by the commander on the forecastle. Scott went to the quarterdeck to try to speak to the duty men there, but they jeered him. Furious at their refusal to listen he ordered the captain of the marines to clear the forecastle, using force if necessary. The captain of marines immediately asked for the order in writing, which halted Scott momentarily. Instead, he sent a note by an officer in a boat to his admiral, French in *Warspite*, asking for permission to open fire. Meanwhile, all loyal marines were ordered below to collect their rifles and ammunition. Because there were so few of them, Lieutenant Ralfs took up two Lewis machine-guns. While all this was going on, Scott ordered the bosun's mate to go around the ship, piping that anyone who was not on the quarterdeck within five minutes would be treated as a mutineer. Soon after, French arrived on board and instructed Scott to put persuasion before force, but by then the crew had assembled on the quarterdeck and agreed to sail.[71]

Not all the *Hood*'s insubordinates were giving in, however. When the cable party were piped to go to the waist, only one able seaman arrived to report to Lieutenant Commander Longly-Cook, the cable officer. They went to the forecastle and were greeted with loud cheers and laughter by a large group of men; several were sitting on the lashed cables and it was obvious that the anchor could not be weighed without a full party. Longly-Cook was politely told that the sailors would not move without the use of force and he reported this to Captain Patterson. It seemed that the first injury, or possibly death, of the mutiny was about to occur, for Patterson fully intended to keep to his word of parting the cable.[72]

When Tomkinson was appraised of this he altered his orders for each squadron to sail together and signalled every captain to leave independently. He had made the break-through.

One of the first to move was the *Adventure*. In the engine-room tasks normally assigned to stokers were taken over by officers. One anchor was being raised by other officers when a gang of sailors dashed on to the forecastle to obstruct them. To prevent the marines being called out with fixed bayonets, other ratings had battened them down in their mess-deck. This seemed to reassure the men and they were soon in a mood to accept the order to steam away.

Exeter was the next ship to proceed, but there had been little trouble on board her. Tomkinson was jubilant when he saw that Astley-Rushton's flagship, the *Dorsetshire*, was also under way, although the mutiny committee on the *Norfolk* had been shouting 'no, no, no' at her crew. This negative cry soon became positive as the *Norfolk*, too, steamed slowly from the anchorage at 9.30. But as she left Tomkinson could hear the cries of 'no, no, no' being repeated around him in the *Hood*.

However, the sight of the *Warspite* departing dowsed the fire of mutiny in the *Hood*; gradually the men returned to duty, the anchor was weighed and the battle cruiser began to move.[73]

A relieved Tomkinson surveyed the anchorage. Only three ships were left – the *Centurion*, her escort the *Shikari*, and the *Nelson*. Belatedly, the former commander-in-chief's flagship unshackled and followed the fleet.

For some obtuse reason Tomkinson did not signal news of his success immediately and when he did it crossed with an Admiralty query. At ten minutes to midnight Their Lordships, who by now had sent intelligence agents to Invergordon, asked: 'Unofficial reports received that fleet have sailed. Request report forthwith.'[74]

Although late in giving this information, Tomkinson had forestalled the Admiralty, for five minutes earlier he had informed them: 'Atlantic Fleet ships have all sailed from Invergordon, except HMS *Centurion*, which is boiler cleaning and will sail with HMS *Shikari* at 1100 tomorrow, Thursday.'[75]

17
UNOFFICIAL INQUIRY

On the passage south Tomkinson had a great deal to occupy him. First he had to ensure that the various units' arrival at their home ports would be in time to prevent more unruliness; then he had to compile one of the most momentous reports of proceedings in modern naval history.

Through the BBC radio on Thursday 17 September he heard news that was to send his spirits to a low ebb and then raise them again. Reports of the mutiny had spread worldwide and had made a bigger impact in the United States and in France than in Britain. Navies had been the hub of revolutions in Germany and Russia; now to the outside world Britain seemed to be on the brink of communism if such a long-established institution as the Royal Navy was in revolt. The devaluing of the navy – always regarded as the senior diplomatic representative of Britain and her Empire – brought a run on gold reserves. On the previous day £5 million had been withdrawn to support the pound; now this day the figure doubled.

As the sullen sailors in the *Hood* obediently went about lighter tasks specially devised for them, lip-service to Tomkinson and the fleet was being paid in the House of Commons.

Captain Hall, a former army officer, who had received a copy of the mutineers' manifesto, appealed to First Lord Austen Chamberlain in an impassioned speech not to punish the offenders in any way. He went on: 'Another thing that emerges is that the commander-in-chief [Tomkinson] in the absence of Admiral Hodges . . . acted with great promptitude, with dispatch and with great commonsense. We remember previous incidents in the navy when officers in charge have perhaps not seen their duty as clearly as the present commander-in-chief [Tomkinson].'

A.V. Alexander, Chamberlain's predecessor, supported this acclamation. He described it as 'very great service in the crisis', and added: 'The sympathetic and tactful action which the acting commander-in-chief of the Atlantic Fleet has taken is only what I have expected of him from my knowledge of him.'

Chamberlain, who had not taken office until nineteen days before the mutiny and who had failed to appreciate the seriousness of the Cabinet's decision on the pay cuts, did not attempt to distance himself from Tomkinson. 'I was particularly glad to hear the honourable and gallant member pay a tribute to the Senior Officer, Atlantic Fleet

[Tomkinson]', he said. 'The Admiralty have already conveyed to him their full approval of the action which he took and of his service during these times. The compliment is well deserved and will be well received by the men of the fleet.'

He agreed that Tomkinson had acted with 'great promptitude and great commonsense'. Then came a statement, which would not be forgotten by the men or their officers in the mutiny. 'The past is past,' Chamberlain said. 'It is in the interests of everyone in the navy – and out of it – to forget it. I am not going to look back. I am going to look forward and I count confidently on the traditions of the service and of the men of today to loyally uphold them.'[1]

Tomkinson did not just read what he wished to see into the words, for later he received a congratulatory letter from his friend C.W. Dyson Perrin, of Ardross Castle by Alness, which eulogized: 'Surely no man has ever yet had the unanimous expression of praise which you received in the debate in the House and which all your friends must have been as pleased as I to read.'[2]

In fact, Chamberlain was diplomatically caulking the cracks in the Admiralty's foundering vessel, for his 'general amnesty' and support of the praise for Tomkinson had gone further than the sea lords intended.[3]

This renewed confidence in the navy's future did not restore Britain's economic position and, as the *Hood* neared Portsmouth, yet another £18 million was wiped from the gold reserves.

The main concern of Tomkinson on this day was to ensure that all the ships entered their home ports by noon on Saturday 19 September. Then maximum weekend leave could be granted to defuse the still simmering controversy of pay cuts. In the morning Tomkinson signalled that usual weekend leave would be granted to one watch and night leave to half of the other watch.[4] Just before this message went out the Admiralty confused the situation again by ordering 'usual leave',[5] but this meant that half of one watch would not get ashore on Saturday or Sunday. It took almost twenty-four hours before the Admiralty agreed to a turn around.[6]

In order that the *Rodney*, one of the leading ships in the mutiny, could get to her home port of Plymouth in time, Tomkinson detached her and she went ahead. It was later revealed that during the passage south mutineers on the *Rodney* had signalled their colleagues in the flagship: '*Nelson* will now take over pivotal ship; keep your end up and do not forget 0800 next Tuesday.'[7]

Tomkinson also had to ask the Admiralty what speed the *Hood*, *Repulse* and *Rodney* could steam at because of economy restrictions.[8] This was eventually put at a fraction over 12 knots, but after running into fog later it had to be cut; when visibility cleared Tomkinson had to order more of the Hood's boilers to be lit, so she could steam at 14 knots to make up time.

As if to signify that most of the sea lords were not in accord with their civil lord, that evening the Admiralty, to Tomkinson's annoyance, signalled all ships of the Atlantic Fleet that they viewed with 'the greatest concern the injury which the prestige of the British Navy has suffered', and that they relied on personnel to do their 'utmost to restore confidence of the country by their future behaviour'.[9]

Tomkinson, who was still preparing his report of proceedings, received an unexpected snub from Admiral Field, the First Sea Lord, the next day. First he signalled him that he proposed to visit the Admiralty on the Saturday, when the *Hood* was due to dock,[10] but within four hours – quicker than the Admiralty had replied to his more urgent signals at Invergordon – Field answered: 'Although I shall be glad to see you at any time, I suggest you remain at Portsmouth so far as necessary to assist C-in-C Portsmouth in his investigations.'[11]

It left Tomkinson mystified, if not amazed, because he had already examined cases of hardship extensively. Then the uncertainty of Field was brought to his attention again when he received a 'personal immediate' signal indicating that the First Sea Lord would be 'very glad' to see him on the Saturday.[12]

Any doubts that he might be blamed for the mutiny were again dispelled when the *Hood*, with the crew behaving correctly and orderly, arrived at Portsmouth at 5.30 a.m. Among his mail was a letter from Field, dated the previous day, which opened: 'My Dear Tomkinson, I congratulate you on the very able way you handled a most difficult situation and the least we could do was to back you up.'[13]

After revealing that it had taken him an hour to persuade the Cabinet to send the ships to their home ports, Field's last tribute was: 'Well done. All the board consider you handled the job with great ability and tact – yours ever, F. Field.'

It was a letter that never left Tomkinson's possession, for on it he considered his future depended.

Already the post-mortem examination on the mutiny and his actions had begun, for the three commanders-in-chief of the home ports, Admirals Sir Hubert Brand, Sir Arthur Waistell and Sir Reginald Tyrwhitt, all friends of his, had been called to the Admiralty for a conference.[14]

There is no record of Tomkinson's Saturday conversation with Field at the Admiralty, although from his report of proceedings, dated 19 September, there is little doubt that Tomkinson gave his honest, if over-exaggerated, summing up that 'for two days the ships at Invergordon of the Atlantic Fleet were in a state of open mutiny. The conditions of affairs and the general tension that existed are not easy to describe.'[15]

He considered that there was an 'undoubted organisation' in the outbreak and preparations must have been made over a considerable period. 'It seems likely to have originated in *Rodney* and *Valiant* and concerted action was effected at the meetings at the canteen on the evenings of Sunday and Monday.' He claimed that persuasion in some cases appeared to amount to 'almost intimidation', but stressed that he had not ordered the use of firearms, which 'would have led to a much worse state of affairs'.[16]

He sided with the men by saying 'the cause of complaint was well founded', but added: 'I deplore the fact that this disgraceful episode should have occurred during my temporary command of the fleet.'[17]

Chamberlain studied Tomkinson's report and observed on 4 October that he reserved any expression of opinion as to responsibilities. 'In these matters I think that we of the board of Admiralty must accept some measure of blame,' he admitted.[18]

Based on Tomkinson's fears that the mutiny was not spontaneous, Special Branch detectives and MI5 agents were sent to Plymouth and Portsmouth that weekend.[19] Reports were vetted by the board of Admiralty throughout this period, as they kept in almost constant session. The sea lords were convinced that a more serious outbreak was imminent, with a mass desertion from ships seemingly planned for 8 a.m. on Tuesday 22 September. They visualized the men of the home ports marching out in their thousands into towns, rioting and inducing other sections of the community to join them. On the Monday, the Cabinet and the king were informed of this highly coloured prediction, which the Admiralty suggested – almost in a form of blackmail – could be averted only by halving the pay cuts to 10 per cent.

On Monday 21 September, a few hours after it was announced by the Government that Britain had been forced to go off the gold standard and that the value of sterling had plunged by 4s in the pound, the Atlantic Fleet heard through premier Ramsay MacDonald in the Commons that they had won a victory. All ships and establishments were informed that the 'simplest way of removing just grievances' was to limit reductions in the three services to not more than 10 per cent.[20]

Soon after, Field, in a 'let's get tough' letter to Tomkinson wrote: 'If the men are not satisfied with the pay now and what has been done for them, the sooner we know it the better, and those who wish to make trouble must be dealt with seriously.'[21]

Tomkinson was still designated Senior Officer, Atlantic Fleet, but after 24 September, when Hodges resigned as the commander-in-chief because of his thrombosis, it was a possibility that Tomkinson would be appointed in his place. An old colleague, Rear-Admiral George Chetwode, the Naval Secretary, who listed other candidates, including Keyes, no longer on the active list, Admiral Tyrwhitt and Admiral John Kelly, also pointed out in a memorandum that Tomkinson could be promoted to acting vice admiral in advance of his formal elevation to that rank in the spring. Seemingly, Chetwode was an ally; he agreed with Tomkinson, who had told the Admiralty that he would not attempt to distribute blame or praise captains or any other officers at Invergordon. In a letter on 26 September 1931, Chetwode wrote to him: 'My Dear Tommy [Tomkinson's affectionate nickname by friends], I think myself that it would be a great mistake to attempt to find scapegoats – either in the fleet or at the Admiralty – and I hope this wretched business will be forgotten, or at any rate put out of all our minds, as soon as possible.'[22]

Chamberlain, however, had no intention of appointing any of the four, but after an internal battle the Cabinet and the king favoured Kelly, who had been passed over by Field when considering the vacancy of Second Sea Lord a year earlier. He accepted the appointment for a year, with Tomkinson reverting to Rear-Admiral of the Battle Cruiser Squadron.[23] The last order he was to make in his exalted position as acting commander-in-chief was for the Atlantic Fleet to prepare for a resumption of their interrupted autumn cruise north, but not to Invergordon. In an effort to make the men face the anchorage of their disgrace, he favoured a return there, but he was overruled by Kelly, backed by his chief of staff Colvin, and the destination became Rosyth.[24]

In spite of this disagreement, Colvin admired Tomkinson and wrote to him about the mutiny in negative fashion just before the fleet sailed: 'There are two things that cannot truthfully be said. One – that you acted without taking everyone's views into consideration and Two – that your decisions were made against the advice of those you called upon for their views. I don't mean by this that you relied entirely upon other people's opinions, but that whatever criticisms there are, apply equally to me in my humbler capacity and that I am not in the least afraid to meet them.'[25]

The letter was based on 'Notes of Refusal of Duty of Six Ships of the Atlantic Fleet at Invergordon', which Admiral Dreyer had taken on himself to prepare – mainly in defence of the Admiralty. Captain Stephen Roskill, who served under Dreyer, described him as an extremely ambitious man, with a marked streak of ruthlessness', targeted at becoming the First Sea Lord.[26] As a lieutenant he had attracted the Admiralty's attention when he invented the Dreyer Table, a complicated range-finding machine, which computed the course and speed of an attacking ship, together with that of the enemy, to produce a plot, which was fed to the director and guns. In HMS *Dreadnought* he had served under Bacon, whom Keyes had superseded in charge of the Dover Patrol, and thus was a member of the Admiralty faction who were against Keyes and his friends. At the Admiralty, Dreyer was prone to write long involved memos and notes, with heavy underscoring and italicizing. In spite of his industriousness he was 'too much of a paper man' and was not liked, or trusted, by his closest associates in Whitehall, but he held sway over Field.[27]

In a covering letter to his memorandum, Dreyer wrote that it did not 'ascribe fault to anyone, except the agitators and the foolish men who took their advice'. He thought the men should be taught that the 'damned agitators have caused them to lose caste and they should have trusted their officers'.[28]

The notes brought instant complaint from Tomkinson, who on his copy ringed the figure six and wrote 'Nonsense', because he had suggested in his report of proceedings that all ships were in open mutiny. He wanted the word 'some' deleted and substituted with 'nearly all'. Later, in a reply to Dreyer, he criticized: 'Your memo may be of some use to officers, but with all of which I, for one, am not in agreement.'[29]

His bluntness did not endear him to Dreyer, who was still writing in terms of 'My Dear Tommy.'[30] However, Dreyer did strike out six in the opening sentence and wrote in 'some', although later in his memo the phrase a 'small band of discontented agitators in a few ships' crept in.[31]

On 7 October, the day before the *Hood* sailed to Rosyth, ten of her crew were sent to Portsmouth Barracks, for interviews with Naval Intelligence officers to decide whether they should be discharged. At the barracks were a total of 121 ratings from the fleet, but the Admiralty had issued the strict instruction that no one was to be discharged 'services no longer required' until after the General Election on 27 October.[32] Tomkinson and Kelly had insisted that the fleet could not go on the cruise with known agitators still in ships.

Kelly put the fleet through rigorous evolutions and exercises at Rosyth. Neither he nor Tomkinson were amused in one practice, which called for the *Hood*'s marine band to lower a boat, put their instruments in it and row to the flagship *Nelson* to 'play a popular tune'. The bandmaster led them into 'Has Anybody Here Seen Kelly?' The new commander-in-chief was met later by seamen with fixed bayonets to repel boarders on the *Hood*,

136

when a message that he was inspecting all action stations was misinterpreted as 'enemy is on the boat-deck'.[33]

In spite of these slip-ups in Tomkinson's command, when the *Hood* returned to Portsmouth on 19 November, Kelly reported that the fleet was at a high level of cleanliness, smart and efficient, with leave-breaking almost non-existent and 'other offences small', although the behaviour of the men ashore and their saluting of officers was 'below standard'.[34]

In the aftermath of mutiny Tomkinson had recommended that the *Hood* should be paid off and recommissioned with a different crew,[35] but this suggestion was overruled again. Instead, Christmas leave began in the middle of November. Many admirals were wondering why Tomkinson had not recommissioned himself, or at least put his own affairs in order.

Certainly the Admiralty were trying to put their own house in order, for during the fleet's second autumn cruise Kelly was instructed in a secret letter on 17 October from Sir Vincent Baddeley, the assistant secretary at the Admiralty, to 'make a careful examination of the state of discipline' in the ships of the fleet and into the 'whole circumstances of the recent failure of discipline, in order to bring to light, as fully as possible, all contributory causes and any defects that may exist in methods available for detecting and checking undesirable movements before they have time to spread through a ship, or from one ship to another'.[36] He was told he was not to hesitate to recommend the removal of officers, or men, from ships; he was not to conduct his investigations as a court of inquiry and was to report as rapidly as possible.

Field had activated the investigation by informing Chamberlain that he had 'received one or two letters from some naval officers and also visits from one or two others, expressing a very strong opinion that some sort of inquiry should be made.'[37] Chamberlain had hesitatingly given his approval, as long as it was not called a 'court of inquiry', because this would imply that disciplinary action might be taken[38] – and that was contrary to his amnesty statement in the Commons.

Kelly, with the help of Captain James Somerville, later to become one of the most successful admirals in the Second World War, and Captain John Tovey, a future commander-in-chief of the Home Fleet, took three weeks to complete his probe, managing most of it when the ships were in close proximity at anchorage. He had several friendly conversations with Tomkinson – the two of them had been at the centre of the *Royal Oak* fiasco – and asked him to write down his views.

In a letter headed 'State of Discipline in Atlantic Fleet', Tomkinson asserted: 'It may be possible, perhaps, that trouble would have been averted, but it is my firm conviction that discontent, not only in the Atlantic Fleet but in the whole of the navy, would have remained and would have manifested itself sooner or later – probably in a more widespread revolt, certainly in a discontented, unpopular and weakened service.'[39]

He did not go as far as blaming the Admiralty for mishandling the situation, but gave these reasons for it:

1. Suddenness of pay cuts to the men, the short time before they became effective and inadequate methods of representation of complaints.

2. A subversive organization, which existed in 'certain ships', although there was no evidence that it existed, he admitted lamely.

3. Disposition of ships – they were close together and there was little to do during shore leave at Invergordon, which led to powerful persuasion, intimidation and threats of personal violence.

4. The complaints of the men about breach of contract by the Government were so well founded that officers found it difficult to explain.

He noted that the expression 'failure of discipline' had been used in the terms of reference to Kelly, but he stressed: 'It must be remembered that maintenance of a form of discipline was made a necessary condition of the concerted action, which was proposed to the men and that, except for refusal to take ships to sea, discipline to a great extent was in fact maintained.'

Tomkinson was already hearing gossip that his command was being compared with other fleets, or bases, which had not mutinied, so covered himself by insisting: 'Men serving abroad were not aware of cuts in full until after Invergordon. When leave is given at home shore establishments the bulk of men disperse to their homes and therefore the subversive elements among them were not in this case afforded the opportunities which obtained at Invergordon.'

A great deal of Tomkinson's opinion was incorporated into the Kelly Report, consisting of sixty-four sections, which the Admiralty received on 10 November.[40] Kelly had fired a warning salvo to Field, a fortnight earlier, when he wrote that the 'officers and men alike, from the highest to the lowest, appear to attribute the mutiny directly to the action of the Admiralty in accepting the cuts as at first promulgated'.[41] His enquiries also led him to believe that complete confidence in the board of Admiralty would not be restored 'so long as the present board remain in office'. Field instantly replied that he did not consider he was to blame and that he had offered to resign, but was told it would be 'quixotic'.[42]

Evidently the board gained Kelly's sympathy, for in his final report, although trenchant, pointed and accusative, there was no suggestion that the board should resign. Nevertheless, he found the Admiralty guilty, fairly and squarely, something that no British admiral had ever had the audacity to do.

Tomkinson's conduct was examined in four sections of the report, and his decisions were questioned on these two issues:

1. Whether he had ordered large enough shore patrols at Invergordon.
2. Whether he should have insisted on exercises continuing, or cancelled them.[43]

Kelly did not pronounce Tomkinson guilty; neither did he exonerate him, but considered that there were 'three decisions for examination'. These were:

1. The decision as to a normal patrol and the absence of measures to prevent subversive meetings – 'in the light of what followed this decision was clearly

wrong, but my inquiries made it perfectly clear to me that there was no appre-
hension among senior officers, or other officers, generally that serious trouble
was afoot. Furthermore, though it might have postponed events for a short time,
it would not have avoided the inevitable outbreak.'

2. The decision by SOAF to bring matters to a head – 'this was not discussed with
Tomkinson and my opinion of any action which might, or should have been
taken, must be purely conjectural. Subject to these qualifications, I consider the
sailing of the fleet should have been cancelled and an order issued to commanding officers to investigate hardship and report to SOAF to represent these to the
Admiralty forthwith.'

3. The decision to order ships at sea to return to harbour – 'SOAF alone was in a
position to appreciate local atmosphere and circumstances. Actually the decision
had little, or no effect on the issue.'

Kelly's commentary on Tomkinson's tact came in the finding that 'use of force' would
have changed the men's passive attitude and probably have led to 'extensive sabotage and
possibility of violent mutiny'.

He also pointed out that Tomkinson had only hoisted his flag in the preceding May and
was 'practically unknown' outside his own comparatively small command. 'He, I understand, considered therefore that he was unable to rely on his personality to influence the
men unless he had definite assurances that their grievances would be redressed. These
assurances he was clearly unable to give and he decided after full consideration to bring
matters to a head.' Kelly thought that these decisions were perfectly correct.

He had already told the king[44] that the board of Admiralty should resign and this was
not lost on Their Lordships, as Dreyer began drafting long, vitriolic memoranda in their
defence.[45]

Meanwhile Tomkinson took his Christmas leave, and blissfully made preparations for a
cruise in the *Hood* to the West Indies, in company with the *Repulse, Delhi, Norfolk* and
Dorsetshire.

The gale which battered the Hood off the Lizard, when they left on 6 January, 1932,
presaged the storm ahead for him. Massive seas forced the speed of the flagship to be
reduced to 8 knots to prevent flooding, but the seaplane and quarterdeck catapult were
washed out of action.

Tomkinson was dogged by bad weather all the way to the Azores, where, even at
anchor, the *Hood* was 'taking it green'.[46] Morale was low, but on passage to Barbados it
warmed under the strength of the sun. By the time the *Hood* arrived the men were fit in
mind and body, while the festivities arranged improved their temper. The visit lasted a
fortnight, then it was on to St Vincent, Grenada and Trinidad.

18
THE AXE FALLS

Another night of a mixture of diplomatic conversation, polite yarning and social small talk lay ahead of Tomkinson as he dressed in his cabin in the *Hood* for a dinner ashore at Government House, Trinidad. But this evening of 16 February on his West Indies idyll began in impending dishonour, when he read a routine transcript of a BBC news broadcast, picked up by the ship's communications department.[1]

This revealed that he had been superseded by Rear-Admiral Sir William James as commander of the Battle Cruiser Squadron. There had been no prior warning that he was to be relieved, and from the précis of the broadcast he was unable to ascertain when it was to occur.[2]

In this troubled state of mind he attended the dinner, but next day, still without further news, he signalled the Admiralty: 'British official press W/T announces appointment of flag officer to relieve me in the 2nd Battle Cruiser Squadron. Request I may be informed if this is correct, observing that I was definitely offered the appointment for a period of two years and have not (repetition not) received any intimation from Admiralty as to my supersession.'[3]

It was another twenty-four hours before the Admiralty replied mysteriously and ominously: 'The position is explained in personal and confidential letters dispatched on February 5.'

Tomkinson's suspense lasted for another two days, when he received two letters from Whitehall, both marked 'Personal and Secret', and both bearing the date stamp 2 February – apparently Their Lordships had little idea of when they were sent. The first was a mixture of good and bad news; it informed him that five days earlier he had been promoted to vice admiral, then came the blow that he would be reappointed for only another six months as commander of the squadron, which meant that his original two-year term was being truncated by eight months.[4]

The second letter was virtually the announcement of the end of his naval career, as the brunt of the blame for the Invergordon mutiny was transferred to him. He read this censure:

After making every allowance for the difficult and unusual circumstances in which you were placed, Their Lordships are unable to relieve you of responsibility for a

140

serious error of judgement in omitting to take any decided action on the 13th and 14th September, when dis-satisfaction had begun to show itself amongst the men. If the situation had been well handled on those two days, instead of being allowed to drift, Their Lordships consider it improbable that this outbreak would ever have occurred.[5]

Unknown to Tomkinson, the sea lords had unanimously decided as early as their New Year's Day board meeting that he had failed to appreciate the seriousness of the canteen meetings, failed to 'close the canteen entirely', failed to delay the order to go to sea on the Tuesday and failed to address the men himself. Linked to these decisions was the recommendation that he should be reappointed for only another six months after his promotion. Field had decided that no reason should be given for this curt dismissal, but that the Invergordon censure should be contained in a separate communication.[6]

Retribution was heavy in the tropical air that day, for Captain Patterson, still in command of the *Hood*, had also been informed bluntly that he was to be relieved at the same time as Tomkinson, and with him were to go the captains of the *Rodney, Valiant, Adventure, Nelson, Norfolk* and *York*. Invergordon had scythed through the navy's potential admirals.

The morale of the *Hood* descended,[7] just as the gloom of despair and disgrace cloaked Tomkinson during the voyage home to Portsmouth. In Britain, friends, led by Keyes, who had kept remarkably quiet during the aftermath of the mutiny, were rallying to support him. In the House of Commons on 24 February, Lieutenant-Commander R.T. Bower, MP, asked what was the normal procedure for the appointment of the commander of the Battle Cruiser Squadron. He was told by Lord Stanley, Parliamentary and Financial Secretary to the Admiralty, that it was customary for it to be for two years, if the holder were a rear-admiral, but when an officer was promoted to vice admiral the question of retention of the command for the two full years was 'specially reviewed'. This did not satisfy Bower, who, without referring to Tomkinson, asked whether the supersession of an officer ten months before his appointment was due to end was usual or normal, or would there be special reasons. Stanley denied there was any ulterior motive for the alteration of command of the squadron.[8]

When he arrived back in Britain, Tomkinson was surprised to learn of the intrigue to saddle him with the consequences of the mutiny and to save the faces of Their Lordships. It had begun as early as the previous October, with Dreyer acting as the prosecutor in his series of memos and comments on Invergordon.[9]

Although Kelly had taken good care not to apportion blame on Tomkinson in his report, many admirals, including Keyes, were surprised at Tomkinson's inactivity at Invergordon.

For five weeks the notorious and explosive Kelly Report had gone the rounds of the desks of the sea lords and their assistants and, on 1 January 1932, came the first hint of disciplinary action against Tomkinson when after a meeting it was minuted: 'The board is unanimously of the opinion that Admiral Tomkinson's handling of the situation calls for a censure.' The board's pronouncement of guilty was based on three of Kelly's points –

failure to appreciate the seriousness of the canteen meetings; failure to close the canteen; his decision to adhere to the order to send ships to sea on the Tuesday. And for good measure they threw in their own fourth – failure to address the men himself, although he must have realized that their grievances had considerable justification.

There was also the underscore that their conclusion was 'on the basis of Admiral Kelly's report, which definitely finds fault with the action which Admiral Tomkinson took'.[10]

The minute of their meeting added that an unnamed member had raised the question of whether it was fair to take censure action against Tomkinson when 'the men, whose behaviour was infinitely worse, were allowed to go unpunished'.

As if to indicate that they were playing fair, the minute also stipulated that it was preferable to appoint Tomkinson as Rear-Admiral of the Battle Cruiser Squadron for another six months because 'considerably less stigma' would attach to him than if he were removed immediately. They considered that 'being relieved only six months short of his full two years would be unlikely to cause public comment of any sort outside the service'.[11]

Again, the sea lords were wrong and reckoned without Tomkinson's many allies, including the redoubtable Keyes.

Field had acquired unanimous approval for these decisions and with such support it was hardly necessary for him to obtain endorsement from more senior admirals, yet five days later he was chairman at a rare meeting of the navy's 'elder statesmen', the three commanders-in-chief of the home bases – Brand (Plymouth), Tyrwhitt (The Nore) and Waistell (Portsmouth), all personal friends of Tomkinson.

Every aspect of the mutiny was discussed and the general consensus of opinion was that the Admiralty was to blame by not being firmer with the Government when the pay cuts were increased. They all condemned Tomkinson's handling of the mutiny, although Field did not reveal that two messages of approval – one from him – had originally been sent.

Brand, the only admiral to have prepared for the meeting with a written statement, said: 'I feel that Tomkinson allowed matters to drift . . . that he should have asked permission to resign his command on the arrival of the Atlantic Fleet at home ports; whether he acted rightly, or wrongly at Invergordon, I fail to understand how any officer in command of a fleet could have remained in command after what had happened.'[12]

The blunter Tyrwhitt had always thought that Tomkinson had 'made a balls of it through sheer inactivity' and never altered his opinion.[13]

Tomkinson's old colleagues were fading fast, for all three agreed that he should be axed, but then came the realization that as he was the representative of the board, the sea lords should also be sacked. To prevent this happening, the minutes contained the phrase 'Rear-Admiral Tomkinson should be relieved, but only if it is possible to issue an Admiralty statement sharing the blame.'[14]

Later Tyrwhitt wrote to Kelly: 'A good drop of blood was spilt. . . . It is quite true they [Admiralty] were let down by the Government and as I told him [Field] if he had only told the navy exactly what had happened he would have cleared his yardarm, more or less. . . . We decided that the navy should be told what happened. I have not seen the work of art yet, but an apology will, I understand, be included.'[15]

He never did see the 'work of art', for it never materialized for full circulation.[16]

The board considered the recommendation linking Tomkinson with an Admiralty statement sharing the blame – and ignored it. Three weeks later Kelly was informed by the board they could not concur with his opinion that the outbreak was inevitable owing to circumstances and causes beyond the control of Tomkinson. They still maintained that the course of events might have been different if, after the receipt of the 3 September telegram, action had been taken in the fleet, completely ignoring the fact that Tomkinson did not see it until four days later. Their letter to Kelly went on:

Even more regrettable was the omission by the senior officer [Tomkinson] to take any decided action on 13 and 14 September, when dissatisfaction had begun to show itself among the men, and after making every allowance for the difficult and unusual circumstances in which the senior officer was placed, Their Lordships are unable to relieve him of responsibility for a serious error in judgement . . . in allowing matters to drift during that critical period.[17]

Tomkinson mulled over these lately discovered revelations and on 13 March from the *Hood*, which was being repaired at Portsmouth, he sent a letter of protest to the Admiralty, via Kelly. He concluded that it was obvious from the curtailment of his appointment that he was being punished for the mutiny, although he did not call it such, and then pointed out: 'There has been no inquiry, public or otherwise, into the Invergordon incidents and that in the absence of such inquiry and without evidence of those who were present and responsible for any course of action and who alone were in a position to judge whether the other measures were at any time advisable, or not, no correct, or fair, conclusion can be drawn.'[18] It must be stressed here that when Tomkinson referred to 'an inquiry' he meant a properly promulgated board of inquiry, or court martial, composed of several high-ranking officers. Kelly's inquiry had been a secret one-man investigation, although he had helpers.

The letter continued: 'I request therefore that Their Lordships may be asked to reconsider their censure of me and the curtailment of my appointment and that their decision may be communicated to me at as early a date as possible.'

But the Admiralty had no intention of relieving Tomkinson's state of mind with an early reply. The likeable, yet weak, Field who had his way smoothed to the top of the Admiralty by the anti-Keyes faction there, had little compassion for an admiral who was a friend of Keyes. Field was now sixty-one and suffering from a stomach ulcer,[19] which had haemorrhaged recently, and he had no taste for the feud that Keyes was about to embroil him in.

Field had already told Admiral Ernle Chatfield, his eventual successor as First Sea Lord: 'Tomkinson let down the side by not taking immediate action to stop agitation at the canteen and should be relieved of his command at once.'

Dreyer was still on a 'My Dear Tommy' level with Tomkinson, but behind his back had said: 'No-one has ever been better treated than he was.'

Kelly, who was on poor terms already with Field by virtue of his refusing to absolve the sea lords of any blame for the mutiny, worsened relations with his covering remarks on Tomkinson's protest letter. He reminded the board in contradictory style that his investigations were 'purposely carried out in such a matter as to be in no sense an inquiry' and that he had not investigated the conduct of Tomkinson. Then came this timely memory-jogger: 'Furthermore, as the First Lord of the Admiralty had already expressed in the House of Commons the full approval of this officer's [Tomkinson's] action and service, I could not but regard it as outside my province to investigate this particular respect of the case further than was necessary to gain a clear impression of all the happenings.'[20]

The Admiralty's ploy now was to let their recalcitrant, yet newly promoted, vice admiral cool down, but in the meantime Field, in an obsequious and hypocritical private letter to Kelly, maintained that the board could not change their decision, unless Tomkinson 'alters his attitude'. He stressed that the Admiralty had preserved a dignified silence and had accepted guilt as much as anyone to 'shield the officers of the Atlantic Fleet from any victimisation or blame'.[21]

Field did admit, however, that neither he, nor any of his colleagues, professed that they would 'have done any better than Tomkinson. It is just the bad luck of force of circumstances and the feeling that such wholesale refusal of duty was inconceivable that prevented drastic action being taken at once by him.'

The next move by Tomkinson was to ask his golfing friend Admiral Waistell, the Commander-in-Chief Portsmouth, for his opinion on the controversy. Waistell read the letter of censure and suggested that he had reasons for complaint, because 'having administered the censure, the Admiralty did not tell him of the grounds and evidence on which it was based'.[22] Poor Tomkinson unfortunately was unaware at that time that Waistell had endorsed the instrument of his sacking at the meeting of the 'elder statesmen'.

In the wings, however, Keyes, as loyal as ever to anyone who served with him, was huffing and puffing, although privately he could never understand why Tomkinson had not 'hauled down his flag immediately after Invergordon'. In the middle of Tomkinson's letter campaign against the Admiralty Keyes wrote to him:

It is an absolute outrage. How Field can have the face to make scapegoats – and in such a cruel way beats me. Interpreting the gutless spirit of his board Austen Chamberlain said let 'bygones be bygones'. Moreover, he praised you in the House. I would go to him and Baldwin, if I were you. You know very well that I would not have hesitated to supersede you if I had thought it in the best interests of the service – and I do think – and feel very strongly that the ships that mutinied ought not to have gone to sea again manned by the mutineers under the officers who had been unable to maintain discipline – whether they were initially to blame or not. . . . They [the Admiralty] have declared in the House that no man has been punished for the mutiny – that the SNLRs [services no longer required men] were for misconduct after. How they dare have one reading of AC's [Chamberlain] undertaking for the men and another for you – or to take action against you NOW – having sent you on a cruise with the squadron that mutinied – which I thought all wrong.

What do they know now that they didn't know then? I don't see how they can any longer avoid a real inquiry – and I expect your treatment will bring it to a head. I have a real heartache for you, my dear Tommy. You were put by fate into a cruel position at Invergordon – and I thought you, the senior officers, captains and others would have to pay for it – including, of course, the whole board. Field seems to have thrown one after another to the wolves.[23]

It was typical of the Keyes spirit that he should write these lines of support for his friend at a time when his wife was seriously ill with acute colitis and when he was 'horribly frightened' about her condition.

Another friend, Admiral Dudley Pound, due to take over as Second Sea Lord in charge of personnel, in place of Admiral Fuller, who had been sacked after Invergordon, was also offering advice. Back in Britain after being in the naval delegation to the League of Nations, Pound wrote to Tomkinson that the shortening of his appointment with the battle cruisers was a 'drastic step'.[24] The letter continued:

Whether for the good of the service it was necessary to sacrifice you or not, it seems to me that you have been asked to suffer too much and the board too little, unless some action regarding some of the members of the latter is contemplated, of which I have no knowledge. . . . Some people after your treatment might feel inclined to chuck the whole business, but I am sure with your determined and courageous outlook on life, you would never think of doing so. Whatever your fault may have been considered to be, you will have paid for it a hundred times by giving up the BCs [battle cruisers].

Unwisely, Pound concluded that Tomkinson's future career should not be affected and the 'same appointments which were open to you before should be open to you now'.

It is possible that he may have heard a rumour that Tomkinson intended to ask for a court martial, for three days later, although advising him not to quietly accept the censure, he suggested that Tomkinson should make it known he originally sought a trial, but his private feelings had given way to the 'good of the service'. This would make Tomkinson's position stronger with the board, he suggested. Mysteriously his last sentence directed: 'Stuff this advice in a waste paper basket.'[25] Tomkinson did no such thing and the letter remained in his private papers.

Keyes was pressing Tomkinson to let him take his complaint to friendly MPs, who would raise the issue in the Commons. But Tomkinson would not allow him to do it and instead went along with Pound's advice because this approach would not prejudice his chance of obtaining another appointment.

Six weeks went by and still he had not received a reply to his protest. On 25 April he wrote a reminder to the Admiralty that they had not answered; such was his anguish that he wrote '1922', instead of '1932' as the date.[26] This triggered the swiftest reply ever in his correspondence with Whitehall. Kelly forwarded the letter on the same day to the Admiralty, who immediately replied on the same day. This stated that the decision could not be altered and 'Their Lordships are of the opinion that it is in the best interests of the service that ships which were principally concerned in these incidents should be paid off as soon as conveniently possible and should make an entirely fresh start. In addition to this consideration the battle cruiser force has, by a recent decision, been reduced to two ships and Vice Admiral Tomkinson has also been promoted to higher flag rank.'[27]

The board repeated that after reading all the reports of the mutiny it had become evident that nothing was done to prevent further mass gatherings on shore, 'although it was known on the Sunday evening that there had been meetings at the canteen, which eventually, by their continuation on Monday, incited the men to refuse duty'.

Field did offer to see Tomkinson, but the vice admiral was now on an irretractable course and said conversely that an interview would 'serve no useful purpose', yet if the First Sea Lord sent for him, that 'would be a different thing'.

The Field–Dreyer alliance on the board considered that Tomkinson had not been strong enough and because of this there was a chance of more revolts. During April 1932, all commanding officers were informed that they were 'expected to put down any further disturbances . . . with a strong hand'.[28] Later there came the Admiralty's 'Notes on Dealing with Insubordination', which signified that although 'prompt action must be taken', it should be made clear to the men that complaints would be investigated and, if found genuine, remedied quickly. There were eight suggestions for ending massed disobedience. The last one was the use of force, which the board declared innocuously must 'depend on circumstances'. It ended: 'Shooting to kill should only be resorted to as a last extremity.'[29] Tomkinson had considered using force, but not the possibility of killing.

He next attempted Pound's 'inquiry blackmail'. On 2 May he wrote to the Admiralty that their censure clearly indicated that they considered him guilty of a serious offence under the Naval Discipline Act. He warned that it had been his intention of applying for a court martial, if his request for withdrawal of the censure was not met, but he had changed his mind because the trial would damage the navy 'in the eyes of the public and the loss of prestige of the board of Admiralty'.[30]

Kelly, who was in correspondence with George V, must have intimated to Tomkinson the fact that the king did not want the mutiny to be exhumed. Now Tomkinson asked that it be placed on file in Admiralty records that he had been censured without an inquiry and without his being given an opportunity to answer any charge. Kelly tried in vain to persuade him to withdraw this last letter and reluctantly sent it on without comment. Tomkinson explained to his commander-in-chief that the only way he could have prevented the canteen meetings was to have stopped all leave on the Monday. 'I did consider doing this, but I am still convinced that it would have been a great mistake and am quite sure I should not have been backed by the Admiralty, had I done so,' he insisted.[31]

Keyes now became the rallying point for his cause and in a succession of letters gained support from powerful friends. Beatty,[32] Churchill and Lord Linlithgow, a former civil lord, promised their backing and maintained that the Admiralty, when threatened with an inquiry, would cave in and reinstate Tomkinson. William Boyle,[33] now head of the Royal Naval College, and Austen Chamberlain joined the sympathizers, but Baldwin,[34] a friend of the Tomkinson family, who was to become premier again within three years, chose to stand aside.

146

By now Keyes was causing trouble for the Admiralty and he was confusing the Tomkinson issue with his own pressure to be appointed First Sea Lord in place of Field. He ranted to Baldwin that Madden, when First Sea Lord, had sidetracked him and all the 'war-tried proved leaders', like Tyrwhitt, Kelly, Boyle and Meade, by filling the principal appointments at the Admiralty with his own friends – Field, Fuller, Hodges, Dreyer and Im Thurn.[35] Later he was able to make a personal appeal on Tomkinson's behalf in a thirty minute chat with Baldwin, who was 'intensely interested, but it was obvious he does not mean to get mixed up in it'.[36]

Boyle, Tomkinson's mutual friend, had thought it through more calmly than Keyes, who was about to discuss the case with Sir Bolton Eyres-Monsell, the First Lord. He attempted to rein in Keyes by warning: 'Your object being to get a measure of justice for Tomkinson, I suggest that . . . you limit yourself to his case. If you introduce other matters, particularly your own affairs, it would, in my opinion, prejudice Tomkinson and give them an excuse for shelving his case, hinting or saying that you were using it as a smokescreen under which to reopen a question already settled against you.'[37]

In lucid language Keyes passed on to Tomkinson a report of his meeting with Eyres-Monsell, who both of them loathed and regarded as a Baldwin toady. Eyres-Monsell had been a commander, but, after marrying a wealthy woman, had left the navy. Tomkinson always maintained that he was not an experienced officer and did not know the service. 'He took all he could out of it for his education, then left to make his name as a politician. It was her wealth and not his brains.'[38]

Keyes reported: 'He [Eyres-Monsell] said everybody inside the service and out had demanded your head on a charger – a most insistent demand – I said I thought a much more insistent one was that the board who had let you, poor devil, and the navy down so disastrously should be swept away and how could he expect to restore contentment and trust in the administration of the service. . . . He is a rabbit and completely under Field's thumb.'

Keyes thought he showed Eyres-Monsell to be a 'b—y liar'. 'Monsell had no idea he [Field] wrote to you, I am sure; he told me the only communication commending you was a telegram before you got back to Portsmouth – that the commendation you received in the House was given before they knew the facts – that directly they knew them they decided to relieve you – that is a lie of course – but they will stick to it.'[39]

With his fuses lit, Keyes now asked Tomkinson to 'provide me with the ammunition' – Field's private letter of congratulations, and a full account of the mutiny, with copies of letters and signals.

The crusading Keyes, loving these exchanges before the big battle ahead, now flushed out Pound, Tomkinson's alleged friend and his own protégé. He 'sent' for him and asked why he had given the bad advice of not actually asking for a court martial, because he must have known that once Tomkinson accepted the censure he would be 'broken forever', with no chance of further appointments. 'He [Pound] admitted this and said, hard luck though it was, you had failed and must be a victim,' Keyes wrote. 'My dear Tommy, you'll get no help from him or Joe Kelly. DP [Pound] has got the Geneva [League of Nations] bug well under his skin and the Admiralty outlook of hushing things up –

regardless of justice and fairness. This may seem severe, but it is true and gave me a sick feeling.'[40]

Tomkinson was also sickened by Pound 'making a most outrageous statement behind one's back without knowing the full facts' and was determined to have it out with him,[41] but not before he posted a prickly reminder on 9 June to the Admiralty that they had not replied to his request for the censure to be placed on record.[42]

There is little doubt that his case would have been treated more reasonably and possibly more leniently if he had not been linked with Keyes, whose opinions, not just on Tomkinson but also about the sea lords, were being broadcast loudly and clearly in many quarters and bringing contempt to the Admiralty. His rumbustious lobbying for support among officers and MPs caused Eyres-Monsell to complain to Beatty that Keyes was making it 'more difficult for them to administer the navy'. Keyes' allegations against Field were singled out as undermining discipline.[43]

Beatty warned Keyes that it was a very serious charge and that he must be careful with his accusations. 'I think before you take any further action, it would be as well if you would discuss it with me,' he admonished. 'I still support you, when and where I can, if I think there is sufficient cause and you can produce the necessary material. But it has to be done in the right way and not lay oneself open to the attack of being disloyal to the administration, no matter how much one may dislike it.'[44]

Keyes would not be silenced and, despite this advice, he wrote another tactless letter to Eyres-Monsell, repeating much of the Tomkinson controversy. He also denied the 'monstrous charge' that he was undermining the navy in his efforts to become First Sea Lord, and hinted that he would try another tack – by becoming an MP.[45] It was no coincidence that soon after this threatening missive had been received the Admiralty broke their silence again and told Tomkinson there was nothing to add to their previous letters, but the whole correspondence would be placed 'on permanent record' as he had requested.[46]

It was still not explained to him why the Admiralty had waited five months to censure him, and proved to him that they were not sure of themselves, for even after agreeing about it on 1 January, a month went by before they moved against him. Not until that spring was Keyes able to find out that another naval hero, Captain Gordon Campbell, who won the Victoria Cross for Q-ship actions in the First World War, had spurred the Admiralty into action.

At the end of January, when Tomkinson's promotion had been gazetted, Campbell and several other naval MPs in the Commons met to find a way of raising the whole question of the mutiny and the possibility of a public inquiry. Afterwards Campbell met Eyres-Monsell in the lobby and said he would ask the following questions:

1. Did Tomkinson command the fleet when it mutinied?
2. Had Tomkinson been promoted?
3. Had Tomkinson been reappointed?

When he received answers to them Campbell threatened to ask this supplementary: 'Was it the policy of the Admiralty to reward officers who command fleets that mutiny?'[47]

Eyres-Monsell had 'rushed off in a temper' and it was alleged that on that very evening, Rear-Admiral Sir William James was contacted and invited to succeed Tomkinson.[48]

Campbell's questions were never asked, however, and afterwards he was blamed for inspiring Tomkinson's relief. Meanwhile Eyres-Monsell had asked Campbell to write him a 'personal letter' on his thoughts about Invergordon. One paragraph stated that the senior officer of the Atlantic Fleet was 'so little known and was held in such small respect by the personnel that he carried no personal influence and had not confidence enough to go onboard the ships of the squadron'.[49]

It became a double irritant to Tomkinson when he heard of this. He was never a man to harbour a grudge, but in his current state of mind his anxieties overflowed into a caustic letter he wrote to Campbell on 6 July, when the *Hood* was in Guernsey. Although he did not think of himself as a 'popularity Jack', with the lower deck, he wrote, he doubted whether many officers had more friends amongst ratings than he. For several years he was the chairman of welfare conferences, the closest ratings could get to forming a trade union. He raged that Campbell had been 'mean and backhanded to attack an individual officer's reputation, without letting him know anything about it'.[50]

Campbell appeared innocent of these charges, however, for he was in sympathy, and in a reply registered his 'complete disgust' that Tomkinson was relieved while the sea lords retained their seats, or other appointments. He stressed that it was a private letter and should never have been 'leaked'.[51]

Eighteen days before he was due to haul down his flag as Rear-Admiral of the Battle Cruiser Squadron, Tomkinson had his first confrontation with Field at the Old Admiralty Building in Whitehall since the previous September. He began the interview by asking how could Field reconcile his personal letter of congratulations and Chamberlain's tribute in the Commons to his subsequent agreement to censure and virtual dismissal. Field refused to be drawn and did not answer.[52]

Tomkinson pressed on and asked what was the 'serious error of judgement' he was alleged to have committed and how was it considered that further ratings' meetings on shore could have been prevented without stopping leave. Field at last intervened to say that shore leave should have been cancelled on the Monday. Tomkinson replied: 'I had weighed this carefully at the time and with senior officers on the spot and we considered it to be quite out of the question. It would have precipitated the mutiny and might have made it worse in execution.'

He asked whether the board would have backed him in this decision; again Field did not reply. Tomkinson claimed that in the absence of an inquiry it was 'entirely unjust to make a scapegoat out of me'. Field argued that the board had not taken any disciplinary action against him and the interview ended with Tomkinson pointing out that although this might be the ruling of the Naval Law branch, in the eyes of the service to 'censure me and to suspend me in my command is very decidedly disciplinary action'.[53]

On 15 August at Portsmouth his flag was lowered in the *Hood* to mark the end of a disastrous appointment. Tomkinson handed over to Rear-Admiral James, who soon found the condition of the ship 'far from satisfactory' in which he had never encountered 'a more unhappy party'. He claimed that Tomkinson and Captain Patterson had been at dag-gers drawn' and that Commander McCrum had 'lost all interest through being hunted by Tomkinson, whose habit was to find fault with everything'.[54] This bore out Tomkinson's view that the *Hood* should have been recommissioned immediately after the mutiny.

19
LAST CONFRONTATIONS

With no appointment offered him, Tomkinson escaped from the intrigues of command to his home at Mansfield House, Iver Heath, Buckinghamshire, still believing he would be found another job by Pound, now Second Sea Lord in charge of personnel.

It was known that Field would retire as First Sea Lord by the New Year and there would be a new board, with Chatfield at the head. After a chat with Keyes, Tomkinson, who appeared not to be downhearted, or vindictive and was bearing up well under the strain, agreed it would be preferable to rely on a fresh board for fair play.

But, inadvertently, Keyes surrendered the initiative to the 'enemy'. He had refused to withdraw his charges of favouritism by Madden and Field, but in an effort to quell animosity with Eyres-Monsell promised him: 'After my talk with Tomkinson I am content, as he is, to leave his future in the hands of Chatfield and your new board.'[1]

As a compromise seemed to be in sight, Eyres-Monsell agreed to see Tomkinson on 29 September, 1932. Tomkinson found the First Lord attentive and sympathetic, but could force few comments from him or persuade him to ask questions. Far from being apologetic for the mutiny, Tomkinson emphasized: 'I had done and left undone nothing what I regretted and if I were placed in a similar position tomorrow I would act in a similar manner.'[2]

Because Eyres-Monsell was not in office until after the mutiny, Tomkinson's only grievance with him could be: 'Why did the Admiralty wait five months to censure me, when they had no further reliable information than was available a few days after the mutiny.' The First Lord insisted that it was to avoid certain questions – obviously by Campbell – being asked in the Commons, which would have been 'very awkward' for him – implying that it was done in Tomkinson's interest. 'That's absurd,' Tomkinson replied. 'There was no question that could be asked that I should mind in the least.'

After the meeting, Tomkinson was aware that time was no longer on his side, although he believed that after six months on the sidelines he was certain to be employed again. Behind the scenes Eyres-Monsell would not take on the onus of deciding whether the Admiralty had future plans for him. Not until February 1933 – more than two years after the mutiny – was Tomkinson asked to report to Chatfield, who had only been in office for a month as First Sea Lord.[3]

Chatfield went straight to the point and told Tomkinson the sea lords were unanimous he should not be offered another position because of his 'inaction' on the Tuesday and Wednesday when the mutiny had broken out.

Tomkinson refused to accept this and said that Field had maintained he should have stopped leave on the Monday. He asked whether Chatfield agreed with this opinion and received a 'no' for the first time from a senior officer. So what would Chatfield have attempted in similar circumstances? he asked. The new First Sea Lord replied that he would have got together the officers and petty officers in the flagship and driven the mutineers below from the forecastle, but without using force.

Tomkinson commented later: 'This was an astounding suggestion to make . . . and only shows how entirely he has misjudged the situation as it was and how great a mistake was made by the board of Admiralty in not instituting an immediate inquiry.'[4]

Another month later he requested at last a court martial. His defence was that he had been censured and superseded in command and now it appeared that he was to suffer again at the hands of the reconstituted board. Therefore, he requested a thorough and impartial inquiry into circumstances leading up to the mutiny and into the conduct of officers of the Atlantic Fleet during that period.

With this last attempt to obtain justice he realized that he had few friends at the Admiralty and he said as much to Pound, who, feeling hurt because Tomkinson was 'seeing red and trying to hit out at anybody', tried to ameliorate by claiming he did not have the full knowledge of the mutiny before writing previous letters and giving advice.[5]

'I have never taken the line, neither have I suggested it to you at any time, neither I hope have I ever given the impression that I agreed with what you did at Invergordon,' he wrote. He agreed that the criticism of the shore patrols was not justified and that the reasons for the censure were 'most unfortunate'.

Nevertheless, Pound stressed:

I have never been able to understand you bringing the ships outside into harbour – when one has got the plague, one isolates it. But what has always seemed to me incomprehensible was that when faced by active mutiny you took no drastic steps to deal with it. If anyone else had been there and done nothing I should have said: 'I wish to God Wilfred had been there.' . . . Had you taken drastic action and succeeded, the service and all it could give was yours. Had you taken action and failed you would have had everyone's backing. But frankly the service has never understood the British navy mutinying and nothing being done to fight it.[6]

Only then did Tomkinson realize his cause was a lost one. Yet in a hopeless and uncharacteristically bad-tempered reply, he claimed: 'None of the facts have changed since April 1932 and any further information that was then available can only be hearsay.' It seemed obvious to him that if the ships outside had not been called in, mails would have been cut off and investigations could not have been made.

'Please don't imagine that I'm seeing red and wanting to hit out at anybody and everybody, as you put it,' he wrote. 'I hope I am able to keep my head whatever the circumstances. Your position, as you say, may be a damnable one, but what of mine? Would you like to exchange?'[7]

He did not get a reply. Most of his friends were entering into the shadows of doubt now.

Pound, eventually to be First Sea Lord during the Second World War, was to become renowned as a 'waverer'. Although Kelly was inclined to be over critical or over enthusiastic about his colleagues, he described Pound as being 'not quite a gentleman – a disastrous lacuna in a First Sea Lord'. He also maintained he was too pigheaded and unwilling to recognize that there was 'another side to a question'.[8] Pound suffered from dangerously high blood pressure and was eventually to die from a tumour of the brain. Although no one knew when the tumour developed, he was not considered to be fully fit for many years, for he also suffered from a long-standing osteo-arthritis of the left hip and shortening of the left thigh, a painful condition which prevented comfortable sleep and rest.[9] He was a diversely different personality to Tomkinson, so it was odd they had set up a friendship. He had few intellectual interests or social graces, although his recreations of fishing and shooting were similar to those of the man he had suddenly turned against. Tomkinson had a sense of humour; Pound had not.

With Tomkinson now on half pay and imminently due for retirement, the campaign for reinstatement entered the Parliamentary lists. In January 1934, Keyes surprisingly agreed to stand as the Conservative candidate in a by-election for Portsmouth North. He was reticent to accept because his stutter precluded him from making an acceptable public speech, but he realized that this new forum would be an outlet for criticism of the Admiralty.

Like most things he touched, the campaign was a success and he was returned to Parliament with a substantial majority over his opponent, a Socialist teacher. Keyes had vowed to assist Tomkinson and it took a great deal of moral courage on his part to resurrect the mutiny, which most senior officers were only too glad to bury and forget.

As the months went on, it was obvious that neither Eyres-Monsell nor Chatfield would help Tomkinson, who was rapidly becoming a forgotten cause. In a heavily critical letter of the new board to Eyres-Monsell, Keyes raked over the controversy again and warned that he was about to exhume the way his friend had been treated. His final paragraph almost pleaded: 'In the event of it being considered impossible to hold an inquiry now, you could surely find some good employment for Tomkinson, who is the only officer, or man, against whom disciplinary action has been taken.'[10]

But Tomkinson and Keyes had played into Eyres-Monsell's hands earlier when they had assured him they would be willing to adhere to decisions of the new board. Eyres-Monsell was quick to remind Keyes of this and that there was no point in Keyes having a meeting, either with himself or Baldwin, who was virtually sharing the premiership with Ramsay MacDonald.[11] But Keyes persisted and argued:

An accused has certain rights and privileges; these have not been accorded to Tomkinson and it is absurd to talk of a careful and exhaustive inquiry. I do regret, however, that Tomkinson and I agreed to leave his naval future to Chatfield and the new sea lords since I am not free to question their decision, for I ought to have realised that it was too much to expect them to reverse the policy they inherited, or to hold an inquiry which could only have condemned their predecessors and officials still serving in the Admiralty. Unfortunately Tomkinson put too much faith in his friend Pound, but for whose ill-considered advice the matter would have been settled long before Chatfield took office.[12]

Tomkinson was prepared to accept that he would not obtain a further naval appointment, but he did not wish to be under any obligation to Eyres-Monsell, or Baldwin, for civil employment. All he desired was to have his name cleared and the Admiralty to withdraw their censure, so that he could remain on the active list until he was promoted to admiral, a rank he would have been certain to reach but for the mutiny. Keyes put these wishes to Eyres-Monsell,[13] only to receive what he described as an 'intolerably insolent' reply.[1] The First Lord charged back with:

> You are under a great misapprehension if you suppose the board are not prepared, if necessary, to state plainly in public the reasons for their decisions in regard to Vice Admiral Tomkinson. They are fully prepared to do so and therefore any idea of striking a bargain on the assumption that they are afraid of publicity had better be given up at once and I am surprised that it was put forward.
>
> I deprecate the action which you propose [in the Commons] to take, solely because I am convinced that it cannot benefit Vice Admiral Tomkinson in any way and that the effect of reminding the navy and the public about Invergordon will be harmful both in and to the service.

He added that it proved Keyes was acting in consultation with Tomkinson, who 'knows the standard of loyalty which he himself has expected and received when he has been in a position of authority'.[15]

A furious Keyes could only reply in these few words: 'It is clearly impossible for me to have any further communication with you . . . and I only write to give you notice that the Speaker has promised to allow me to raise the matter on Tuesday [31 July] and I will do so.'[16]

Eyres-Monsell was worried by the Keyes threat becoming reality and persuaded Chatfield to bring his authority to bear. 'I am very sorry you have made this decision, which to me is putting Tomkinson's grievance too high,' he told Keyes. 'I do not see it is defensible for him to put up a Member of Parliament to fight the Admiralty in the Commons. If other officers did that where would discipline be?'[17]

But Tomkinson had never sought Keyes' aid as an MP and had protested to his friend about his efforts to obtain further employment for him.[18] Nevertheless, Keyes had set the stage for his grand parliamentary *coup de grâce* and no one could stop him going ahead with it.

He was never a great political orator because of that stutter and hesitancy, which had remained with him since boyhood. He was also a slow thinker in debates and allowed political opponents to take the initiative; it therefore took a great deal of courage from him to get on his feet and make the longest speech so far of his political career in the Commons on 31 July 1934. It was now two years and nine months since Invergordon; few naval officers wished to be reminded of it, fewer MPs were interested.

Keyes chose his words very carefully and not once during his fifteen minute speech[19] did he use the word 'mutiny'. Instead he substituted 'disturbance', 'disaffection' or 'outbreak'. Having underlined that it was with great reluctance that he brought up the subject, he insisted it was to call attention to the grave injustice done to Tomkinson.

After recapitulating the events of the 'disturbance', he compared it with the Spithead mutiny of 1797, when in similar circumstances, Lord Bridport had assumed command of the fleet, owing to the failing health of Lord Howe, and had sent his chief of staff to the Admiralty for help and, in response to his request, three members of the board had investigated on the spot. The parallel suited Tomkinson's case, for he had made a similar request and not been granted it. Keyes went on to paraphrase the words of the current day's board: 'Lord Howe had warned the Admiralty that the men had intolerable and legitimate grievances but the board of Admiralty had allowed matters to drift.'

Keyes argued that in 'these days of quick transport it would have been quite possible for, say the First Sea Lord . . . or other members of the board . . . to have flown to Invergordon.'

He reminded the House that members of the Admiralty had approved Tomkinson's action by signal and had praised him the day after the mutiny ended, while Austen Chamberlain had promised that no one would be penalized; Field had also personally commended Tomkinson by letter. He stimulated memories by describing how Tomkinson had been superseded, having left England without being given a 'hint of any sort that his conduct of the affair at Invergordon had anything but the full approval of the board of Admiralty'.

He maintained that it was not too late to hold a judicial inquiry at which Tomkinson could defend himself; failing this it would be only fair to withdraw the censure and allow him to remain on the active list until he attained the rank of full admiral.

Commander Arthur Marsden, who represented North Battersea and who had commanded the destroyer *Ardent* at the Battle of Jutland, at first supported Keyes in the retelling of the mutiny and the injustice to Tomkinson but at the end of his speech he came to the rescue of the Admiralty with: 'Now that the gallant Admiral of the Fleet has ventilated the case in the House and brought forward the facts in a manner that they have never been brought forward before and the House realises that whatever Admiral Tomkinson may have committed as an error of judgment, at least he behaved through as an officer and a gentleman. If the House is of that opinion and this case having been ventilated, it might be as well now to let the matter rest where it is.'[20]

Members took his advice, for no one else thought it worthwhile catching the Speaker's eye. Eyres-Monsell, however, leaped up in defence of the Admiralty with the opening shot that Keyes had instituted the debate to criticize the board. He denied that the

Admiralty signal had approved all Tomkinson's actions, but insisted that all it endorsed was the previous message. 'The reply which the Admiralty sent to that message, 802, which everybody in the navy knows means the specific information contained in the telegram was "Your 802 received. Their Lordships entirely approve of the action you have taken." ' He also insisted that at the time of the original Parliamentary debate there was almost a complete lack of information about what had occurred at Invergordon.

To Keyes it was a classic case of ambiguous hair-splitting.

Eyres-Monsell denied – and lied – about knowledge of Field's private letter of praise to Tomkinson and then to continue his argument in double standards, quoted Keyes' private letter to himself, which stated Tomkinson was content to leave his future in the hands of Chatfield and the new board.

Then for the first time he quoted an Admiralty minute about Tomkinson's super-session, which stated: 'It is in the best interests of the service that ships which were concerned in these incidents should be paid off as soon as conveniently possible and should make an entirely fresh start. For the same reason Their Lordships decided that it would not be expedient for the flag officer who was in command when these incidents occurred to remain in the same appointment for a protracted period.'

He also disclosed that he had conducted his own inquiry with officers and civilian advisers and on their advice had approved the letter of censure. His last official words on the matter were:

An inquiry by the Sea Lords of the Admiralty is the highest authority that you can get. It is the supreme court of the navy and there is no appeal whatsoever from it. The new board, whom the honourable and gallant gentleman trusted so much, upheld the decision. I put it to the House that I am bound to accept these decisions and I think the House will agree with me that these questions of employment must be left to the responsible and serving members of the board, who alone are in possession of the facts.[21]

Tomkinson had lost, but Keyes would not be deterred and consulted Churchill, who was 'very pleased with my effort – said he had heard from two or three who were there that I displayed great Parliamentary agility'.[22]

Churchill advised him that the best way to deal with Eyres-Monsell's 'misleading and unsatisfactory reply' was to raise Tomkinson's case again in the next session of Parliament after the summer recess. Keyes wrote to his friend: 'I am going to have a blazing speech absolutely on the tip of my tongue. . . . There is no such thing as a forlorn hope, if one believes in the Almighty – knows one's cause is just and has the guts to fight.'[23]

Keyes was rattling too many naval skeletons, however. Two former commanders-in-chief thought he had gone far enough. 'I admire your courage in tackling the House on the question,' Brand wrote, 'but I hope you will not mind an old friend saying that he is sorry you brought it all up again, as I believe it may cause a certain amount of restlessness in the navy and a possible lack of confidence in the present board of Admiralty, which is the last thing one wants.'[24]

156

In a milder voice, Waistell said that Keyes 'had to' raise the question of Tomkinson's treatment, which put the 'case clearly before navy and public', but stressed the effort was 'foredoomed to failure'.[25]

Tomkinson was deeply dismayed, yet showed little outward anxiety to his family, and throughout that summer enjoyed the company of Joan and his daughters. To them 'daddy was just home on leave'.[26] The fact that he was out of a job was never recognized. For many hours he meditated on the Hansard report of Eyres-Monsell's speech and decided to seek one more interview with him, but this time he did not ask Keyes for any advice.

Throughout their meeting at the Admiralty on 26 September 1934 Eyres-Monsell was clearly embarrassed and uncomfortable and objected to many of Tomkinson's outspoken remarks.[27] The discussion opened with Tomkinson complaining that some of the statements made about him in the Commons were 'very unfair' and he wished to tell Eyres-Monsell why they were. The First Lord refused to debate the subject, but when Tomkinson argued that allegations had been made about him to which he could not reply, Eyres-Monsell agreed to listen to the criticism.

The touchy subject of Field's letter of commendation was raised, with Tomkinson reminding him that he had told him of it and the contents a year earlier. Eyres-Monsell remained silent.

Turning to the excuse that he had lost command of the Battle Cruiser Squadron before the end of his appointment because he had been promoted to vice admiral, Tomkinson pointed out that Admiral James, his successor, had been allowed to stay for the full two years, even though during the last eleven months he, too, was a vice admiral. Eyres-Monsell remained silent.

Of his censure, Tomkinson reminded him that it was contingent on action being taken against the sea lords. Eyres-Monsell still remained silent.

'What is meant when you say that an exhaustive inquiry was made by naval members of the board?' Tomkinson queried. 'As far as I know, and I have asked many senior officers also, no witnesses were examined. If this is not correct and witnesses were examined, then I should have been given an opportunity to be present, in accordance with the usual custom. Were any witnesses examined?' Eyres-Monsell remained his silent, stoic self.

When Tomkinson had finished his questioning, Eyres-Monsell condescended to speak and then only to say that Keyes had taken the matter to the Commons and out of the hands of the Admiralty, who could take no further steps.

'But they could withdraw the letter of censure,' Tomkinson insisted.

'I am advised by the sea lords that this should stand,' Eyres-Monsell replied.

'But on what grounds?' Tomkinson wanted to know.

The First Lord retreated into silence again.

In the next session of Parliament Keyes began to warm to the cause again and told Baldwin that he had better instruct Eyres-Monsell to reconsider Tomkinson's complaints, or he would bring it all out again in the Commons.[28] The next day in the lobby Eyres-Monsell spoke 'fearfully friendly' to him, while Churchill told him he could not carry the war into private life, and would get what he wanted by personal contact. Keyes appeared to have taken this advice, for instead of 'cutting' Eyres-Monsell socially he went to one of his parties.[29] Time and expediency cooled the atmosphere between the two. By the end of 1934 they were allies with Chatfield, who had been avoiding Keyes, in a campaign to shake off Air Ministry control from the Fleet Air Arm. The politicians had won.

For six months the issue was dormant, then just before the end of two years on half pay and with retirement from the navy looming, Tomkinson made his last attempt to clear his name. He sought an interview with Chatfield, who, unknown to him, was his real enemy. Chatfield wanted to know why another meeting was necessary.[30] Tomkinson replied that he had had a 'very unsatisfactory interview' with Eyres-Monsell the previous September. He continued: 'It may be a matter distasteful, or of small importance, to you, but you must realise I feel sure that it is one which has altered my career completely and in a very drastic way. . . . The unfair treatment that I have received at the hands of the present board has been ever present in my mind for nearly three years.'[31]

Chatfield gave the letter a great deal of thought, for it was a month before he replied, but there was no comfort in his words. 'It is no use coming to see me to reopen the case,' Tomkinson was told.[32]

Although small of stature, quietly spoken and seemingly timid because of his gentle manner, Chatfield had a will of steel and was one of the navy's toughest negotiators, not prone to compromise.[33] Later, when writing of Invergordon, he revealed: 'The First Lord asked me to go into some cases and give him my opinion of them; he would accept my judgement. It was a painful affair; one of the most prominent cases came before Parliament. I do not wish to dwell on this unpleasant labour, superimposed as it was on other pressing work; to do so would be unavailing now and would revive painful recollections. I gave my decisions and the First Lord and I stood by them.'[34]

It was the end of Tomkinson's paper and verbal war, and signified the termination of his peacetime naval career.

EPILOGUE

The months of fighting a losing battle to clear his name, and the years of Admiralty intriguing, left Tomkinson unmoved in his loyalty to the navy. He bore the service no malice and loved it to the end. On his retirement he decided to leave Mansfield House at Iver Heath and move deeper into the country. Just outside Devizes in Wiltshire he and Joan found Stert House, the home of their desires.

They had shifted house so many times since their marriage that they agreed never to move again. Tomkinson became a devoted countryman and home-lover. With the help of his loyal gardener, Mr Ellis, who worked for the family for more than forty years, he tended the four acres of garden and fruit trees; he maintained the tennis court on which he often played against his daughters; he cleaned the gutters of the house; rarely was he seen sitting in a chair. He went salmon fishing every year to Scotland; he shot grouse there; he was chairman of the Archers, the well-known wandering tennis club; he taught his youngest daughter Susan how to play golf – yet still found time to be the county director for the Red Cross.[1]

To his family and friends he rarely spoke about his naval deeds, or what happened at Invergordon.

The mutiny was forgotten by the Admiralty at the outbreak of the Second World War. All the captains who had been cast aside by it were brought out of retirement, and with them went Tomkinson, who at sixty-two was recalled with the rank of vice admiral and given the desk-bound job of Flag Officer, Bristol Channel, with living quarters at the Royal Hotel, Cardiff, and an office at the Imperial Buildings, Mount Stuart Square. He held the appointment for nearly three years, during which time he motored home to Stert House whenever possible. Then after a bout of pneumonia he was permanently retired.

Even then, when Keyes, who was appointed Director of Combined Operations by Churchill, heard of it, he wrote in high dudgeon to his friend: 'I can't bear you being relieved like that. I know how it was done – and how some like that fat ass Maxwell [Rear-Admiral Sir Wellwood George Maxwell] at Newcastle stay on. . . . Alexander and D.P. [Dudley Pound] must be got rid of.'[2]

In fact, Pound, whom Keyes referred to as Tomkinson's 'evil genie', was to become the only First Sea Lord to die in office, when on 21 October 1943, aged sixty-six, he did not recover from a brain tumour.

Field, Tomkinson's other two-faced accuser, survived two more years. Tomkinson, always prepared to forgive and forget, attended the memorial service, but Keyes, now a baron, did not go and he explained to his colleague: 'You are bigger minded than I am and I don't think if I had been fit enough to come up I would have gone . . . he used to run me down and I hated the way he allowed you to be made a scapegoat at Invergordon. I am being rather petty and I ought to be ashamed of myself. Well may he rest in peace. He was a charming fellow as I remember him best.'[3]

After writing this 'petty' tribute, Keyes was to live only another fifty-three days. His heart had been strained through lack of oxygen in a flight at high altitude over Leyte in the Pacific and doctors had advised him to slow down. He tried, but his condition did not improve. He died early on Boxing Day 1945.[4]

Tomkinson's children carried on his service tradition. Peter, a lieutenant-commander and destroyer captain, won the Distinguished Service Cross and bar; Joyce was a second officer in the Wrens; Susan, a flight officer in the Women's Auxiliary Air Force, was mentioned in dispatches and appeared in the propaganda film *Coastal Command*, while his eldest daughter, Betty, was regional administrator for the Women's Voluntary Service and was awarded the MBE and OBE. His son-in-law, Henry Hogan, Venetia's husband, commanded 501 Squadron in the Battle of Britain, in which he won the DFC.

Tomkinson was also delighted to hear that his nephew Christopher Tomkinson, an RNVR pilot, had won the DSC for leading an air attack on oil refineries on Sumatra, but was much saddened to learn later that he had been killed in a bombing raid on Sakishima.[5]

As the years went by Tomkinson became a forgotten naval curio. In spite of all the trauma, the heart-searching, the accusations and the unproved ignominy of Invergordon, he outlived most of the senior officers associated with it. Dreyer, whose ambitions of becoming First Sea Lord disintegrated when he was 'rusticated' to China as the commander-in-chief, was recalled as Commodore of Convoys during the war. Pound then brought him back to the Admiralty to organize the training of Merchant Navy crews in anti-aircraft gunnery. Pound was still unable to see Dreyer's limitations, and in July 1942 appointed him Chief of Naval Air Service, of which he had no experience or knowledge. He was quickly relieved and returned to his mien of Invergordon by writing long letters of self-justification to Pound. He died in 1950, aged seventy-eight.[6]

Neither of the rumbustious pair of Kelly and Astley-Rushton lived long enough for war service. Kelly, after being favoured by the king with promotion to Admiral of the Fleet in 1936, died just four months later. He was sixty-five. Astley-Rushton was also 'elevated' to Vice Admiral of the Reserve Fleet in HMS *Hawkins*. He was responsible for the correct anchoring and smart appearance of the fleet at the Silver Jubilee review by George V in 1935. Afterwards every flag officer in every fleet was decorated, except Astley-Rushton. He decided to protest to the Admiralty, and as soon as he was able to leave Portsmouth after the review he rushed to London by car to make his feelings known in Whitehall. He was motoring home when he was killed in a crash. He was fifty-six.

Hodges, whose illness propelled Tomkinson into national importance and blame at Invergordon, came out of retirement for three wartime appointments at Folkestone, Trinidad and Teignmouth. He died in 1951 aged seventy-seven.

160

Chatfield held the appointment of Minister for the Co-ordination of Defence when war began, with a seat in the Cabinet until 1940, when the office was abolished. His strong opinions that big naval guns held the key to winning the war at sea were soon submerged by U-boats and aircraft; when out of the political field he wrote two autobiographical books. As the years went on he was admired more for his integrity. As a retired adviser to the Admiralty, his death at the age of eighty-four in 1967 was considered a great loss.

Eyres-Monsell was created first Viscount Monsell of Evesham in 1935 and faded from politics. He became a regional commissioner for Civil Defence of the South Eastern Region from 1941 to 1945. He was eighty-eight when he died in 1969.

Colvin, Tomkinson's chief of staff at Invergordon, was knighted soon after the mutiny; he became president of the Royal Naval College at Greenwich, was first naval member for the Commonwealth Naval Board and from 1942 to 1944 was naval adviser to the High Commissioner for Australia. He died in 1954, aged seventy-two.

Tomkinson remained remarkably preserved both in body and mind. At eighty he was still playing tennis at Stert House, as meticulous as ever, always insisting to his children and grandchildren that he must measure the distance of the posts and the height of the net before the game could begin. Through Joan, who had a deep understanding of successive generations and the changing ways of the world, he was able to adjust to the liberated life of post-war Britain. They were fortunate that Betty lived at home to help them and latterly looked after both of them; this she managed to combine with being a magistrate, and a hospital and school governor.[7]

He accepted the divorce of his son, Peter, who to his delight had joined Tomkinsons Limited as director of sales and design and won for the company three industrial design awards for carpets in three successive years.[8]

He also followed with interest the athletic prowess of his grandson, Michael Hogan, which culminated with his running for Britain in the Olympic 400-metres hurdles in the 1964 Tokyo Games.[9]

By the time he was ninety he had twelve grandchildren – he organized the weddings of many of them – and five great-grandchildren; he had attended the funerals of four of his brothers and three of his sisters. Although he had outlived his hour, his time, his scapegoat disgrace, he still maintained an image of lofty disengagement, to justify his actions at Invergordon. Indeed, when he died at the age of ninety-four at Stert House on 7 October 1971, there were many people – several letters appeared in *The Times*[11] – who believed that he had been sacrificed on the Admiralty's high altar.

NOTES

Chapter One

1. Michael Tomkinson's *The Tomkinson Story* (privately published, 1985; copy at Kidderminster Library).
2. Ibid., pp. 1–3.
3. Ibid., p. 5.

Chapter Two

1. *The Times*, 30 Sept. 1891.
2. S.W.C. Pack, *Britannia at Dartmouth* (1966), pp. 75–96.
3. Ibid., pp. 75–6 and p. 99.
4. *The Times*, 30 Sept. 1891.
5. Pack, pp. 98–9.
6. Author's interview with Tomkinson's daughters.
7. E.A. Hughes, *The Royal Naval College, Dartmouth,* p. 17.
8. S. Roskill, *Admiral of the Fleet Earl Beatty* (1980), pp. 21–2.
9. Pack, pp. 76–9.
10. Roskill, pp. 21–2.
11. *The Tomkinson Story*, p. 3 and p. 5.
12. *Navy List*, 1895.
13. Ibid., 1897.
14. Ibid., 1898.
15. R. Keyes, *Adventures Ashore and Afloat* (1939), (hereinafter referred to as *Adventures*), p. 37.
16. J. Winton, *Jellicoe* (1981), p. 65.
17. Ibid.
18. R. Connor, *The Boxer Rebellion*, pp. 9–10.
19. Ibid.; C. Tan, *The Boxer Catastrophe* (1955), p. 32.
20. Tan, pp. 43–6; D. Bloodworth, *The Chinese Looking Glass* (1967), pp. 150–5.
21. Connor, p. 17.
22. *Adventures*, pp. 151–2.
23. Ibid.

24. Ibid., p. 159.
25. Ibid., p. 164.
26. Ibid., pp. 165–6.
27. Ibid., p. 167.
28. Ibid., pp. 168–73.
29. Ibid., pp. 177–82.
30. Kelly to Tomkinson, 28 Oct. 1899 (Tomkinson Papers/6, hereinafter referred to as TOMK)
31. *Adventures*, pp. 188–9.
32. Ibid., pp. 190–5.

Chapter Three
1. J. Winton, *Jellicoe*, p. 65.
2. *North China Herald*, 19 May 1900.
3. Winton, p. 66.
4. *Adventures*, p. 196.
5. Ibid., p. 198.
6. Winton, pp. 67–8.
7. *Adventures*, p. 200.
8. Winton, p. 83.
9. R. Connor, *The Boxer Rebellion*, p. 217.
10. *Adventures*, pp. 205–7.
11. Ibid., p. 208.
12. Winton, p. 83.
13. Connor, p. 107.
14. *Adventures*, pp. 211–13.
15. Ibid., pp. 209–10.
16. Ibid., p. 211.
17. Ibid., pp. 216–27.
18. Ibid., pp. 228–31.
19. Ibid., p. 268.
20. Ibid., pp. 288–95.
21. Ibid., pp. 310–15.

Chapter Four
1. M. Tomkinson, *The Tomkinson Story*.
2. Tomkinson to C.O., HMS *Hibernian*, 23 April 1910 (TOMK/1); *Navy Lists*, 1901–07.
3. *The Tomkinson Story*, p. 3.
4. Author's interview with Tomkinson's daughters.
5. Keyes to Tomkinson, 3 Oct. 1907 (TOMK/3).
6. Ibid., 1 Jan. 1908 (TOMK/3).
7. Ibid., 26 Nov. 1908 (TOMK/3).

8.   Ibid., 17 Nov. 1910 (TOMK/3).
9.   C. Aspinall-Oglander, *Roger Keyes* (1951), p. 83.
10. R. Hough, *The Great War at Sea* (1983), p. 177.
11. Keyes to Tomkinson, 17 Nov. 1910 (TOMK/3).
12. Ibid.
13. E. Gray, *Few Survived* (1986), pp. 69–71; Hough, p. 177.
14. P. Kemp, *Oxford Companion to the Sea* (1976), p. 840; Gray, p. 71; Aspinall-Oglander, pp. 83–4; Hough, p. 177.
15. A. Coles, *Three Before Breakfast* (1979), p. 10.
16. Aspinall-Oglander, p. 16.
17. Gray, pp. 69–71.
18. Aspinall-Oglander, pp. 86–7.
19. *Evening Standard*, 11 Feb. 1914.
20. Ibid.; *The Times*, 11 Feb. 1914.
21. Gray, pp. 69–71.
22. Ibid.
23. Aspinall-Oglander, p. 87.

Chapter Five

(All Tomkinson's war diary entries are contained in TOMK/2, (I), (II), (III), (IV) and (D.191). Many unnumbered pages are listed here under their respective dates.)
1.   TOMK/2 (I), 3 Aug. 1914, p. 1.
2.   Ibid.
3.   4 Aug., p. 2.
4.   R. Keyes, *Naval Memoirs* (hereinafter referred to as *Naval Memoirs*), Vol. I, 1910–15 (1933), pp. 60–1.
5.   Ibid., p. 62.
6.   C. Aspinall-Oglander, *Roger Keyes*, p. 92.
7.   *Naval Memoirs*, p. 67.
8.   Ibid.
9.   P. Halpern, *The Keyes Papers*, Vol. II, 1914–18 (1980), p. 2.
10. Aspinall-Oglander, p. 90.
11. A. Coles, *Three Before Breakfast*, p. 31.
12. 4 Aug., p. 2.
13. Aspinall-Oglander, p. 90.
14. 5 Aug., p. 2.
15. *The Keyes Papers*, p. 1.
16. *Naval Memoirs*, p. 68.
17. 5 and 6 Aug., p. 3; *Naval Memoirs*, pp. 68–70.
18. 13 Aug., p. 6.
19. 7 Aug., p. 4.
20. 10 Aug., pp. 5–6.
21. 9 Aug., p. 4.

22.   18 Aug., p. 8.
Chapter Six
1.   *Naval Memoirs*, Vol. I, p. 74.
2.   Ibid., pp. 75–8; S. Roskill, *Admiral of the Fleet Earl Beatty* (1980), p. 82.
3.   *Naval Memoirs*, pp. 82–3.
4.   Ibid., pp. 83–5.
5.   Ibid., pp. 86–7.
6.   David Woodward, in *Warships and Sea Battles of World War I*, ed. B. Fitzsimons (1973), p. 23.
7.   TOMK/2 (I), 28 Aug. 1914, pp. 7–11; C. Aspinall-Oglander, *Roger Keyes*, p. 95.
8.   *Naval Memoirs*, p. 87.
9.   Ibid., p. 88.
10.   Ibid., p. 87.
11.   28 Aug., p. 10.
12.   *Naval Memoirs*, p. 88.
13.   28 Aug., p. 10.
14.   *Naval Memoirs*, p. 89.
15.   Ibid., p. 90.
16.   28 Aug., p. 10.
17.   Ibid., p. 10a; *Naval Memoirs*, p. 92.
18.   *Warships and Sea Battles of World War I*, p. 25.
19.   Ibid., pp. 21–5.
20.   A.T. Patterson, *Tyrwhitt of the Harwich Force* (1973), p. 62; Roskill's *Beatty*, pp. 82–4.
21.   Keyes to Admiral Arthur Christian, 29 Aug., P. Halpern, *The Keyes Papers*, Vol. I, p. 4 (1972).

Chapter Seven
1.   *Naval Memoirs*, Vol. I, pp. 98–9.
2.   TOMK/2 (I), 10 Sept. 1914, p. 1a.
3.   C. Aspinall-Oglander, *Roger Keyes*, p. 97.
4.   22 Sept., unnumbered.
5.   *Naval Memoirs*, pp. 106–7.
6.   A. Coles, *Three Before Breakfast*, pp. 104–5.
7.   Ibid., p. 105.
8.   Aspinall-Oglander, p. 100.
9.   22 Sept., unnumbered.
10.   29 Sept., p. 17.
11.   24 Sept., p. 11.
12.   *Naval Memoirs*, p. 112.
13.   Ibid., pp. 113–14.
14.   8 Oct., p. 23.
15.   Keyes to his wife, 9 Oct. (*Keyes Papers,* No. 19, hereinafter referred to as *KP*).

16. 8 and 9 Oct., p. 23.
17. 14 Oct., pp. 28–9.
18. 16 Oct., p. 29.
19. 22 Oct., pp. 32–3; *Naval Memoirs*, pp. 119–20.
20. 24 and 25 Oct., pp. 34–5.
21. 3 Nov., pp. 40–1.
22. Aspinall-Oglander, pp. 103–4.
23. *Keyes Papers*, p. 4; *Naval Memoirs*, pp. 130–1.
24. 4 Nov., p. 41.
25. Keyes to wife, 4 Dec. 1914 (*KP* 30).
26. Ibid., 7 Dec. (*KP* 32).
27. TOMK/2 (I), 4 Dec., pp. 50–1.
28. *Keyes Papers,* Nos 23, 24, 26, 28; Aspinall-Oglander, p. 106.
29. *Naval Memoirs*, pp. 140–1.
30. Aspinall-Oglander, p. 107.
31. 15 Dec., pp. 53–5.
32. Ibid.
33. Aspinall-Oglander, p. 109.
34. Ibid.; *Naval Memoirs*, p. 145.
35. Ibid., p. 110; ibid, pp. 146–7.
36. *Naval Memoirs*, p. 142.
37. Ibid., p. 143.
38. Ibid., p. 145.
39. Ibid., p. 142.
40. W. Churchill, *The World in Crisis*, Vol. I. (1923), pp. 470–1.
41. Keyes to Chief of War Staff, 21 Dec. (*KP* 37); Keyes to wife, 17 Dec. (*KP* 35).

Chapter Eight
(TOMK/2 (II) references unnumbered, but dated.)
1. *Naval Memoirs*, Vol. I, p. 152.
2. Ibid.
3. A.T. Patterson, *Tyrwhitt of the Harwich Force* (1973), p. 95.
4. TOMK/2 (I), 24 Dec. 1914, pp. 58–61.
5. Ibid.; *Naval Memoirs*, p. 154.
6. *Naval Memoirs*, pp. 154–6.
7. Ibid., p. 157 and TOMK/2 (I) 24 Dec., pp. 58–61.
8. Ibid.
9. Patterson, pp. 96–7.
10. *Naval Memoirs*, p. 157.
11. Keyes to wife, 26 Dec. (*KP* 42).
12. 10 Jan. 1915, p. 64; *Naval Memoirs*, p. 159.
13. 20 Jan. – Tomkinson diary entries unnumbered from this section.

14. *Naval Memoirs*, pp. 160–2.
15. Paul Kennedy, in *Warships and Naval Battles of World War I*, ed. B. Fitzsimons, p. 44.
16. Ibid., p. 49; *Naval Memoirs*, p. 167.
17. Keyes to wife, 31 Jan. (*KP* 55).
18. 28 Jan.
19. 31 Jan.
20. 30 March.
21. 12 Feb.
22. *Naval Memoirs*, p. 167.
23. Fisher to Keyes, 8 Nov. 1914 (Fisher Papers).
24. Keyes to wife, 2 Feb. (*KP* 56).
25. Fisher to Beatty, 3 Feb. (Fisher Papers).
26. Fisher to Jellicoe, 4 April (Fisher Papers).
27. 3 Feb.
28. 9 Feb.
29. C. Aspinall-Oglander, *Roger Keyes*, pp. 112–13.
30. *Naval Memoirs*, p. 299.
31. 9 Feb.
32. 15 Feb.
33. 24 Feb.
34. 3 March.
35. 18 March.
36. 23 March; 6 and 13 May.
37. 30 March.
38. Keyes to Tomkinson, 15 April (TOMK/3).
39. 7 April.
40. 25 March.
41. 16 April.
42. 26 May.
43. 2 June.
44. 7 June.
45. 9 June.
46. 10 and 11 June.
47. 3 July.
48. TOMK/2 (II) – unnumbered, 18 Aug.; following references also unnumbered.
49. 22 Sept.
50. 12 Aug.
51. 11 Sept.
52. 25 Sept.
53. 26 Sept.

Chapter Nine
(Tomkinson Papers TOMK/2 (II) and (III), dates only because of unnumbered pages.)
1. H. Holger, *Luxury Fleet* (1980), p. 172.
2. B. Fitzsimons (ed.) *Warships and Sea Battles of World War I*, pp. 77–8.
3. Holger, p. 172.
4. *Warships and Sea Battles*, pp. 77–8.
5. Hall to Tomkinson, 5 Oct., 1915 (TOMK/3).
6. TOMK/2 (II), 7 Oct. 1915.
7. 6 Oct.
8. 11 Oct.
9. 10 Oct.
10. 11 Oct.
11. 28 Oct.
12. 18 Oct.
13. 29 Dec.
14. 3 Dec.
15. 12 Dec.
16. 25 Dec.
17. 12 May 1916.
18. 2 Jan. and 22 Aug. 1916.
19. 6 June and 19 Aug.
20. 12 Feb.
21. 29 Jan.
22. 31 Jan.
23. 2 and 26 March.
24. 28 Feb.
25. Ibid.
26. 25 May.
27. 3 March.
28. 11 and 18 April.
29. 19 and 20 Dec. 1915.
30. 18 Nov. and 3 Dec. 1915; 10, 11 March, and 11 Aug. 1916.
31. 23 Oct. and 18 Nov. 1915; 16 May, 12 and 23 June 1916.
32. 9 and 31 Aug. 1916.
33. TOMK/2 (II), 26 Nov. and 24 Dec. 1915; TOMK/2 (III), 15 June 1916.
34. TOMK/2 (III), 2 May.
35. Tomkinson to Keyes, 11 July 1916 (*KP* 161).
36. TOMK/2 (II), 5 Jan. 1916.
37. TOMK/2 (III), 21 May.
38. S. Roskill, *Admiral of the Fleet Earl Beatty* (1980), p. 145.
39. 2 June.
40. Tomkinson to Keyes, 11 July 1916 (*KP* 161).

41. 29 July.
42. 31 July.
43. TOMK/2 (IV), 16 and 31 Aug.
44. 23 Aug.

Chapter Ten
(All Tomkinson's diary entries in TOMK/2 (IV), unnumbered, but dated. TOMK/2 (D191) numbered and dated.)
1.   TOMK/2 (IV), 7 Nov. 1916.
2.   5 Dec.
3.   17 Dec.
4.   20 Dec.
5.   25 Dec.
6.   8 and 11 Jan. 1917.
7.   7, 9, 10, 13 March.
8.   23 Jan.
9.   Ibid.
10. Ibid.
11. 24 Jan.
12. 26 Jan.
13. 7 Feb. and 19 May.
14. TOMK/2 (D191), 19 June, pp. 4–5.
15. Ibid.
16. A. Coles, *Three Before Breakfast* (1979), pp. 180–1.
17. TOMK/2 (D191), 12 and 14 July, p. 11.
18. 17 July, p. 12.
19. *Naval Memoirs*, p. 105.
20. 7 Sept., p. 20; *Naval Memoirs*, p. 109.
21. Tyrwhitt to Tomkinson, 11 Sept. 1917, (TOMK/3).
22. TOMK/2 (D191), 25 Oct., p. 29.
23. 28 Oct., p. 30.
24. 18 Nov., p. 34.
25. 10 and 11 Nov., pp. 32–3.
26. J. Winton, *Jellicoe*, pp. 254–60; S. Roskill, *Admiral of the Fleet Earl Beatty*, pp. 229, 242.
27. TOMK/2 (D191), 1 Jan. 1918, p. 37.
28. *Naval Memoirs*, pp. 169–71.
29. TOMK/2 (D191), 14 Jan. pp. 37–8.
30. Keyes to Beatty, 18 Jan, 1918 (*KP* 211); H. Newbolt, *Naval Operations of the Great War*, Vol. 5 (1931), p. 208.
31. *Naval Memoirs*, pp. 158–61; B. Pitt, *Zeebrugge* (1958), pp. 18–19.

Chapter Eleven
(All Tomkinson's diary entries are under TOMK/2 (D191), pages numbered and dated.)
1. G. Bennett, *Naval Battles of the First World War* (1968), p. 269.
2. R. Hough, *The Great War at Sea*, 1914–18 (1983), pp. 314–15; & B. Pitt, *Zeebrugge*, pp. 23–4.
3. *Naval Memoirs*, p. 217.
4. P. Walker, *The Zeebrugge Raid* (1978), p. 24; Pitt, pp. 29–30.
5. Walker, p. 24.
6. TOMK/2 (D191), 26 Feb. 1918, p. 44.
7. 18 March, p. 46.
8. 5 April, p. 49.
9. 10 April, p. 49.
10. 22 April, p. 54.
11. 3 Feb., p. 40.
12. 18 March, p. 46.
13. 15 Feb., p. 42.
14. 11 April, p. 50.
15. Ibid.
16. *Naval Memoirs*, pp. 252–4.
17. 11 April, p. 50.
18. *Naval Memoirs*, p. 255.
19. Ibid., p. 256.
20. 21 April, p. 51.
21. Walker, p. 158.

Chapter Twelve
(Tomkinson diary references TOMK/2 (D191), numbered and dated.)
1. S. Roskill, *Admiral of the Fleet Earl Beatty*, pp. 255–6.
2. TOMK/2 (D191), 22 April, p. 51.
3. Ibid., p. 52.
4. C. Aspinall-Oglander, *Roger Keyes*, p. 238.
5. TOMK/2 (D191), 22 April, pp. 52–3.
6. *Naval Memoirs*, pp. 263–4.
7. TOMK/2 (D191), 22 April, p. 53.
8. *Naval Memoirs*, p. 265; P. Walker, *The Zeebrugge Raid*, p. 155.
9. TOMK/2 (D191), 22 April, p. 53.
10. *Naval Memoirs*, p. 265.
11. Ibid., pp. 277–8.
12. Ibid., p. 278.
13. Walker, pp. 35 and 158.
14. B. Pitt, *Zeebrugge*, p. 121.
15. TOMK/2 (D191), 22 April, p. 54; *Naval Memoirs*, p. 279; Pitt, p. 119.

16. Pitt, pp. 119–20.
17. *Naval Memoirs*, p. 279; Walker, p. 158.
18. TOMK/2 (D191), 22 April, pp. 53–4.
19. *Naval Memoirs*, pp. 279–80.
20. Ibid., pp. 280–1.
21. TOMK/2 (D191), 22 April, pp. 54–5.
22. Walker, p. 158.
23. *Naval Memoirs*, p. 290.
24. TOMK/2 (D191), 22 April, pp. 55–6.
25. Ibid., p. 56; Diary of Surgeon Probationer George Abercrombie in P. Liddle, *The Sailors War* (1985).
26. *Naval Memoirs*, p. 291.
27. TOMK/2 (D191), 22 April, p. 54.
28. Ibid., p. 56.
29. *Naval Memoirs*, p. 293.
30. Walker, p. 159.
31. TOMK/2 (D191), 22 April, pp. 56–7.
32. Ibid., p. 51.
33. Ibid., p. 57; *Naval Memoirs*, p. 295; *Pitt*, p. 136; Walker, p. 59.
34. *Naval Memoirs*, p. 298.
35. Walker, p. 143.
36. *Naval Memoirs*, p. 294.
37. Pitt, pp. 145–7.
38. Walker, p. 27.
39. *Naval Memoirs*, p. 321.
40. TOMK/2 (D191), 8 May, p. 59.
41. Ibid.; *Naval Memoirs*, pp. 321–3; Pitt, p. 148.
42. TOMK/2 (D191), 9 May, p. 59.
43. *Naval Memoirs*, p. 323.
44. Ibid., p. 324; Pitt, p. 149.
45. Ibid.; TOMK/2 (D191), 9 May, p. 59.
46. TOMK/2 (D191), 9 May, p. 59; Pitt, p. 151.
47. *Naval Memoirs*, p. 327.
48. Ibid.
49. TOMK/2 (D191), 9 May, p. 61.
50. Ibid.
51. *Naval Memoirs*, p. 328.
52. TOMK/2 (D191), 9 May, p. 62.
53. Pitt, pp. 158–9.
54. Ibid., pp. 160–3.
55. TOMK/2 (D191), 9 May, p. 62; *Naval Memoirs*, pp. 328–9.
56. *Naval Memoirs*, p. 329.
57. TOMK/2 (D191), 9 May, pp. 62–3; *Naval Memoirs*, pp. 329–30.

58. Ibid.; ibid.
59. T.C. Sanford, *Zeebrugge and Ostend Dispatches*, pp. 165 and 181.
60. Pitt, pp. 10 and 165; Roskill, *Beatty*, pp. 255–6.
61. Walker, pp. 225–32.
62. Roskill, *Beatty*, pp. 255–6.
63. *Naval Memoirs*, pp. 346–7.
64. Walker, pp. 211–24.
65. Pitt, p. 165.
66. TOMK/2 (D191), 11, 13, 15 May, p. 63.
67. Ibid., pp. 63–6.

Chapter Thirteen
1. TOMK/2, (D191), 5 Aug., 1918, p. 68; 13 Aug., p. 69.
2. Ibid., 22 Aug., p. 70; *Naval Memoirs,* Vol. II 1916-18 (1935), p. 350.
3. Ibid., 10 Sept., p. 72.
4. Ibid., 19 Sept., p. 73; *Naval Memoirs*, pp. 356–8.
5. C. Aspinall-Oglander, *Roger Keyes*, p. 256.
6. TOMK/2 (D191), 27 Sept., pp. 74–5.
7. Ibid.
8. Aspinall-Oglander, p. 256.
9. TOMK/2 (D191), 14 Oct., pp. 76–8.
10. Ibid.; *Naval Memoirs*, pp. 368–9.
11. Ibid., 17 Oct., pp. 78–82; *Naval Memoirs*, pp. 369–73.
12. Ibid.
13. Ibid.
14. Ibid.
15. Ibid., 18 and 19 Oct., pp. 82–5.
16. Ibid., 26 Oct., p. 87; R. Keyes, *Outrageous Fortune* (1984), p. 21.
17. Ibid., 9 and 10 Nov., p. 93.
18. M. Tomkinson, *The Tomkinson Story*.

Chapter Fourteen
1. P. Halpern, *The Keyes Papers*, Vol. II, 1919–38 (1980), p. 3; *Naval Memoirs,* Vol. II, p. 387.
2. Tomkinson to Keyes, 6 March 1919 (KP 12).
3. Ibid.
4. Keyes to Madden, 17 April (KP 19).
5. Madden to Keyes, 23 April (KP 20).
6. Keyes to wife, 24 and 25 March (KP 15, 16).
7. *The Keyes Papers*, p. 5; C. Aspinall-Oglander, *Roger Keyes*, pp. 282–3.
8. A. Coles and T. Briggs, *Flagship Hood* (1985), pp. 3–10.
9. Ibid., p. 11.
10. Ibid., p. 12.

11. Ibid., pp. 13–14.
12. Ibid., pp. 15–16.
13. M. Tomkinson, *The Tomkinson Story*.
14. *The Keyes Papers*, p. 5; Aspinall-Oglander, pp. 282–3.
15. Author's interview with Tomkinson's daughters.
16. *The Keyes Papers*, p. 6; Aspinall-Oglander, p. 283; *Naval Memoirs*, p. 393.
17. Aspinall-Oglander, p. 283.
18. Author's interview with Tomkinson's daughters.
19. Aspinall-Oglander, p. 284.
20. *The Keyes Papers*, p. 117.
21. Author's interview with Tomkinson's daughters.
22. *The Keyes Papers*, p. 122; Aspinall-Oglander, pp. 283 and 285; B. Pitt, *Zeebrugge* (1958), p. 176.
23. Ibid; *The Keyes Papers*; B. Hunt, *Sailor– Scholar* (1982), p. 172.
24. Aspinall-Oglander, p. 283.
25. O. Warner, *Admiral of the Fleet* (1969), p. 43.
26. *The Keyes Papers*, p. 121; Aspinall-Oglander, pp. 279–83; Pitt, p. 177.
27. S. Roskill, *Admiral of the Fleet Earl Beatty*, p. 161.

Chapter Fifteen
1. L. Gardiner, *The Royal Oak Courts Martial* (1965), pp. 133–4; Keyes to Admiralty, 11 March 1928 (*KP* 197); C. Aspinall-Oglander, *Roger Keyes*, p. 294.
2. Gardiner, pp. 55–8.
3. Ibid.
4. Ibid., p. 61.
5. K. Dewar, *The Navy from Within* (1939), p. 307; Gardiner, p. 63.
6. Gardiner, pp. 64–88.
7. Ibid., pp. 89–95.
8. Oglander, p. 293; Gardiner, pp. 101–4 and 109–11.
9. Gardiner, p. 198.
10. Aspinall-Oglander, p. 292.
11. Ibid., p. 294.
12. Ibid.
13. Dewar, pp. 313–14.
14. Aspinall-Oglander, p. 294.
15. Gardiner, pp. 139–40.
16. Dewar, p. 316.
17. Ibid.
18. Keyes to Admiralty, 11 March (*KP* 197).
19. Ibid.

20. Dewar, p. 317.
21. B. Hunt, *Sailor–Scholar* (1982), p. 173.
22. Gardiner, p. 160.
23. Gardiner, pp. 195–6.
24. Dewar, p. 344.
25. Aspinall-Oglander, p. 296.
26. Ibid., p. 299.
27. *Keyes Papers*, Vol. II (1980), p. 121.
28. Keyes to Tomkinson, 23 June 1928 (KP 200); Aspinall-Oglander, p. 304.
29. Aspinall-Oglander, pp. 300–3.
30. Ibid.
31. S. Roskill, *Naval Policy between the Wars* (1976), pp. 69–70.
32. A. Coles and T. Briggs, *Flagship Hood*, p. 48.
33. Admiral E. Longly-Cook's speech to the Hood Association, 24 May 1980.

Chapter Sixteen
(All commanding officers' Reports of Proceedings (ROP) are in ADM 178/110.)

1. Admiralty Board minute 2848, 3 Sept. 1931 (ADM 167/83); Admiralty warning signal timed 17.38, 3 Sept.; D. Divine, *Mutiny at Invergordon* (1970), pp. 94–5.
2. Divine, p. 90.
3. Cypher message, board minute 2848, 3 Sept.
4. Divine, p. 90.
5. Ibid., pp. 67–72.
6. Naval Command paper 3920, 31 July 1931, Royal Archives, GV K2330 (3)/20/34/ and 36.
7. Divine, p. 95.
8. Ibid., p. 104.
9. ADM 178/9.
10. S. Roskill, *Naval Policy between the Wars* (1976), p. 94; Divine, pp. 105–6; ADM 178/9.
11. Admiralty Letter CW 8284/31 of 10 Sept. 1931 (ADM 1/8747 and ADM 116/2864).
12. A. Coles and T. Briggs, *Flagship Hood* , p. 52.
13. Ibid.
14. Ibid.
15. Admiralty Fleet Orders AFO 2238 and AFO 2239/31.
16. ADM 116/2864; Divine, p. 109.
17. *Flagship Hood*, p. 53.
18. Ibid.
19. Roskill, p. 98.
20. Patterson's Report of Proceedings (ADM 178/110); Divine, p. 112.
21. Astley-Rushton's ROP (ADM 178/110).
22. Divine, pp. 115–16.

23. Tomkinson's ROP, paragraph 8; Divine, pp. 116–17.
24. Ibid; Divine, p. 118.
25. Tomkinson (hereinafter SOAF) to Admiralty, 1025, 15 Sept. 1931; Elkins' Papers (ELK/2).
26. Patterson's ROP.
27. Watson's ROP (ADM 178/110).
28. *Flagship Hood*, p. 58.
29. Elkins' Papers (ELK/2); K. Edwards, *The Mutiny at Invergordon* (1937), pp. 236–9; Divine, Ch. 12.
30. *Flagship Hood*, p. 56; Elkins' Papers (ELK/2).
31. Roskill, p. 102; *Flagship Hood*, p. 57.
32. Lieut. Cdr. Beresford to Roskill, 30 December 1973, Roskill, p. 102; Tomkinson ROP; Elkins' Papers (ELK/2).
33. SOAF to Admiralty, 2315, 14 Sept. Roskill, p. 103.
34. Scott's ROP (ADM 178/110).
35. Tomkinson's ROP.
36. Custance's ROP, (ADM 178/110).
37. Edwards, pp. 249–50.
38. Dibben's ROP (ADM 178/110).
39. Scott's ROP.
40. SOAF to Admiralty, 0120, 15 Sept.
41. *Flagship Hood*, p. 59.
42. Scott's ROP.
43. Patterson's ROP.
44. Ibid.
45. SOAF to Admiralty, 0916, 15 Sept.; Divine, pp. 156–7.
46. Edwards, pp. 269–70; Divine, pp. 158–9; full text as enclosure to *Norfolk* ROP (ADM 178/110).
47. Cabinet papers – CAB 53(31), 16 Sept. 1931 and conclusion CAB 23/68; *Flagship Hood*, p. 62.
48. Admiralty message to SOAF, 1205, 15 Sept.
49. SOAF to Admiralty, 1340, 15 Sept.; Divine, pp. 164–5.
50. Commodore (D) Rosyth to SOAF, 1725, 15 Sept. (Tomkinson's ROP).
51. Patterson's ROP.
52. Admiralty to SOAF and C-in-Cs, 1910, 15 Sept.; Divine, p. 165.
53. Admiralty to SOAF, and C-in-Cs, 1945, 15 Sept.
54. Ibid., 2035, 15 Sept.; Divine, p. 167.
55. Admiralty to SOAF, 2100, 15 Sept.
56. SOAF to Admiralty, 0053, 16 Sept.; Divine, p. 166.
57. Edwards, pp. 285–6.
58. Admiralty to SOAF, 1117, 16 Sept.; Divine, p. 170.
59. SOAF to Admiralty, 1148, 16 Sept.; Divine, p. 170.
60. Divine, ibid.

61. Patterson's ROP; Pursey to Roskill, 23 April, 1974, Roskill, p. 108.
62. SOAF to Admiralty, 1406, 16 Sept.
63. Tomkinson's ROP.
64. Admiralty to SOAF, 1445, 16 Sept.; Divine, p. 171.
65. Dreyer memo to Chatfield (Chatfield Papers, CHT 2/2); Cabinet Papers, CAB 53 (31) 16 Sept., and CAB 23/68.
66. *New York Times*, 17 and 18 Sept.
67. Patterson's ROP.
68. *Flagship Hood*, p. 66.
69. Divine, pp. 173–4; *Flagship Hood*, p. 66.
70. SOAF to Admiralty, 1947, 16 Sept.; Roskill, p. 109.
71. Elkins' Papers (ELK/2); Divine pp. 175–6.
72. Patterson's ROP.
73. *Flagship Hood*, pp. 65–6.
74. Admiralty to SOAF, 2350, 16 Sept.
75. SOAF to Admiralty, 2345, 16 Sept.

Chapter Seventeen
 1. Parliamentary debate, Commons Vol. 256, col. 1104–22.
 2. C.W. Dyson Perrin to Tomkinson, 20 Sept. 1931 (TOMK/9).
 3. D. Divine, *Mutiny at Invergordon,* pp. 182–3.
 4. SOAF to Admiralty, 1155, 17 Sept. 1931.
 5. Admiralty to SOAF, 1147, 17 Sept.
 6. Ibid., 1350, 17 Sept. (time of receipt 1402, 18 Sept).
 7. C-in-C, Plymouth to Admiralty, 19 Sept.; Cdr. J.H. Owen, *Mutiny in Royal Navy* (Vol. II p. 45 in ADM 178/133); Divine, p. 191; F. Copeman, *Reason in Revolt* (1948), p. 50.
 8. SOAF to Admiralty, 1820 and 1840, 17 Sept.
 9. Admiralty to all ships Atlantic Fleet, 1910, 17 Sept.
10. SOAF to Admiralty, 1347, 18 Sept.
11. First Sea Lord (Field) to SOAF, 1617, 18 Sept.
12. Ibid., 1853, 18 Sept.
13. Field letter to Tomkinson, 18 Sept. (TOMK/9).
14. *The Times*, 18 Sept. 1931.
15. Tomkinson's ROP (ADM 178/110).
16. Ibid.
17. Ibid.
18. ADM 178/110.
19. ADMs 178/66, 178/133; Divine, p. 192.
20. Admiralty to all establishments, 1618, 21 Sept.
21. Field to Tomkinson, 3 Oct. (TOMK/9).
22. Chetwode to Tomkinson, 26 Sept. (TOMK/9).
23. ADM 178/129; Royal Archives GV K2330(3)/13,/17 and /19.

24. SOAF to Atlantic Fleet, 1201, 5 Oct.
25. Colvin to Tomkinson, 7 Oct. (TOMK/9).
26. S. Roskill, *Naval Policy between the Wars*, pp. 119–20; S. Roskill, *Admiral of the Fleet Earl Beatty*, p. 66; Divine, p. 234.
27. A. Coles and T. Briggs, *Flagship Hood*, pp. 45–6; Roskill, *Beatty*, p. 66.
28. Dreyer's Notes on Refusal of Duty (ADM 178/110).
29. Tomkinson to Dreyer, 6 Oct. (TOMK/9).
30. Dreyer's letters to Tomkinson through 1932 (TOMK/9).
31. Dreyer's Notes on Refusal of Duty.
32. Admiralty Board minute 2860, 17 Oct. 1931, ADM 178/114.
33. *Flagship Hood*, pp. 71–2.
34. Ibid., p. 72.
35. Ibid.
36. Baddeley to Kelly, 17 Oct. in ADM 1/8761–240/32, also in Royal Archives GV K2330(3); Divine, p. 221.
37. Field to Chamberlain, 13 Oct.
38. Chamberlain to Field, undated.
39. Tomkinson to Kelly, 26 Oct. (TOMK/9).
40. Kelly Report, 9 Nov., Kelly Papers (KEL/109); ADM 1/8761–240/32; Royal Archives GV K2330(3); Divine, pp. 227–30.
41. Kelly to Field, 22 Oct. (KEL/109); ADM 178/89.
42. Field to Kelly, 30 Oct. (KEL/109).
43. Kelly Report (KEL/109).
44. Kelly to George V, 1 Nov., Royal Archives GV K2330(3).
45. Admiralty Minute, 9 Dec., ADM 178/110.
46. *Flagship Hood*, p. 72.

Chapter 18
1. A. Coles and T. Briggs, *Flagship Hood, pp. 72–3.*
2. Ibid.
3. Tomkinson to Admiralty, 17 Feb. 1932 (ADM 178/111).
4. Admiralty letter MO266/32 to Tomkinson, 2 Feb. (TOMK/3).
5. Admiralty letter NL MO2855/31 to Tomkinson, 2 Feb. (TOMK/3).
6. D. Divine, *Mutiny at Invergordon*, p. 245.
7. W. James, *The Sky was Always Blue* (1951), pp. 13–14.
8. *The Times*, 25 Feb. 1932.
9. Divine, p. 232.
10. Admiralty Board minute, 1 Jan. 1932 (ADM 178/111); Divine, p. 236.
11. Ibid.; Divine, p. 237.
12. A.T. Patterson, *Tyrwhitt of the Harwich Force* (1973), pp. 278–81; Divine, pp. 238–9.
13. Tyrwhitt to Keyes, 21 July 1934 (*KP* 274).
14. Admiralty Board minute, 1 Jan. 1932; Divine, pp. 233–5.

15. Tyrwhitt to Kelly, 12 Jan. (see Patterson, *Tyrwhitt of the Harwich Force*, pp. 278–31).
16. Ibid.
17. Admiralty to Kelly, 2 Feb. 1932 (Kelly Papers 505/HF 003).
18. Tomkinson to Admiralty, 13 March (TOMK/3).
19. S. Roskill, *Naval Policy between the Wars*, p. 126.
20. Kelly to Admiralty, 14 March (Kelly Papers 505/HF003).
21. Field to Kelly, 31 March (ibid.).
22. Waistell to Tomkinson (TOMK/3).
23. Keyes to Tomkinson, 19 March 1932 (KP 244).
24. Pound to Tomkinson, 6 April (TOMK/3).
25. Ibid., 9 April (TOMK/3).
26. Tomkinson to Admiralty, 25 April (TOMK/3).
27. Admiralty to Tomkinson, 25 April (TOMK/3).
28. Admiralty Letter NL 1201/32, 12 Aug. 1932, and ADM 178/133.
29. Admiralty Board minute 2834, 11 April 1932.
30. Tomkinson to Admiralty, 2 May (TOMK/3).
31. Tomkinson to Kelly, 3 May (TOMK/3).
32. Keyes to Tomkinson, 3 May (*KP* 247).
33. Ibid., 2 June (*KP* 252).
34. Keyes to Baldwin, 18 May (*KP* 248); Keyes to Tomkinson, 2 June (*KP* 252).
35. Keyes to Baldwin, ibid.
36. Keyes to Eyres-Monsell, 30 May (*KP* 250); Keyes to Tomkinson, 2 June (*KP* 252).
37. Boyle to Keyes, 29 May (*KP* 249).
38. Tomkinson to Keyes, 8 June (*KP* 253).
39. Keyes to Tomkinson, 2 June (*KP* 252).
40. Ibid.
41. Tomkinson to Keyes, 8 June (*KP* 253).
42. Tomkinson to Admiralty, 9 June (TOMK/3).
43. Beatty to Keyes, 11 June (*KP* 255).
44. Ibid.
45. Keyes to Eyres-Monsell, 14 June (*KP* 256).
46. Admiralty to Tomkinson, 25 June (TOMK/3).
47. Campbell to Keyes, 10 June 1932 (*KP* 268).
48. Ibid.
49. Ibid.
50. Tomkinson to Campbell, 6 July (TOMK/3); Tomkinson to Keyes, 26 Sept. 1934 (*KP* 284).
51. Campbell to Tomkinson, 15 July 1932 (TOMK/3); Tomkinson to Keyes, 26 Sept. (*KP* 284).
52. Tomkinson to Keyes, 28 July 1932 (TOMK/3).
53. Ibid.
54. James, *The Sky was Always Blue*, pp. 13–14.

Chapter 19
1.   Keyes to Eyres-Monsell, 27 Aug. 1932 (*KP* 258).
2.   Tomkinson to Keyes, 29 Sept 1932 (TOMK/3).
3.   Ibid., 26 Feb. 1933 (*KP* 261).
4.   Ibid.
5.   Pound to Tomkinson, 5 March 1933 (TOMK/3).
6.   Ibid.
7.   Tomkinson to Pound, 10 March 1933 (TOMK/3).
8.   Kelly to Chatfield, 30 July 1936 (Chatfield Papers CHT/4/6).
9.   H. L'Etang, *The Pathology of Leadership* (1969), pp. 125–7.
10.   Keyes to Eyres-Monsell, 4 July 1934 (*KP* 270).
11.   Eyres-Monsell to Keyes, 10 July (*KP* 271).
12.   Keyes to Eyres-Monsell, 11 July (*KP* 272).
13.   Ibid., 15 July (*KP* 273).
14.   Keyes to Chatfield, 26 July (*KP* 278).
15.   Eyres-Monsell to Keyes, 21 July (*KP* 275).
16.   Keyes to Eyres-Monsell, 25 July (*KP* 276).
17.   Chatfield to Keyes, 25 July (*KP* 277).
18.   Keyes to Chatfield, 26 July (*KP* 278).
19.   Parliamentary Debates, House of Commons, fifth series, Vol. 292, 31 July 1934, pp. 2,564–6.
20.   Ibid.
21.   Ibid.
22.   Keyes to Tomkinson, 8 Aug. 1934 (*KP* 279).
23.   Ibid.
24.   Brand to Keyes, 8 Aug. (*KP* 282).
25.   Waistell to Keyes, 10 Aug. (*KP* 283).
26.   Author's interview with Tomkinson's daughters.
27.   Tomkinson to Keyes, 26 Sept. 1934 (*KP* 284).
28.   Keyes to Tomkinson, 23 Dec. 1934 (*KP* 288).
29.   Ibid.
30.   Chatfield to Tomkinson, 25 June 1935 (TOMK/3).
31.   Tomkinson to Chatfield, 27 June (TOMK/3).
32.   Chatfield to Tomkinson, 21 July (TOMK/3).
33.   S. Roskill, *Naval Policy between the Wars*, pp. 53–4.
34.   Lord Chatfield, *It Might Happen Again* (1947), pp. 62–3.

Epilogue
1.   Author's interview with Tomkinson's daughters.
2.   Keyes to Tomkinson, 12 July 1942 (*KP*).
3.   Ibid., 3 Nov. 1945 (*KP*).
4.   R.Keyes, *Outrageous Fortune*, pp. 457–60.

5.   M. Tomkinson, *The Tomkinson Story.*
6.   S. Roskill, *Naval Policy between the Wars*, p. 130; ADM 205/12.
7.   Author's interview with Tomkinson's daughters.
8.   *The Tomkinson Story.*
9.   Ibid.
10. Author's interview with Tomkinson's daughters.
11. *The Times*, 9–28 Oct. 1971.

BIBLIOGRAPHY

PRIMARY SOURCES

General

P. Halpern (ed), *Keyes Papers (see* Secondary Sources*)*
Tomkinson Papers (Churchill College, Cambridge).

Invergordon references
Churchill College, Cambridge

Papers of :
    Vice Admiral Frederic Dreyer, DRYR 3/2, 8/1, 8/2.
    Captain Stephen Roskill, ROSK 7/171, 172, ROSK 21/3, 3A.
    Vice Admiral Wilfred Tomkinson, TOMK/9.

National Maritime Museum, Greenwich

Papers of:
    Admiral Lord Chatfield, CHT 2/2, 3/1, 4/1, 2, 4, 5, 6, 7, 11.
    Vice Admiral Sir Robert Elkins, ELK/2, 10, 11.
    Admiral Sir William Fisher, FHR/14, 15.
    Admiral Sir John Kelly, KEL/108, 109, 110, 111, 113.
    Commander Harold Pursey, Pursey/10, 11, 12, 13, 14, 15.

Public Record Office, Kew

Cabinet Papers
    CAB 23/68, 24/223, 23/90B.

Admiralty Papers
    ADM 1/8761–240/32, 1/8747/78 and 87
    ADM 53/70081, 7715, 76044, 78927, 73061, 84906, 85274, 87358, 80288, 81351,
    82565, 88623, 91740, 94203, 83061–3, 74291.
    ADM 116/2864, 2884, 3611.

ADM 167/83, 84, 85, 86, 87.
ADM 179/92.
ADM 182/61; 62, 90, 91.
ADM 230/1.
ADM 178/66, 73, 75, 79, 80, 89, 110, 111, 112, 113, 114, 129, 133, 135, 149, 150, 151, 162, 164.

SECONDARY SOURCES
Aspinall-Oglander, C., *Roger Keyes*, Hogarth Press, 1951.
Bennett, G., *Naval Battles of the First World War*, Pan Books, 1968.
Bloodworth, D., *The Chinese Looking Glass*, New York, 1967.
Chalmers, Rear-Admiral W.S., *The Life and Letters of David Earl Beatty*, Hodder and Stoughton, 1951.
Chatfield, Lord., *It Might Happen Again*, London, Heinemann, 1947.
Churchill, W., *The World Crisis*, Vol. I, Thornton Butterworth, 1923.
Clements, P., *The Boxer Rebellion,* New York, 1915.
Coles, A., *Three Before Breakfast,* Mason, 1979.
Coles, A. and Briggs, T., *Flagship Hood*, Hale, 1985.
Connor, R., *The Boxer Rebellion,* Hale.
Copeman, F., *Reason in Revolt,* Blandford Press, 1948.
Corbett, Sir Julian, *History of the Great War – Naval Operations*, Longmans, Green, 1920.
Dewar, K., *The Navy from Within*, Gollancz, 1939.
Divine, D., *Mutiny at Invergordon*, MacDonald, 1970.
Dreyer, Admiral Sir Frederic, *The Sea Heritage*, Museum Press, 1955.
Edwards, K., *The Mutiny at Invergordon*, Putnam, 1937.
Ereira, A., *The Invergordon Mutiny*, London, Routledge and Kegan Paul, 1981.
Fitzsimons, B. (ed.), *Warships and Sea Battles of World War I*, Phoebus, 1973.
Fleming, P., *The Siege at Peking*, Rupert Hart-Davis, 1960.
Gardiner, L., *The Royal Oak Courts Martial*, Blackwood, 1965.
Gray, E., *Few Survived,* Secker and Warburg, 1986.
Halpern, P. (ed.), *The Keyes Papers*, Vols I, II and III, Naval Records Society 1972, 1980, 1981.
Holger, H., *Luxury Fleet*, Allen and Unwin, 1980.
Hough, R., *The Great War at Sea, 1914–18*, Oxford University Press, 1983.
Hughes, E.A., *The Royal Naval College Dartmouth*, Winchester Publications.
Hunt, B., *Sailor–Scholar*, Wilfred Laurie University Press, 1982.
James, Admiral Sir William, *The Sky was Always Blue*, London, Methuen, 1951.
Jellicoe, Admiral Viscount, *The Grand Fleet, 1914–16*, Cassell, 1919.
Kemp, P. (ed.), *Oxford Companion to the Sea*, Oxford University Press, 1976.
Keyes, Sir Roger, *The Naval Memoirs of Admiral of the Fleet Roger Keyes*, Vols I and II, Thornton Butterworth, 1933, 1935.
Keyes, Sir Roger, *Adventures Ashore and Afloat*, Harrap, 1939.

Keyes, Lord, *Outrageous Fortune*, Secker and Warburg, 1984.
Knight, F., *The Harwich Naval Forces*, Hodder and Stoughton, 1919.
L'Etang, H., *The Pathology of Leadership*, Heinemann, 1969.
Liddle, P., *The Sailors' War*, Blandford Press, 1985.
Marder, J., *Fear God and Dreadnought.*, Cape, 1959.
Marder, J., *Fom the Dardanelles to Oran*, Oxford University Press, 1974.
Moorehead, *Gallipoli*, Hamish Hamilton, 1956.
Newbolt, Sir Henry, *Naval Operations of the Great War*, Vols 4 and 5, Longman, 1928 and 1931.
Pack, Captain S.W.C., *Britannia at Dartmouth*, Alvin Redman, 1966.
Pack, Captain S.W.C., *Sea Power in the Mediterranean*, Barker, 1971.
Patterson, A. T., *Tyrwhitt of the Harwich Force*, MacDonald, 1973.
Pitt, B., *Zeebrugge*, Cassell, 1958.
Roskill, S., *Naval Policy between the World Wars*, Collins, 1976.
Roskill, S., *Admiral of the Fleet Earl Beatty*, Collins, 1980.
Sandford, T. C., *Zeebrugge and Ostend Dispatches,* Churchill College.
Tan, C., *The Boxer Catastrophe*, New York, 1955.
Tomkinson, M., *The Tomkinson Story*, Private publication, 1985.
Walker, P., *The Zeebrugge Raid*, Kimber, 1978.
Warner, O. *Admiral of the Fleet*, Sidgwick Jackson, 1969.
Wincott, L., *Invergordon Mutineer*, Weidenfeld and Nicholson, 1974.
Winton, J., *Jellicoe*, Michael Joseph, 1981.

Other Publications

Navy List, Hansard, The Times, Evening Standard (London), *North China Herald, New York Times, Kidderminster Times.*

INDEX

193